Between WATER AND FIRE

notionpress.com

Between WATER AND FIRE

ASPECTS IN THE HISTORY OF THE PARATHAVAR COMMUNITY

(Collected Articles)

Vinod Vincent Rajesh

Notion Press

Old No. 38, New No. 6
McNichols Road, Chetpet
Chennai - 600 031

First Published by Notion Press 2018

ISBN 978-1-948372-45-9

Dedicated to

MSUFA &
The Non-teaching Staff of MSU

Contents

Dr. G.J. Sudhakar,
Professor and Head, Historical Studies,
C.P. Ramasamy Aiyar Institute of indological Research
Chennai - 600018

Foreword

I am happy to see one of my good students at the Department of History, Loyola College, Chennai, has worked for a thematic book entitled **Between Water and Fire: Aspects in the History of the Parathavar Community** and is publishing through the Notion Press Publications wherein articles published by him in various prestigious journals are collected, edited, and published. As the editor of the Journal of Indian History and Culture, in my observation, he is one of the emerging scholars in the field of social history who writes articles of uncompromising quality using latest techniques of research. We had the pleasure to invite him as a resource person to a National Seminar hosted by the C.P. Ramasamy Aiyar Institute of Indological Research, and he did his role well. I also have come across scholarly people appreciating his intellectual acumen, presentation skill and convincing arguments demonstrated in other seminars.

The present book pertaining to the Parathavar community is an interesting study. Ever since Subaltern studies emerged as part of historical research in India, interest in capturing various facets of groups of people categorized as castes and tribes along with the interest in local history derived scholarly notice. Though great minds like Edgar Thurston attempted to give a bird's eye view on the castes and tribes of Southern India, specialized research had been the domain of the components of other social sciences like anthropology and sociology. Hence, Verrier Elwin produced his pioneering studies on Indian tribes, followed by scholars like Bernard Cohn, Louis Dumont, and others. David Ludden and James Scott explored and gave an impetus to the study of local history. Closely following their line emerged Ramachandra Guha, a historian whose main focus was on environmental history through which he discussed the intertwining of people's lives in the peripheral regions. At present, the academia and the intellect of the developed world have shifted to concentrate on family histories, whereby the term microscopic-study is being given new definition and meaning. However, in India, professional writings of these kinds of investigations have a vast scope, yet serious perspectives have only recently emerged and also only in limited numbers.

The work of Mr. Vinod Vincent Rajesh has to be viewed as containing almost all of the above-mentioned shades and it is left to his readers to bring out specific features of his writing. As an insider, it is normal for a person like him to have internalized the socio-economic processes of the community in his upbringing itself. The history of the said people starts from the Sangam period, if not before, and continues with prominence until at present. From time to time research has been made by scholars on the subject matter with scholarly commitment. A general outline about the community is found in the works of Nilakanta Sastri, P.T. Srinivasa Iyengar, N. Subrahmanian, V. Kanagasabhai Pillai, and others. Further, specialized writings came from the works of Clarence T. Maloney, Patrick A. Roche, Susan Bayly, K.S. Mathews, S. Decla and others. In contrast to the traditional historical writings, the writer of this book lays stress on 'historical memory' based on the creative works of R.N. Joe d'Cruz and attempts to integrate his own memory with inferences from most of the works mentioned above. It is in one way a psycho-analytic approach whereas the writer drafts a theoretical outline with the support of ideas from as great a philosopher like D.P. Chattopadyaya and adopts a comparative Marxist method. In my observation, the articles though independently drafted, are used to ultimately compare which has cumulatively been done well in the last article of the series. Hence for me, the central focus of the study or for that matter the crux of the research appears to be the religious conversion which is placed in the middle of the articles and those placed above are aimed to discuss the life pattern before the adoption of Christianity and those placed after discuss the post-conversion changes.

In my opinion, the sifting of information from diverse primary sources like those belonging to the Sangam period, travelogues of Marco Polo, St. Francis Xavier's letters, signboard information as well as inscriptions in the churches, and folk information collected through field visits and triangulation of all these to provide a neat sketch based on indirectly sensing the new hypotheses emerging out of the existing works is noteworthy. The researcher has used some of the primary sources by questioning them for missing information. It goes to prove the depth of understanding of the writer in the subject matter though he is able to maintain maximum possible objectivity in writing. This apart, also his skill of observing historical elements emerging out of emotional contexts such as that during 'ravage of Tsunami' and 'Anti-Kudankulam Movement' is appreciable. He is able to substantiate these not only with existing contributions in the field of study, but also able to carve out new and original perspectives. It is also interesting to note that he has used updated secondary material for writing this book. Particularly, in the second chapter, he has used a latest article published in 'The Hindu' (June 2017). This alertness is expected of a contemporary researcher. By and large, the book could serve as a significant contribution to the scholarly world. I wish the writer all success in his future endeavours and hope to receive more contributions from his desk.

Chennai
28-10-2017

G.J. Sudhakar

Preface

My parents had an inter-caste marriage. My father belonged to the Parathavar community and my mother was from the Nadar community and a Hindu and needless to say by the ascribed membership into the caste my father was a Christian. They lived happily and my father who was an officer in the Tamil Nadu Fire Service remained away from his caste group. The caste had embraced Christianity almost 500 years before. My father's ancestors seem to have had a key-role as lay leaders of the converts within the Southern Tamil Nadu region. Folklore is that when Devasahayam Pillai was killed as part of state awarded punishment, it was an ancestor of my father in his mother's line who secretly undertook the risk of collecting his dead-body and interned it in the Kottar Church premise. His ancestor's in his father's line were also accorded special status in the St. Xavier's Church of Kottar that they were not only lay-leaders but also had the lone-right to hold the steering of the Church cars known in the Tamil singular as 'Ther' or 'Chapparam.' This continued until my father's generation and his love marriage prevented further succession.

During his childhood, my father had served as an altar-boy and had the chance of thoroughly memorizing the prayers, sacramental tenets and liturgical compositions of the Roman Catholic Church in the Latin language. Until his death, on request, he with excellent rhyming and impressive flow said all that he memorized. Yet he was never fanatical. Before joining government service he had run a Tuition center where 'pooja festivals' were celebrated with much devotion and tremendous fanfare. After marriage, he became a devotee of 'Lord Murugan' and often visited 'Tiruchendur' and with chance paid visits to other holy-abodes of the Lord. He had the capacity to chant 'Kandha Shashti Kavasam' from memory that impressed the elder sister of mine who also evolved the talent in her. He undertook severe penance for 48 days to reach Sabarimala which I also followed in a later stage. He was never discouraged in his spiritual pursuit by his parents or siblings though not welcomed by many of the fellow Christians and the spiritually minded personnel in the Roman Catholic Church. In fact, his siblings have joined us when we offered a sacrifice of a rooster and 'Pongal' to the female divinities of the Hindu 'little tradition.' We celebrated both "Deepavali" and 'Christmas' without variation. Christians of the Roman Catholic denomination normally celebrate 'Pongal' in its cultural setting. They adopt 'Independence Day' and 'Republic Day' in such a way that the Parish Priest hoists the National flag before saying the Holy-Mass.

No matter if the acceptance of diverse faiths among Christians like what has been said above is discounted, but a fabric of such a kind is damaged when the loyalty to the nation-state is questioned for the reason that their holy places are located outside the country, and hence, there is an urge to mingle and mix with the rest of the Christian world as also to convert this country into a Christian-majority state. Though I have observed some 'Born-Again Christians praying to help God to make all Indians accept Christianity, that is not a common and general phenomenon. Christianity is the religion of the majority in the world particularly of the people in the economically developed countries of Europe, America, and Australia who are racially-minded people than spiritually engaging ones. A Christian in India or any other third world country seems to be well aware of this fact. The British government or so to say the Christian masters did not recognize any Christian group including the complete coverts of the coastal region as martial so that they could find employment at the least in the defense force like the navy. To its contrast, there had been freedom fighters from among the coastal Christian people like my wife's grandfather Mr. (late) Vincent Mariadoss.

As far as the Parathavar community was concerned the Tsunami that ravaged the coastal Tamil Nadu was a major rupture that exposed the existence of the community in the observation of other people. An individual in the Parathavar community encounters a complex situation where he sees the opportunities opened by the Church have neither adequately reached his caste members nor has it altered their lives substantially as a reward for their loyalty for 500 years although these contentions are not accepted by other castes particularly within Christianity. A typical representative of this voice is that of R.N. Joe d'Cruz who has urged the community to return to the fold of 'Hinduism', the emissaries of which are willing to offer as and such caste status as the reconverts wish.

Issues of direct confrontation and conflict like what has been stated above demand an interdisciplinary skill. As a student of history, it appeared to me that the questions of why conversion and what are the changes instigated by conversion has to be balanced with the question of what had been the socio-economic and religious status of the Parathavar people before conversion? My readings on sociology and philosophy improved the spectrum of academic perspective to which my mentor and friend Dr. Pavananthi Vembulu who had worked extensively among the fishing folk of Tamil Nadu after Tsunami added the importance of folklore and anthropological angle. Going by his way helped in collecting several local myths and traditions which are structurally identical with that of native religion which categorically drove me toward D.D. Kosambi's 'Myth and Reality.' However, what I realized through these personal experiences is the fact that prayers by individuals had been chiefly performed for economic well-being and religion is often brought to public sphere only to manipulate political power. On his influence, interpretations were made on the basis of the liberal Marxist method though taking of sides with the excuse of it being a minority religion and subaltern class has been avoided.

Under such conditions, I worked in the last decade conducting series of field visits. After Tsunami, yet another rupture that was ignored and very diplomatically handled by the political community was the Anti-Nuclear Protest of the Parathavar people supported not only by the Church but also by several of the caste and religious organizations. In the event of the protest, the living memory of the people that had its mooring at the least from the mythical period of 'the Great Deluge' underwent a vibration and made projections capturing of which has been attempted through these articles. It is in the shade of the memory, other sources were cross-examined. Hence, it is not a conventional type of History Writing which has been made in these nine articles. The first article is based on the influence of sociology and provides direction for overall investigation. The second and the third articles are of separate category and they are on 'Origin' and 'Historical Geography' and they take into account aspects of race as well as genetics and principles of Geography respectively. The next three chapters form another category and were on Economics, Religious Background, and Social formation prior to the adoption of Christianity. The last three chapters were on the Sixteenth Century Ruptures, Arrival of St. Xavier, and Changes instigated by Christianity. In other words, the five chapters beginning from the second represent 'water' and the last three denote 'fire' in the lives of the Parathavar community.

Acknowledgements

I am also a researcher by accident than choice. During my civil services preparatory days in New Delhi, my attending of the sociology classes of Dr. Mahapathra as well as my spending of a few days at the Brahmaputra Hostel of Jawaharlal Nehru University, I realized the importance of social science research. Then one of the most popular names among serious researchers was Jacques Derrida who was most quoted yet completed his university-level teaching career with merely a post-graduate degree. It really attracted me to Derrida and created convictions against opting for official degrees. However, with the death of my parents – Mr. F. Vincent Decruz and Mrs. P. Swarnam Decruz – I cannot hope to support my living and continue with civil services preparation without a fellowship. Therefore, I appeared for the UGC-JRF exams and got only NET eligibility. Sooner, I learned that in India – particularly in the field of history – knowledge is being viewed with degrees than real intellectual attainment.

In such a situation, I landed at the Department of History, St. Joseph's College, Trichy as an M. Phil student where I met Dr. T. Sundararaj, Reader and Head of the Department. Shortly before completing the course, I became a substitute teacher for Rev. Fr. Xavier Arockiasamy, presently Principal of Loyola College, Chennai. Dr. T. Sundararaj had a project with the railways in which I volunteered to join as a 'Research Fellow.' I also registered for Ph.D. under a topic that suited the requirements of the Indian Railways. But before the commencement of the project, I got permanent placement as a lecturer in Manonmaniam Sundaranar University, Tirunelveli. Despite migration from one university area to another, I decided to continue under Dr. T. Sundararaj. I had a great appreciation for his ability as a research guide.

As expected he allowed considerable freedom in choosing the topic and taking my own time what extended beyond usually tolerated. He provided scope for developing self-perception of the concepts I intended to discuss in the course of research. Apart from these, in my short experience in the field of academics, there were several cases of mismatch between the wavelengths of the guide and the research scholar. But in the case of Dr. T. Sundararaj and me, there was a perfect synchronization in the basic understanding of the dimensions of historical research. It made me proud and happy. He had been one of those rare scholars in this part of the world liberated from the obsession of the idea of 'archival materials are the only source of writing history.' As a fellow human-being, I could feel his growth day after day not only through mere reading but by internalizing experiences offered by life. I thank him for creating such an impact on me. But his demise at an unexpected point of time prevented our further collaboration.

There had been a few other people who I remember at this juncture for having considerable confidence in my intellectual caliber. Prof. Dr. Cynthia Pandian, who served as Vice-Chancellor of Manonmaniam Sundaranar University, Tirunelveli between 2005 and 2008 was a visionary and institution builder. She appointed all of her staff members honestly including me to the post of lecturer when I was holding merely an M.A. degree with UGC-NET at a time when Ph.D. was valued more. I thank her for initiating my academic career.

Similarly, Dr. Sadasivan was also instrumental in my selection to the service of the university. All through his life, he had been a patient listener and master critic. During our days together in the university, we constantly discussed historical issues and mutually benefitted. He often used to expose me to the broad academic circle in which he was well recognized not just as a colleague but as his equal. I thank him for the munificent gesture and friendship. He is the only person who had read almost every writing of mine in Tamil and English with patience.

Dr. K.A. Manikumar, my M.Phil guide and colleague at the Department of History, Manonmaniam Sundaranar University offered me several opportunities for my growth including the co-editorship of the book entitled 'Southern Tamil Nadu through the Ages.' Dr. R. PavananthiVembulu, my mentor and decade-long friend who involved me in several projects such as the 'Tirunelveli Corporation Slum Survey' and supported me in the successful conduct of an International Workshop. I was able to realize the demands and expectations that activities of these kinds generated among persons like Prof. Dr. K. Sadasivan, Prof. Dr. K.A. Manikumar and Dr. R. PavananthiVembulu, and therefore, worked hard and gave out the best in me. Therefore I sincerely thank all of them. Particularly, I thank Dr. R. Pavananthi for giving 'foreword' to this work.

I always have the feeling of carrying the great legacy left by my fond teachers Mr. S.A. Thiagarajan, Rev. Fr. Peter Francis, Dr. M.X. Miranda, Mr. Satagopan and Prof. Mahapathra. I make use of this opportunity to remember them. Some of my students also took an active part in the making of the research. Mr. Ananda Kumar and Mr. A. Vijayakumar both M.A. History students of 2009-2011 and 2010-2012 batches of Manonmaniam Sundaranar University respectively and Mr. D. Murugesan, Chairman of the Students Union of the same university assisted me during field visits. With these men in the pillion of my motorcycle, I often felt like Che Guevara. Ms. Shanthi Devi, an M.Phil student of the 2011-2012 batch had the rare capacity to make dialogue with my writings at the student level. She read my scripts and often discussed the issues handled and sometimes even brought out valuable observations. I thank all of these budding scholars and hope they expand the horizon of research from where I leave.

I also place on record the cooperation extended by my colleagues in the departments of History of both Manonmaniam Sundaranar University, Tirunelveli and St. Joseph's College, Trichy. Particularly, during the headship of Prof. Dr. M. Desayar, I conducted most of my field visits. He encouraged my tasks. Faculty members of other departments have also contributed in their own way in the shaping of the research. I thank all of them.

The greatest casualty of the course of research was my family – wife Sonia and sons Rubert and Robert. Most of the time, I deliberately isolated myself from them. I can feel the sacrifice and I remain indebted and thankful to their sacrifice.

'Sundaram'   Vinod Vincent Rajesh
27-08-2017

Introduction

The Parathavar people were the chief residents of the coastal Tamil Country since historical times. They were depicted as master traders, sailors, pearl-divers and fishermen in all coasts inhabited by Tamil-speaking population but ruled by different kings namely the *Cheras, the Cholas* and *the Pandyas*.[1] Even in the later ancient period of the rule of the *Pallavas,* they seemed to possess the same features in their territory. But from an indefinite point in time what seemed to have strongly conditioned by political change, they came to be known under the same title only in the *Pearl Fishery Coast*.[2] Despite mentioned as traders in early works, even *Noburu Karasimha* in his inquiry about the *Valangai* and *Idangai* castes did not deem it necessary to explain how the community disappeared from the *Chola state* and why it was left from these caste categories.

In the 1901 Census, when castes were enumerated Parathavar claim was made also in Kerala and Karnataka regions of the present day.[3] They speak the language of the area they inhabit. They are not always linked with the sea in these regions. From where these people migrated was lost from their memory as in the case of those within the native land. Since many of these categories identify themselves with seafaring the probable chance of tracing their roots was from the coast of Bay of Bengal although a higher concentration of the said population was observable from the *Pearl Fishery Coast*. Water and Fire are the chief aspects that played key-roles in their lives. The outward appearance of the sea was alike in several places. But the sea is more complex in geographical traits than land that marked the local difference. There were also issues pertaining to freshwater in the coast ranging from water scarcity to flooding. All of these were part and parcel of the tropical climate predominantly characterized by extreme heat metaphorically said as fire in the present work. The dialectics between water and fire had guided the course of cultural formation.

In fact, the cultural formation of the people who were involved in maritime activities since at the least from I Century A.D. cannot be limited by enquiring merely their place of departure – for that matter the Tamil coast. The possibility for their spread throughout the length and breadth of the world had to be taken into view. Literary and archaeological evidence points to wider exposure of the people and culture. Maritime trade was carried out with *Africa, Europe, China* and *South East Asia*. They took an active part in the inland trade as well. The changes in the trade activities either independent of geographical changes or owing to it, caused the shift of focus area from time to time.[4]

At one point of time, within the *Pearl Fishery Coast*, the *Yelu Urs* meaning seven towns emerged into the limelight. Thus the study brings into focus earliest place like *Adichchanallur* as also more recent settlement like *Amalipuram.* To state exactly, the study revolves in time in the regions in and around the *Pearl Fishery Coast.*

As far as the *Parathavar* people, in general, were concerned, they were believed to have chosen *Christianity* only for the sake of economic benefit and development by the non-converts. In a country known for its diversity and multi-cultural moorings particularly marked by ignorance and illiteracy, such blunt understanding can only be normal and not shocking.[5] This can be viewed from the larger axis of the history of the majority-minority separatism also. The argument of this kind shall not be treated as reluctance in accepting the presence of *rice-conversion* in the past. It was true that *Christianity* most often than not capitalized on the poverty of the people in backward regions of the world. But here the problem had been one of generalizing of this pattern to all forms of conversions which largely was a common man's logic of relating change of faith with overall development through time. Hence it was believed that the *Parathavars* were a well educated and wealthy people since they converted near about 500 years before. However, only after the ravage of *Tsunami* that occurred on the 24th December 2004 the backwardness of the community came into limelight much to the shock of the rest.

Albeit *Tsunami* turned the attention of scholarly minds towards the coast of Tamil Nadu – which had until then largely ignored except only for a few exemptions – it did not contribute to studies coming out of a comprehensive understanding of the coastal social system. Many scholars have put forth their views on the people settled at the coast as constituting a single caste and did not distinguish between one and another. Historical inquiries based on Sangam literature tended to set a conventional background standing on the premise of the inhabitants of the *Neydal* region viewed as *Parathavars.* In reality, the social formation in the coastal area was as complex as that of the plain. There were apart from the *Parathavars,* communities like *Mukkuvar, Nulaiyar, Arayar* and so on within a brief geographical area, suggestive of the possible variations in the entire *Tamil Nadu* coast.

Whatsoever, *Christianity* had played a major role in the lives of the *Parathavars* and *Mukkuvars* than any other coastal communities. In the case of the *Parathavars,* they were known to have historically undergone several experiences in the socio-economic and religious spheres that culminated in the characterizing of certain unique features in their caste system. With the conversion, Christianity emerged as a major religious force among them that almost denuded the internal diversities and sought to fence the oscillating tendencies directing the caste to operate in particular ways.[6] As it appeared to be a fertile ground for research, the present researcher intended to pursue caste related historical inquiry in the conviction that it would enrich the existing scholarship on the subject or the theme concerned.

Influence of various historical forces that were responsible for bringing forth changes in an established pattern of social life cannot be effectively studied within a briefly demarcated time period as said already. To understand the process of change, one has to know in detail the elements that form the composite culture as well as the roots of each separate element. After all, history is a dialogue between the past and the present. Therefore, the dialogue of one point of time with another – both situated in different periods in a linear pattern – has to be minutely observed in order to carve out a holistic picture of the social life in a general and cultural setting in particular. At the same time, while creating a broader canvass or time-frame for writing the history, it would be highly ambitious to bring in minute detail of all the information pertaining to the focus area. Nevertheless, major currents that condition the course of history have to be given adequate space along with the parallel developments.

While dealing with conversion into Christianity or Islam one has to bear in mind that they are foreign religions. Particularly, Christianity in its second wave – if one accepts early conversion during I Century A.D. – reached India via Europe. The scriptures and sacraments were largely adopted in the Latin language while the missionaries who came to spread the religion spoke in *Portuguese, French,* and other *European languages.* Even the caste documents at the *Parathavar Jati Thalaivanar's* house are available only in these languages apart from the native language Tamil.[7] Translated works whatsoever that are available such as *Documenta Indica, Letters of St. Francis Xavier and other Jesuit Missionaries* are limited. Learning these languages and translating these documents is not a simple work that could be performed by an individual researcher. The present researcher is conscious of the fact that without thoroughly exploring and examining such documents, even hypothetical justice cannot be achieved. Therefore, the present perspective has only the advantage of professionally viewing the particular people's history from their angle.

The present subject of research – the Parathavars – was chosen when the research scholar was an M. Phil scholar at *St. Joseph's College, Trichy* in August 2004. Being partially exposed to the community's life, the researcher looked for secondary sources to expand the horizon of understanding on the subject concerned and found a very less number of scholarly works. Significant among them was Patrick Roche's, *Fishermen of the Coromandel-A Social Study of the Paravas of the Coromandel* which informed about the *Parathavar* history since their conversion in the first quarter of the 16th century. As a lay insider, the researcher also shared the common notion of the community attributing the conversion process as an initiative of *St. Francis Xavier* – an idea built and spread parallel to that of the concept of chosen people. But it was the work of *A. Patrick Roche* which for the first time informed the present researcher the fact that the *Parathavar* conversion was an event that took place before the arrival of *St. Francis Xavier.* Being a work of anthropological nature, it evoked interest in knowing the past of the Parathavars before the event of conversion and comparing it with the socio-cultural changes that took place after conversion. An important work that enabled a comparative understanding of the social life of the *Parathavars* with fishing folk was *Dhananjayan's Kulakuriyeealum, Meenavar Valakarugalum.* In the capacity of a folklorist, the scholar was able to provide useful hints on the worship patterns that existed before *Sangam* period.

During the M. Phil research period, many important works in the field were beyond access though they provide invaluable information about the people under study. Of late, these are easily available owing to the advancement in technology. Despite certain limitations, these web-based resources like *jstor* and *google book* search have made researching easier.[8] An article entitled *Remarks on the Origin and History of the Parawas* published as early as 1837 by *Simon Casie Chitty* in the *Journal of the Royal Asiatic Society of Great Britain and Ireland* (Vol. 4, No.5) gave sufficient introduction about the subject matter. Similarly, *S.B. Kaufmann's* article, *A Christian Caste in Hindu Society: Religious Leadership and Social Conflict among the Paravas of Southern Tamilnadu* published in the journal *Modern Asian Studies* (Vol. 15, No.2) was also a significant work. *Susan Bayly's*[9] *Saints, Goddesses and Kings Muslims and Christians in South Indian Society* published in the year 2003 was another major work in thematic book form that cannot be ignored. All the above said inaccessible resources are now easily accessible.

Though there remained a few number of works before the year 2004, they are by no means extensive. It prompted the spirit of inquiry resulting in the serious observing of the social system of the coastal people in order to academically enrich the understanding about them. In a parallel time, a similar spirit was efficiently translated into a Tamil novel by *R.N. Joe D'cruz* who published his work *Aazhi Soozh Ulagu* by November 2004. When in December 2004 *tsunami* ravaged the Tamil Nadu coast the sympathetic world started looking for literature that could well inform about the life pattern of the *Parathavars*. A novel that was released just a month before served a great purpose in a short period of time. The ripples caused by *Tsunami* in the academic circle led towards the publishing of two important books in Tamil both edited by *A. K. Perumal* and published in December 2005. The names of the books are *Kanalam Perunthrai* and *Alaigalinoode* and *N. Ramachandran* and *N. Stephen* have co-edited them with *A. K. Perumal.* Subsequently, *R. N. Joe D'cruz* also released his voluminous novel *Korkai* in December 2009.

Apart from the books mentioned above, *D.P. Chattopadyay's* translated book *Madhamum, Samugamum* was instrumental in shaping the design of the research. A Marxist by ideological disposition, *D.P. Chattopadyay* with his thorough reading of the works of archaeologist and historian *Gordon Childe* and anthropologist like *L.H. Morgan* was able to arrive at certain definite conclusions about the evolution of socio-religious life in India from the ancient times. The nature of his observations was overarching and highly applicable to the study of religious conversions. Therefore the present researcher in that sense was indebted to him.

The secondary works of diverse disciplinary backgrounds are significant in their ability to provide clues for the gap that exists in the historical process. Particularly, the chief primary sources that inform about the history of the *Parathavars* are not available without a break. *Pattupattu* and *Ettuthogai* collections which are chiefly categorized as *Sangam* literature have parallels coming from foreign notices. Works of *Pliny,* the anonymous author of the *Periplus of the Erythrean Sea, Strabo, Arrian, Megasthenes* and others shed light on the early life pattern of the people settled at the coast. Apart from these *copper plates* and *archaeological evidence* chiefly based on ceramics attain importance as source material. Nevertheless, valuable information of these kinds is not available to develop continuity of historical explanation for the subsequent periods. Primary sources that appear after periods of gaps such as *Periya Puranam* from where fragments of *Parathava Puranam* and *Valaiveesu Puranam* are traced, *Muthollayiram, Travels of Marco Polo* and *Jesuit Letters* are suggestive of the opinion that there could only be certain episodes in the history of the *Parathavars*.[10]

The gaps that stem out of source material can be mended by using clues that come out of the creative and imaginative capacity of the individual authors. *G.A. Oddie* in his editorial note in the book *Religion in South Asia* mentions about the challenge of *Robin Horton*[11] to scholars to survey the mode of life before conversion and relate it with changes after conversion of religion. A challenge of this kind can effectively be handled only by researchers in the field of history. It also would contribute towards a holistic study of the subject.

In order to connect various articles published during different time periods the thread that possibly weaves them together has been traced. Apart from others, the major link is provided by religion. Hence research questions chiefly based on religion and religious conversion have been asked. They are like whether or not the religious conversion of the *Parathavars* was a directed social action imparted by the needs generated in the sphere of the economy? Whether or not religious conversion tended to bring forth structural changes in the cultural-core of the *Parathavar* people? Whether or not the adoption of a new religion by a defined group of people can be geographically mapped? Whether or not prior to the adoption of *Christianity,* the *Parathavar* people had an independent and vibrant economy? Whether or not the access to *Brahminical* gods remained within reach for the *Parathavar* people before conversion into *Christianity?* Whether or not despite economic development, the nature of the society remained tribal. Whether or not the liberal approach of the *Portuguese* towards the natives was instrumental in causing religious conversion? Whether or not there were identifiable parallels between the Bhakti Movement and the activities of St. Francis Xavier? Whether or not since there was no substantial change in the basic tools of production, the socio-cultural changes brought about by religious conversion were only marginal?

New interpretations like what has been argued by *Robin Horton* cannot be arrived at merely through an intensive re-reading of the sources. Further to that, meeting of the people in their historical setting and outside of it is equally pertinent. In that way, it becomes an interdisciplinary writing involving elements of literature and anthropology. Historical research carried out by peers and contemporaries are predominantly cautious about chronology. But in the present book neither strict adherence to *chronological narration* nor a thorough *back-walking* method is followed. Since the articles are based on elusive dialogue between the past and the present overlapping of both methods of presentation naturally emerge. By that, history writing could be prevented from becoming more particular on certain elements than the overall sketching of the course.

The inductive method based on *Cartesian* style of historiography dominates and guides research in contemporary academic life. Observations whatsoever recorded in the past tend to suffer certain limitations. Such observations converted into letters are neither the voice of the people from the below nor the outcome of the dialogue between them and the elite. In the case of conversion, the chief sources are foreign notices and Jesuit letters. It may throw some light on the general livelihood but not their entire and exact history. When one conducts field work and deducts data from the past, a clear gap between the actual life and depicted life is found.

In an argument with as great a historian as *Ranabir Chakravarthy*[12] narrated the following event in the life of yet another significant historian, 'Ashin Das Gupta.' In his own words "Ashin Das Gupta completed his master's degree with flying colours and approached one of his favourite teachers for registering his Ph. D. degree. His teacher who is usually a kind and patient man shouted at him and said to get out. Das Gupta did not crack an argument with his teacher. Rather, he gave a patient thought over why his teacher was shouting at him and attempted to find meaning to his teacher's words. Then he was convinced that his teacher is expecting him to get out of the nation for research. Ashin Das Gupta left for *Europe* and viewed the Indian coast from the archives in *Portugal."*

In the present researcher's opinion, it is from the coast one has to go to the Archives as far as maritime history is concerned. Archival records are many a time deceptive and too elitist in nature. Thorough understanding of the lives of people by constant observation and interaction facilitates cross-referring of information gathered from archival material. In yet another discussion with *Harbans Mukhia*[13], another historian of standing, the present researcher learned the importance of popular history. By that he means that there is common sharing of certain information about the past in any society – particularly organically united developing societies – which is believed to be the most authentic source of history. It may grossly differ and stand in contrast with research based academic history and it would be very difficult to convince the people on what they believe are not true. Nevertheless, there remains some important meaning within the information which a historical researcher cannot ignore.

In the case of the present research, one of the informants – a retired teacher and presently successful businessman – when asked why the town was named as *Veerapandianpattanam,* he related it with *Veerapandya Kattabomman* who lived by the end of 18th Century A.D.[14] *St. Francis Xavier* who visited this town in mid-16th Century A.D. mentions it as *Veerapandianpattanam.* When the informant was given an explanation about the difference in time he was not able to argue while at the same time he is not also changing his views. However, a significant aspect that has to be observed is the penetration of the icon of *Veerapandya Kattabomman* into the memory of the respondent. This may even be an impact of folk tales or a famous feature film. The researcher's ability lies in connecting the memory of individuals, and thereby, outlines the memory of the collective wherein he could relate his own memory as well.

Human brain looks for a space to accommodate a historically important person within the geographical sphere to which it is well acquainted. *Veerapandianpattanam* is located between *Panchalankurichi* and *Tiruchendur,* the former place is *Kattabomman's* headquarter and the latter is his guardian deity's abode frequently visited on pilgrimage. Here, though *Veerapandyan* of the *later Pandyas* on whose commemoration the place is named is forgotten. Yet another icon replaces it; which can be related to the caste system on the one hand and on the other with the national movement.

In contrast to popular history, the spirit of renaissance – that ushered in the era of colonialism – evoked a sense of scientific history in Europe. Since then adequate works that have dealt with the nature of every colonial country and their motives have been published. Whether or not introducing of their faith among natives was part and parcel of their exploiting mechanism or not? was in itself a major question handled differently by scholars of varied backgrounds and ideologies. However, the basis of present research is religious conversions can be best explained through what can be termed as '*encounter historiography*' in this case between the *Parathavar's* on one-side and the *Portuguese* and other *Europeans* on the other side.

The influence of *D.P. Chattopadyay's* arguments based on 'discoveries impacting upon other activities of man' tends to guide the course of research. In the case of the coastal areas, though the production of common salt did not require exploring of the sea, the diversified economic living style seemed to have begun with the boats. The selection of wood for the making of boats of higher durability was not always available locally and required the dependence on forests located far away. In the *Pearl Fishery Coast,* apart from fishing, *pearl* and *chank* diving emerged as important occupations responsible for the flourishing of internal and external trade what eventually caused encounter among various civilizations and cultures.

In a lecture programme, *Rowena Robinson* elaborated upon the usefulness of the comparative method in understanding religious conversion.[15] The present researcher asked her about the nature of comparison that she was speaking about – whether it is comparing the elements of the social life before and after conversion or it is just comparing the elements of the social life of converts and non-converts or it means comparing of different denominational followers of the same religion? Being a sociologist *Rowena* seems to have not laid much stress on the first part of the present researcher's question. She gave a thought about the comprehensive nature of the question appreciatively and remarked what made the researcher think in such a way? In social sciences, only historians could think about the comprehensive nature of events like conversion. Particularly, the *French Annales School* of thought outlines the importance of *Comparative History.* Eminent historian *D.D. Kosambi's* success is grounded in such an approach. Inspired by the trends as said above, the present researcher also seeks to give adequate scope for the *Comparative Method.*

With these convictions, the present researcher undertook four seasons of field visits in the *Pearl Fishery Coast.* Important coastal settlements between *Vembar* in the North and *Manapad* in the South were visited. The researcher most often masked his identity as an insider and at times revealed it. A thorough understanding of the contemporary issues[16] affecting the community was made prior to the field visits and discussions were initiated on them. Instead of a monotonous discussion, an argument was put forth by making critical remarks while cautiously maintaining a balance to check the course of the discussion turning into offensive. The different modes on which the discussions were made guided to reach the fabric of their cultural core. It was realized that the ideas collected in such varied emotional backgrounds would help in examining the effect of the encounter with the west.

A logical sequence has to be established in order to accommodate a series of articles published in different time period into a single book. As such, the search is made in every article pertaining to the core subject matter they deal with. In that search, it was found that the articles provide answers to certain basic questions like how, who, why and what. History is an unending dialogue between the past and present. The very title of the book is suggestive of a momentum towards Latinization from a Utopian beginning. Moreover, it is the identity in the present which assumes importance the past as it is a subject matter of social sciences in general and interdisciplinary research in particular. Hence, the theoretical study on 'how' is logically placed first. The article entitled **Religious Conversion of the Parathavars: Towards a Theoretical Understanding** published in *South Indian Folklorist* examines the character and nature of the factors that culminated in Latinization. Whatsoever, it does not deviate from the method and approach followed by researchers in the field of history as it incorporates sufficient level of primary data.

The identity of people directly traceable from a remote past provides scope for debate. In the case of the Parathavars, they were commonly referred at the least from the Sangam Period. Yet, scholarly minds from within the community attempted to view beyond Sangam period and explored the possibility of either being trajectory to Aryan culture or part of the Dravidian way of life. Unfortunately, they were not able to arrive at a unanimous and definite conclusion. However, given the fact that the cultural life holds impact of different ancient streams one cannot altogether ignore the debate. Therefore, this researcher also located himself in the debate and took a pertinent angle in an article. In 2011, he along with Prof. Dr. K.A. Manikumar edited and published the book **Southern Tamil Nadu through the Ages** wherein his personal article dealt with the subject. Nevertheless, while he preferred to entitle the article as **Historiography on Origin: the Aborigine Vs Foreign Debate in the History of the Parathavars** the co-editor when bringing out the book changed the title as **History of the Parathavar: A differing Interpretation.** In this book, the said article has been updated and accorded the former title.

People irrespective of wherever they originated tended to settle in particular regions with the evolution of technology that was followed by geographical loyalty. The Sangam literature projects the Parathavars as chief inhabitants of the coastal stretch of the Tamil country that included the Malabar Coast. But with time only those who settled on the *Pearl Fishery Coast* carried the Parathavar identity. It is not to state that there was a total absence of migration among them. A considerable number of Tamil people who resided on the Sri Lankan Coast parallel to the *Pearl Fishery Coast* called themselves *Parathavar*. Issues and ideas pertaining to this remain largely untouched by scholarly minds. Hence, in October 2012 an article entitled **Time, Space and Life: Early Parathavars of the Pearl Fishery Coast** was published in the journal *Indian Historical Studies* taking into purview aspects pertaining to historical geography.

Unless economic factors support, settling down in a geographical area could not be imagined. Supply of fish – a rich source of protein the consumption of which was thought to be a parameter of rich life by several ancient societies – over and above sustenance level contributed initially for barter.

Subsequently, manufacture of salt played an important role in the preservation of the mainstay of food as also inland trade. These developments were followed by *Pearl-diving,* trade, etc and the power axis based on that. Developments as such – as chiefly Marxist ideology states – had severe impacts on socio-religious and political life. Hence, this article on economy entitled **Surplus Formation and Beyond: Understanding the Economic Life of the Parathavars before Conversion** published on September 2013 in the *Journal of Indian History and Culture* is placed after articles on Origin and Historical Geography and before articles on Religion and Society.

Economic development is dependent on the improvement of tools of production. Tools contribute for the shifting of lifestyle with considerable bearing on the belief system. As several kinds of tools withstand time and coexist with the specific tools of the time, the belief system also is marked by variety and coexistence of different ideas pertaining to the external. They further play a vital role in the construct of individual identity and identity of groups within larger society. Such difference in identity constructs is characterized by alliance and conflict in society. Hence, observing of the aspects of religion is a precondition to the study of social formation and change. This observation was attempted in the article entitled **From Totemic Worship to Sanskritic Gods: A Study of Religious Practices of Early Parathavar** published in the book **Images and Imprints in History** released in 2015.

One of the chief tools of from the Sangam period that survived the onslaught of time is the catamaran. As Marxist historians like D.D. Kosambi and R.S. Sharma perceive without the change in the basic tool of production there could be hardly any change in the social system. Even if there appears to be a change in the social system without change in the tools of production such change could only be accounted as superficial. Therefore, literary evidence of the past pertaining to change can be cross-examined by conducting field visits and assessing the life pattern of the people. With such an approach the article entitled **Class Structure, Social Values, Gift Giving: An Ethnographic Study of the Social Life of the Parathavars** was published in the journal *Indian Historical Studies* of April 2015.

Coastal life was constantly exposed to external influences and gradual change was evident. The cultural pattern was such that it accepted factors suitable for the people and rejected unsuitable elements. However, sixteenth century for the *Pearl Fishery Coast* was unique. The *Christian-Portuguese* and *Muslim-Arabs* who carried the scars of the crusade wars assumed new positions in the *Pearl Fishery Coast* and attempted to monopolize trade to their advantage. This adversely affected the *Parathavars* to which the invasion of *Vijayanagar Empire* added injury. All of this culminated in a riot to the response of which the *Parathavars* sought diplomatic ties with the *Portuguese* and offered to adopt *Christianity*. Trends as such were discussed in the article entitled **Embracing Christianity: Tracing Parathavar Conversion in the Light of Sixteenth Century Socio-Political Ruptures** published in the *Journal of Indian History and Culture* of September 2014.

Once after adopting *Christianity* the new converts remained largely unaware of the tenets of the new religion. Priests with missionary zeal were the demand of the time for *Roman Catholic* sect prescribed life rituals like *Baptism, Holy-Communion,* etc which can only be attained through them. *Xavier* was one among the *European* volunteers who offered to spread the religion to remote places like India at the call of *Ignatius Loyola* who founded the order of the *Society of Jesus*. No doubt, *Xavier* served the people with dedication and initiated reformative measures, but his being accorded sainthood caused the evolution of folklore on his personality comparable with *Jesus Christ* himself and developed an image that surpassed the services of other missionaries. An exploration into St. Francis Xavier's contributions have been attempted in the article entitled **St. Xavier: A Lesser Known Reformer of the Parathavar Community** published in the book **From the Fathoms to the Front: Lesser Known Facets of Social Reform in South India** of 2012.

Whether or not the adoption of *Christianity* at the aegis of the *Portuguese* instigated far-reaching change and took the *Parathavar's* closer to the former's level of development is a pertinent question that examines the logic behind religious conversion. *Parathavar* families with *Portuguese* titles emerged as the latter came forward to play the role of *Godfathers* during *baptism*. Though gestures like these depicted the *Portuguese* as people standing above the *colonial* idea of *racism*, the inner motive could be one of exploiting the proceeds of the *Pearl Fishery Coast*. Thus the adoption of *Portuguese* family names would remain only superficial. In the place of economic change based on the introduction of newer and advanced tools and trading ideas by the *Portuguese* that had repercussive effect on the spheres of religion and society, the evolution of colonial ambition that revolved around the economic benefit of the *Pearl Fishery Coast* could have caused adverse effects. Inquiry of such aspects has been made in the article entitled **Latinization at Crossroads: A Study of Post-Conversion Changes among the Parathavars of the Pearl fishery Coast** published in the journal **Indian Historical Studies** of October 2015. The findings of every article are assessed in the common conclusion wherein logic of continuity of articles published in different time periods is attempted.

Endnotes

1   K. Rajan, *Situating the Beginning of Early Historic Times in Tamil Nadu: Some Issues and Reflections*, Social Scientist, (________) p. 47; the scholar explains the difficulty in designating archaeological finds either in the name of kingdoms or as the Sangam culture. He even states that it is difficult to brand them as belonging to Tamil Culture.

2   Edgar Thurston, *Castes and Tribes of South India Vol. VI* (Madras: Government Press, 1909), pp. 140–146; although the community spread out to other parts of Tamil Nadu, Kerala, Karnataka and Sri Lanka they trace their origin from the Pearl Fishery Coast.

3   Edgar Thurston, *Castes and Tribes of South India Vol. Vii,* (Madras: Government Press, 1909), pp. 140–146.

4   During the heydays of trade, there were migrations from the coast to the plains chiefly guided by trade. Graphic detail of Parathavar trade in the city of Madurai was found in Maduraikanci. Korkai was the major port and capital of the pearl-fishing activities. But now sea has receded by about 7 kilometers that gave prominence to port like Kulasekarapattinam. As far as the inland

trade was concerned, even today Parathavar settlements can be observed in places away from the coast like Palayamkottai, Pettai, Kottar, etc.

5   V. Sridhar, Op. Cit., p._, the author states that the Christians have had better access to health and education in contrast to others that resulted in the control of deaths resulting in physical longevity and better living standard respectively. This in the eyes of others has created suspicion and misunderstanding.

6   Prior to the conversion to Christianity, Islam was the major religion that attracted a good number of the coastal people. Important settlements of the Muslims in the coast are Kayalpattnam and Keelakarai. Their pre-conversion kinship is maintained by mutual addressing of the male members by the term chacha although both communities form separate endogamous groups.

7   S.B. Kaufmann, A Christian Caste in a Hindu Society: Religious Leadership and Social Conflict among the Paravas of Southern Tamil Nadu, *Modern Asian Studies*, Vol. 15, No. 2 (1981), p. 208.

8   These search engines facilitate in referring back-issues of important journals. But many social science based journals, proceeding volumes, etc published from India in general and Tamil Nadu in particular, are not converted into e-format. Yet ignored are the articles that appear in Tamil languages whose value cannot be underestimated. It is a handicap in research which has to be addressed.

9   The expansion of the initial of the author *S.B. Kaufmann* is *Susan Bayly* probably both denote the same person.

10   D.D. Kosambi, *An Introduction to the Study of Indian History*, (Bombay: Popular Prakashan, 2002) p. 1.

11   G.A. Oddie (ed.), *Religion in South Asia,* (New Delhi: Manohar, 1991), pp. 8–9.

12   He is the author of books like *Trade in Early India*. The argument took place during the Refresher Course mentioned above also at UGC – ASC, JNU, New Delhi between 24/08/2009 and 18/09/2009.

13   Discussion with him also took place during the Refresher Course at UGC – ASC, JNU, New Delhi between 24/08/2009 and 18/09/2009; he spoke about the fieldwork he conducted in a slum near Qutb Minar where the local community identified a place where Qutb-ud-din Aibek was supposed to have been born.

14   Interview with Mr. Joseph Gregory Babylaus Fernando (72), Resident of Veerapandianpattanam on 02/01/2010.

15   She is the author of important books like *Christians of India* and *Sociology of Religions in India*. The present researcher had the opportunity of meeting her during a Refresher Course at UGC – ASC, JNU, New Delhi between 24/08/2009 and 18/09/2009

16   Contemporary issues include educational backwardness of the community, limitations of the modernization of the fishing industry, development of ports such as Tuticorin and Collachal, perils of being gunned down by Sri Lankan Navy in the sea, conflict between fishermen of

mechanized boats and country boats, conflict between coastal hamlets on the using of certain types of nets etc. By the time of crafting this thesis in ink, a massive movement sparked at Idinthakarai against the nuclear power plant at Koodankulam in Tirunelveli District. The present researcher twice visited Idinthakarai as an observer.

I

Religious Conversion of the Parathavars:
Towards a Theoretical Understanding

Introduction

The study of 'the choice of religion' pertaining to individuals and groups remain a complex area in the field of research in social sciences. It becomes more so in a multi-layered society like that of India, what is structured on the basis of caste. In such a social context, adherence to a particular religion by individuals is suggestive of their psychological positioning within the ascribed caste as well as the broader society. Similarly, as far as the relocation of a caste from one religion to another is concerned, what has to be remembered is the fact that, it takes place in the presence of other castes. Scholars are of the opinion that within these two broad outlines, there could be overlap and unpredictable stages.[1] For a researcher in history, the historical background in which the event of conversion takes place and its possible effects are important aspects of the study. The issue of the conversion of the Parathavars contains a historical cause and effect, the latter being not adequately dealt.[2]

In the first quarter of the sixteenth century, the Parathavars who are chiefly located in the Pearl Fishery Coast converted to the Roman Catholic faith under the aegis of the Portuguese. The conversion of the Parathavar community has been conventionally treated as mass conversion. It is widely viewed both as the reaction to the onslaught of the Muslims and as the rebellion against the fellow Hindus. Yet theoretical understanding about the religious conversion of this particular kind is also limited. While bringing the study of religious conversion within the purview of social history, the particular elements have to be stressed in the broader canvass provided by the general. The idea of 'particular' discussed here specifies the rise of a new form of regularity in human behaviour within the broader society. In the opinion of the present researcher including of the irregularities, if any, apart from the regularities alone would guide drawing of a holistic picture of history. An attempt has been made in the present article towards capturing that. Such realization has to be substantiated with theorization, in order to broaden the understanding of religious conversion as the component of economy and polity. The complex nature of the subject matter cannot be effectively addressed without adopting an inter-disciplinary approach.

Over and above all that has been discussed, the present article is drafted in reaction to the introduction written by G. A. Oddie in his edited book entitled Religion in South Asia revised and published in the year 1991. In the introduction, he discusses important scholars who have researched on religious conversion namely, A.D. Knock, W.H. Clark, Hardy, Robin Harton, Richard Eaton, Downs, Zelliot, Duncan Forrester etc. Among them except Robin Horton, all others have ignored the importance of pre-conversion background. Oddie also discusses the conversion of the Parathavars whose views suffer certain limitations, for in his judgment the community was staunchly Catholic and he is ignorant of reconversion.[3] In reality, there had been reconversion into Protestant faith among the entire Parathavars of Pazhyakayal and into Hinduism among a section of Parathavars belonging to Idinthakarai apart from what remain independent conversions of individuals into the multitude of denominations born in the recent past. In such a background, the present researcher intends to explore and test the applicability of some of the ideas of religious conversions indirectly while narrating the history of Parathavar conversion chronologically.

Though convinced of the role of the economy in conditioning events like 'religious conversion,' the individuality of the researcher has been asserted by way of using social factors of evaluation such as power,[4] conflict,[5] accommodation,[6] acculturation[7] and assimilation.[8] This may again help in identifying the comprehensiveness of the issue under focus as crucial part of social history.[9] The primary sources that have been used for the study include the Travel Accounts of Marco Polo, Letters of Francis Xavier, Notice board information from some of the Churches located in the Pearl Fishery Coast and a few interviews. In the course of the writing, the terms missionary and priest are indiscriminately used. Scholarly writings of B.D. Chattopadyaya, Patrick Roche, A. Sivasubramanian, S.A.A. Rizvi, Rowena Robinson, George Mathew, David Mosse and others have guided the elements of discussion. The article has been structured on the basis of contextualizing conversion followed by inquiries based on the economic dimension of conversion, and discussions on cult worship. Through such classifications, chief questions like, whether or not the Portuguese attempted to acculturate the Parathavars, how the community adjusted itself in the conversion process and how conflicts were resolved at the group level when it was branded as 'mass conversion' were evoked in the article.

Contextualizing Conversion

From the beginning of the historical period, every man and woman in the sub-continent were born into a faith that conditioned both their world view and beyond that. The Vedic religion that had its spread in the northern part of India in the centuries before the Christian era evolved ideas of admitting the members through conducting a ceremony at childhood known as Upanayana. Excepting the Sudras and the outcastes, the members of the first three varnas enjoyed the privilege of Upanayana wherein a sacred thread was twined across the body. In short, a differentiation on the basis of Aryan vs. non-Aryan was created. The Aryans developed several other practices which became their exclusive perquisite. It attracted the rest of the population who were excluded from this process. They had their own pattern of worship marked by regional variation. These people of the local cult worship firmly believed that with their ability to adopt the practices of the Aryans their social status improved. This process was denoted as Sanskritization what was suggestive of the fluid nature of the social system.

The Aryans and non-Aryans constituted a way of life what came to be later called Hinduism. The Vedic fire-cult and the Brahmanic rituals found their easy way into Hinduism and tended to dominate. It incorporated the local gods and equated them with the Vedic divinities based on common attributes. Within this broader category, a prescribed method of admitting the members was not evolved.[10] Even after the emergence of heterodox sects, a formal system of converting the followers of other religions was not thought about. However, the fluidity of the system allowed travel between various sects without much difficulty. The predominance of the idea of Karma linked the diverse sects than separating them. Though there were six chief schools of philosophy within Hinduism, the idea of Karma came to dominate the minds of the followers. The fundamental philosophy of the heterodox sects that emerged as protest movements did not shift from it. The incorporation of deity worship in the heterodox sects had its own impact on Hinduism what reacted by accommodating the icons of the former in its own pantheon that developed over a period of time. Therefore there was no real need for religious conversion at one period of time.

The very fluidity responsible for free mobility between religions at the level of the common man was put to effective check with the concretization of the caste system. Being a fundamental social reality in the sub-continent, caste attributed duties for every member within it. At the level of the individual, the caste infused a certain degree of independence. But families have to essentially confirm to its commands. A father of a girl who was believed to have violated the rules of caste cannot hope to get his daughter married. Therefore, those who believed in the principles of other religions remained 'secret disciples'[11] and it was doubtful whether they were taken seriously in the case of being revealed.

Through the description above, a positive impression about the relatively tolerant nature of the society was only normal. The absence of a fully recognized spiritual head[12] sitting over the shoulder of the ruler and compelling him to frame orthodox religious policy added to the tolerant appearance of the society and state. This matrix was believed to have changed with the arrival of the Muslims into the sub-continent. But in fact, the first bhakti movement that occurred in the South took Hinduism not only to an intellectual plane and undermined the importance of other religions, but also caused religious bigotry.[13] The developments in the south had its repercussive effect in the north. Particularly with the end of the era of powerful states compounded with the invasion of the Muslims in the early medieval period, the religious policy gradually turned orthodox. There was a high frequency of conversion to Islam and recantation.[14] In response, the process of reconversion was made difficult[15] and the social texture became more martial.

The Muslims who established their rule in India were not sons of the soil and they brought with them new religion and language and thereby introduced a new culture. They gave back seat to martial exploits over diplomacy which projected them in a darker shade in the observation of the natives. They ruled the land according to the tenets of the Hanafi law and extended protection to the infidels or the non-Muslims after collecting the Jaziya tax. Proselytization[16] remained a mechanism in the arm of the state to check religious excesses. They resorted to force, discriminatory laws, threats and inducements to spread the faith.[17] The primary motive of such efforts was to have an allegiance of at the least a handful of natives but not converting all the people, and thereby, founding a thoroughly Islamic state.[18] In reality, those who converted to Islam for the sake of political or economic benefits did not find wide favor from the Muslim rulers. This was not to say that there was no systematic effort of conversion at all. But the chief target groups were the followers of local cults rather than members of established religions.[19] These converts rarely became immediate contestants for access to political power.

In the perception of the non-Islamic population, every individual Muslim was viewed in terms of the military power of the Muslim rulers. In order to check the influence of the majority from going beyond control, the Muslim rulers resorted to desecration of their holy places from time to time. There were present certain mechanisms to ease out the possible tension that would have ensued from out of the differences between the followers of different religions. The local converts who could not ignore the social reality of caste looked back into their respective communities for the purpose of marriage. Over and above all these developments, the second bhakti movement that started in the north and the spread of the idea of some of the Sufi thinkers created a favorable climate for social harmony.

It can be inferred from the discussions made above that 'religious conversion' was linked to the secular stand of the state as well than merely impinging on the social fabric. But there was always a wavering tendency in terms of the state policy. For instance, during the rule of the Mughal emperor Akbar, the Jesuits were able to orally get consent for preaching the tenets of Christianity and convert the people. But the official who was responsible for issuing the imperial order refused to perform the work saying, 'whatever the monarch thought he decrees, but we officials apply rationality to his thoughts and issue or do not issue orders according to the need of the prevailing situation of the nation.'[20]

The Pearl Fishery Coast was not an exemption to the diversified trend that characterized the subcontinent. It was a land that also witnessed the contestation of several castes. From its very inception, Islam had its impact in the region via Arab traders[21] followed by Muslim invaders who at one point of time founded the Sultanate of Madurai. In the period under focus i.e. the first half of the sixteenth century, the Battle of Tamiraparani divided it into two with Punnaikayal as the boundary between the state of Kayathar Pandyans and the state of Travancore.[22] The policy of the former state did not suit the conversion agenda[23] of the Portuguese missionaries whereas the latter provided favorable space. The differential treatment stemmed chiefly from the economic needs. The Portuguese were able to pulse the weakness of some of the states and by virtue of their superiority in the economic front placed themselves like their Muslim counterparts and modeled their conversion pattern in the shade of the latter to have loyal supporters.[24]

Economic Undercurrent of Conversion

Changes that occurred in the economic structure – in this context changes that were brought about with the arrival of the Muslims and Portuguese – had its own reflections in the socio-religious processes.

While explaining the link between economy and religion, D.P. Chattopadyaya propounded that there had been only two historical stages in human life; one based on mystical performances and the other marked by the faith of a god's spirit coming in contact with men.[25] He also opined that the priests were only experts who alter the superstructures according to the need of the economy.[26] When these ideas were applied in the context of the Pearl Fishery Coast, what can be observed was the fact that it mostly remained a lucrative spot of thriving trade wherein almost every enterprise required group effort inclusive of the role of the priests. In the period prior to conversion, excessive wealth generated by the trading activities caused arrogance and degeneration at various levels and the priests related themselves in the process chiefly as shark-charmers and took a handsome share in the harvest of the pearls.[27]

The first bhakti movement to an extent was responsible for social changes that could not perfectly synchronize with the developments in the sphere of economy.[28] It provided scope for the Muslims to establish their sway over the Pearl Fishery Coast. Their arrival to the Pearl Fishery Coast was the major encounter experienced by the Parathavars that caused a level of acculturation notably before contact made with the Portuguese. A section of the Parathavars converted to Islam through which they established access to the resources of the larger Muslim community and consequently were able to come out of the degeneracy.[29] The Muslim population was pooled at Kayalpattinam which emerged as a major port known for its wealth.

Islam introduced powerful symbols in the day to day life of its followers that not only distinguished them from others but also constantly and indirectly spread the message of their trade potential and military might. A lifestyle akin to the Arabs what can be termed as Arabization gradually evolved. It was reflected in the dress pattern of men and women, everyday worship pattern, food habits and architectural style. Through these, they developed a sense of brotherhood above the caste structure the idea of which stood on the grounds sharing fortunes and misfortunes in the economic front as it was present among the tribes. Every Muslim was trained to address his fellow member of the religion as a brother. The culmination of all these over a period of time inverted the socio-cultural practice of the converts to the extent of making them adapt to parallel-cousin marriage.[30]

A situation of confrontation in the first quarter of the sixteenth century with the Muslims forced the Parathavars to take serious decisions.[31] They were convinced about the prevailing insecurity in the faith with which they were associated. They could have surrendered to the Muslims offering themselves to convert. But voluntary surrender would have caused sudden and unexpected changes in the cultural pattern to which they had developed an aversion over a period of time earlier.[32] The only hope was to get the support of a power equal in capacity to that of the Muslims. The Portuguese were the only available option. Interestingly, before the Battle of Tamiraparani held in 1532, the Parathavars inhabited an undivided land and constituted a nation unto themselves[33] within the framework of one of the Pandyan kingdoms.[34] They had a leader popularly known as Pandyapathy who exercised control over the village level local leaders. The Pandyapathy seemed to have taken an active role in negotiating with the Portuguese and guided the Parathavars into the process of conversion.[35] Thus the community en masse politically negotiated with the Portuguese who in turn came forward to protect the Parathavars if they accept to embrace Christianity.

The nature of the 'political negotiation' between the Parathavars and the Portuguese stood beyond the conventional understanding of the trends of conversion. Firstly, it was believed that the Christians had better access to economic resources[36] meaning they had a better chance of modernizing and thereby improving the life standards. But the encounter with the Portuguese might have created a few affluent men on the coast but it did not cause the modernization of the fishing enterprise wherein majority of the Parathavar people were engaged. The viewing of the powers of the Portuguese as their own was only symbolic. Secondly, historians like Richard Eaton were of the opinion that, medieval conversions took place in slower phase among groups against individuals, and therefore, did not attract the attention of the rulers.[37] The conversion of the Parathavars took place overnight and was swift. It did not attract the immediate attention of the rulers owing to the unstable political situation. However, by the time of the arrival of Francis Xavier, the army of the Vijayanagar rulers attacked the Parathavars for their adopting Christianity.[38] The Portuguese defended them during such attacks.

The consolidation of the process of conversion was envisaged by the Jesuit priests among who Francis Xavier was the earliest. As said already, the key role of the priests in society was to modify the lives of the people according to the need of the economy. In fact, they believed that through conversion, the economy of the converts was linked with their own and did not concern about whether it was made subservient to the colonial economy and undermined the native interests or not.[39] At that point of time, there was the imminent need of loyal and disciplined followers who would support the cause of furthering the interests of the Europeans at large. For example, the habit of consumption was common among the males and females of the Parathavar community. But the habit affected the overall manpower and the basic discipline and loyalty. Whether conscious of this or not, the habit was severely attacked by Francis Xavier.[40] After a generation since Xavier left the Pearl Fishery Coast, the church capitalized on the loyalty of the Parathavars and collected a share of the pearls harvested.[41] Even the traditional practice of attributing a day's yield for a collective cause was used by the Church for its own growth.[42] By and large, unlikely of the Muslims, the Christians were not able to infuse a spirit of unity pivoting on the economy. Rather its priests sowed the seeds of disintegrating the tribal characteristics of the society.

Apart from the not accounting of the offerings made by the Parathavar community to the colonial powers including the Portuguese, it was also widely believed that they were exempted from taxation. It was not true. Collector Lushington in a letter addressed to a missionary clarified it and clearly stated the fact that they were equally bound by the laws of taxation.[43] He also requested the missionaries to propagate the sayings of Jesus about taxation.[44] However, views that postulated the Christians in general, being exempted from uppu-uzhiyam[45] and allowance of property inheritance and succession in favor of women would have been incentives for the Parathavar converts also. Similarly, the chance for evolving their own clothing pattern among Christian converts in contrast from the other lower castes improved their status.[46] Trends like these were instrumental for perceiving Christianity as a Brahmanized religion as viewed by Ambedkar. Above all, the ability of the missionaries and some of the followers to attack the symbols of local power and religion either prompted conversion or retained the converts within the fold.[47]

Role of the Missionaries

The Portuguese in general and the missionaries in particular, attacked the local religions and cults as they considered them pagans.[48] However, their perception was not shaped by a strong understanding of the dynamics of the indigenous faith system that was characterized by mutual transaction among several religions.[49] At the one hand, the foreigners could not identify the practices of the native Christian converts[50] that entered the faith prior to their arrival as part and parcel of their spiritual life and on the other confused the local mother goddess cult as worship of Virgin Mary.[51] In such a complex situation, the question of guiding the faith of the new converts definitely stood on the equilibrium of instability. Although more than a generation's time passed before the arrival of Francis Xavier, the new converts learned only to call themselves Christians and had no knowledge of the basic teachings and doctrines of the religion.[52]

In fact, a sharp distinction was expected at the Portuguese side for the Parathavars shared their living environment with the Muslims with who the former had waged the crusade wars.[53] They even attempted to reform the practices of the early Christians by evolving uniformity among all the Christians by way of introducing Padroado.[54] But these reforms tended to shrink the differences between the Muslims and Christians for both were in essence opposed to iconography and laid much stress on canonisation. Nevertheless, the uniqueness of Christianity rested on its ideas on death and life thereafter. The life message of Jesus Christ on not only death but also on redemption from sin and life after death had contextual relevance for the people of the coast. The Parathavars who chiefly preferred to identify themselves as fishermen always placed their life on the halfway towards death. Their understanding of the uncertainty and brief nature of life made them conscious of the mundane vices to which they had been susceptible to.

The Christian missionaries and priests who represented Christianity introduced the respective domains of the sacred and profane and underlined elements of sin in their life.[55] They cultivated fear in the minds of the followers and capitalized on their ability to forgive the sins. They projected Jesus Christ as the Savior of the oppressed and sinners. The eternal nature of heavenly life at the reach of the suppressed and downtrodden was highlighted.[56] There were initiatives to strike uniformity of social values purged of what the priests thought as wrong.[57] They enforced a system and order among the followers or converts, the foundation of which was erected on making them accept the supremacy of the church above all. Loyalty to the faith was expected to be expressed through attending the holy mass and other sacraments at the minimum on every Sundays and proper payment of the levies imposed by the church. The priests also were able to derive the allegiance of individuals who could either dedicate their time[58] or contribute a part of their wealth to the growth of the church.[59]

The sincere adherents probably were called 'Principal Christians' who remained as prioritized members in the good books of the priest.[60] Being a 'Principal Christian' mattered much in shaping the image of families and individuals.[61] Such image had social implications as well, for it determined the intra-community transaction like marriage.[62] Apart from these, the service personnel employed by the priests such as translators and teachers for the everyday conduct of the activities of the church[63] and the local delegates such as the Adepans and Pattangattis who represented the people to the priest possibly formed part of the 'Principal Christians.'

The social environment was gradually structured with the ideas of the priests and the adaptation and violation of the rules had positive and negative consequences respectively. Nevertheless, it was not without a certain degree of adjustment and accommodation that the priests were able to pull the followers in their line. They were in the realization of the fact that spreading of the doctrines among ignorant people alone was not sufficient to prevent defection from faith. The overarching character of religion as understood by ordinary people rested in its potential to offer remedies for problems external to them. Particularly in a tropical region wherein mother goddess worship developed with its uncompromising ability to cure dreaded disease like chickenpox, the dislocation of that was almost not a possibility.[64] By any means, mother goddess worship can only be replaced. Thus the worship of Mother Mary became central on a parallel mode to the iconography of local cults and of Hinduism. By 1580's the cult of 'Our Lady of Snow' was firmly established at Tuticorin[65] which emerged as the major port town among the Yelu Urs,[66] just forty years since the departure of Francis Xavier.[67]

The priests while making compromises on certain fronts as said above as well as on accommodating sensitive socio-cultural issues like allowing cross-cousin marriage among the natives, maintained even these 'adjustment zones' within the purview of their strict control. They schemed techniques of furthering their control for which even the 'adjustment zones' at times provided opportunity. Importantly, they created an opportunity after the completion of the annual festival of 'Our lady of Snow' at Tuticorin, wherein the 'Principal Christians' were offered the privilege of dining on the table with the priests and thereafter came to be known as Mesakarar. This created a permanent bifurcation on the community and evoked another class of people called Kamarakarar that remained the commoners. The Mesakarar became an endogamous group and the Kamarakarar aspired to reach the status of the former. Since it was believed that the priests had the capacity to reassign the status of groups, both remained loyal to the priests and the church. Most often than not, it reached the extent of undermining the powers of the secular authority at the local level.[68]

The priests also created effective linkages with the power centers and gave an impression of using all of them for the benefit of the community at large that sheltered under their guidance. These power centers included the King of Portugal, Portuguese officials, the native kings who did not stand as a stumbling block in the process of conversion and the business class within the community.[69] These linkages were important to generate the economic resources needed for the establishment of the church. This also improved the image of the priests whose pivotal role within the faith was commonly accepted and hardly challenged. With the strength of these elements at hand, the priests innovatively adopted methods to organize the followers and derive their loyalty. In the local situation, cult worship on various deities was found to be suitable for that purpose.

Adjustments and Compromises

The introduction of cult worship within Christianity was inevitable owing to the differences that emerged among the vested colonial interests on the one hand and the dynamics of caste on the other. The priests of the Roman Catholic order were supposed to respect a hierarchy – except during a brief period in which Portuguese Padraodo was in vogue[70] – at the height of which stood the Pope. Until the emergence of reformation period hardly any king of Europe contested the spiritual authority of the Pope. But the missionaries and priests were not dependent on the Pope for the expected expenses towards the spread of Christianity in general and the cause of conversion in particular. Rather, they relied on the support of the king and his officers. For the officers who professed their first loyalty to the king, conversion of the local population in areas where they established their colonies, was a matter of diplomacy than an official policy. Therefore, most often than not, the aspirations of the missionaries clashed with that of the authorities.[71]

Over and above these limitations of the missionaries rested the fact that they cannot confine their activity only on those areas conquered and directly held under the control of the officers. For reasons of trade, the Portuguese established their centers even in areas where native rulers held sway. The missionaries aspired to penetrate into these regions at the first stretch and aimed at expanding into all places where pagans inhabited. It had to be understood that, every individual missionary was ambitious of expanding the area under the spiritual control of the congregation to which they belonged and thereby spread the holy rule of the Pope despite financial and other assistance coming not directly from the latter.

In places where the Portuguese established a trade center – as in the case of the Pearl Fishery Coast – conversion cannot be made as the missionaries wished.[72] It may be different in the case of the Parathavars for they voluntarily offered themselves for conversion in an utterly chaotic situation characterized by communal strife, riot and severe crisis. With that, the Portuguese took total control of the community to the extent of subsequently making them direct subjects of the Portuguese king.[73] Nevertheless, when the law and order were in place, the native rulers exercised their control over the territories and checked intrusions of all kinds for one of his most important duties was to maintain the status quo in social life. Therefore, the catholic priests understood the limitations before them, identified the priority group, came forward to adjust in certain spheres and schematized strategies of control while adjusting. The cult worship emerged on such accounts.

In fact, the introduction of cult worship provided a harmonious space for the smooth sail of the converts. It was one of the novel strategies as the cult worships had parallels with the native religion and features of legitimizing caste and local leadership was effectively present within it.[74] Some scholars were of the opinion that Hinduism was a multi-tiered system hence the introduction of cult worship and thereby evoking a parallel was impossible.[75] There cannot be a better Brahmanical view than this. Because, for a scholarly community such as the Brahmins at the highest level of society, the multi-tiered dimension of religion was comprehensible. But for the people living on the coast whose priority of religion was only secondary – at least until conversion – it was doubtful whether there had been any such understandings. A non-Brahmin related him with religion only as a two-tiered system. One belonged to the superior class of people i.e. the Brahmins, and another was his own. The integration of the folk-form of worship into a larger body of Hinduism was difficult, for the general tendency of all communities was to reject the faith of those who are considered inferior in the social ranking.[76]

If viewed from the perception of the higher castes, the preaching of the missionaries was highly inflammatory in content. It was very common among the Christian missionaries to question the religious beliefs of the natives if not directly attacked. Irrespective of whether or not, the motive and meaning of such preaching was understood by the target group, by virtue of scholarly understanding of both the religions to a certain extent i.e. Hinduism and Christianity, the higher castes had the capacity to foresee the consequence,[77] for conversion contributed for the cultural assertion of the people of lower castes against the interest of the higher castes. In the case of the Parathavars, there were certainly some differences. Even the Brahmins were dependent upon the share that came out of pearl fishing and both of their settlements remained separated. Therefore the caste domination for which the practitioners of other unclean professions were subjected was not extended upon the Parathavars in the same degree. However, the social position of the traders was checked by introducing curfew on sea-voyage. Ritually they attributed the role of Palanquin bearers[78] in some of the important temples which remained important for the conformation of the subordination of the community to the Brahmin and some of the non-Brahmin castes.

The higher castes in their potential as pressure groups would have provoked the native rulers against the missionaries and the converts. But the nature of the political situation during Parathavar conversion marked by frequent battles demanded every ruler to have trade and military alliance with the Portuguese in which the missionaries meddled – if not on their self-interest on request from the native rulers.[79] As a compromise, the rulers had no choice than allowing at the least conversion of the coastal people whose integration with the mainstream society was not complete although changes of higher magnitude started from the coast.[80]

In such a context, the cult worship was a creative adaptation[81] of both the catholic priests and the followers; insofar it struck a compromise between the Portuguese version[82] of Christianity and the local system of caste. In the early phase, priests like Francis Xavier were against iconography although they permitted prayers on Mother Mary.[83] However, iconography on Our Lady of Snow at Tuticorin, St. Peter and St. Paul at Alandalai, St. Joseph at Veerapandyanpattinam, St. Antony at Oovari, Our Lady of Ransom at Kanyakumari and etc. emerged as one tier of the pattern.[84] Even St. Xavier became an important icon and several myths were evolved on his visit to the Pearl Fishery Coast. More importantly, a hierarchical structure as in Hinduism did not evolve in this pattern of worship. The iconographic approach culminated in the formation of 'cult worship' and some of the cults emerged famous than other. Thus the cult of St. Antony attracted more followers than any other cult. The priests for reasons not clearly known, maintained subtle boundary on cult worship, for the cult of John De Britto that was famous in areas in and north of Ramnad did not penetrate into the Pearl Fishery Coast.

Though followers of a cult could be geographically categorized, a pilgrimage from one church to other during feast occasion was most common. The conducting of feasts by a village was but continuity from the past and they collectively took the god in the Palanquin reflective of their tribal background. In some of the churches, the death of Jesus Christ was represented by maintaining an image of his body in a lifeless state.[85] It enabled to bring the mood of the followers to the basic premise of the religion – death. Nevertheless, the instruction of the principles of the religion remained difficult. Fr. Henri Henriquez attempted to print and circulate the tenets of Christianity.[86] But in a place where literacy was limited to a marginal section of the people, the introduction of drama was thought to be effective. Importantly the life message of Jesus Christ through his death and resurrection was performed occasionally.[87] It gave an impression of returning to the early form of performance based worship pivoted on the devil dancers.[88]

The second tier of the worship pattern was at the individual or family level. Most of the families had the practice of ancestral worship. The souls of persons that died in the recent past were reverentially venerated. Particularly, the worship of dead female girl children and virgins was believed to bring good luck. Therefore, the worship of these dead was made alongside the Christian cult deities. As far as Christianity was concerned, it allowed scope for remembering the dead during 'All Soul's Day' observed every year on 2nd November. But the veneration of the dead by the families was a constant affair and every occasion including in several cases 'every Friday' became an excuse for performing oblations. It was reflective of their belief in life after death without the presence of the idea of 'remaining dead and inactive until the day of judgment.' Unless the attendance of these people to the proceedings of the church was affected, no mechanism seemed to have ever attempted to cleanse these practices of the home.

Throughout the period since conversion, there had been also men who evoked doubts about the rationality behind conversion. These minority sections of people did not altogether reject Christianity. But they secretly accepted the divine power present among the mother goddesses of the local cult such as Kumariamman,[89] Santhanamariamman[90] etc. There were also persons who believed in black magic and at times of economic crisis they turned towards magicians for improving their life condition.[91] But this was again not on a permanent basis and they swiftly returned to their original faith. Since this did not come in open, stemming these practices was also difficult.

Conclusion

The multi-dimensionality of the irregularities present within religious conversion was so intangible that only a brief and general outlook could be sketched. The continuance of belief in karma and life after death compounded with the inability of Christianity to make inroads in the cultural life of the people made clear that the attempt towards uniformity that can be termed as Latinization was really in crossroads. In their role as spiritual mentors, the priests were able to attack the symbols of local cults and religions and tried to have a definite impact on the minds of the followers. But what has to be remembered was the fact that, other communities in the later periods made a promise to convert to Christianity in the very name of the mother goddesses of these backgrounds.[92] Their frame of mind was reflective of the common psyche of the converts.

The Parathavar conversion has to be observed as an adjustment to a situation of conflict wherein they were threatened by the Muslims, followers of the local cults and the Telugu rulers. The only choice with which they were left was to seek protection from the Portuguese. If that was to actually work in order to express their loyalty, they necessarily had to make some compromises or adjustments. Therefore after a political negotiation, they adopted Christianity. But real change at heart remained a perplexing question.

The 'politically negotiated' mass conversion of the Parathavars most possibly did not give expected incentives. The division between the Church and the Portuguese officials failed to capture the true expectations of the people. But the powerful mechanisms that were evolved after the conversion to derive the loyalty of the people prevented them at least for a period of time from converting to other faiths.[93] Therefore, when the Dutch replaced the Portuguese and established their power in Tuticorin, they provoked the Parathavars to reconvert to the Protestant faith. But the internal power created, recognized and left behind by the Portuguese effectively checked defections.[94] There could also have been a realization after the reduced quantum of confrontations with the Muslims that reconversion would not contribute to their improvement. Therefore, the factor of power standing on the premise of access to economic infrastructure had played a major role in conditioning the choice and course of religious conversion when viewed through the Parathavar model.

By any means, conversion did not amount to the extent of altering the total cultural characteristics of the group though there had been attempts in the early phase. The assuming of the Portuguese title by the Parathavars remained symbolic to their adoption of Christianity. But they did not either lose their cultural identity or acquire that of the Portuguese, for, sooner cult worships and other practices patterned on the native style emerged. In that level, it can be ascertained as the mere change of fellowship.[95] This underlines the fact that the conversion did not actually patch up the Parathavars with the Portuguese and until last the native element in religion tended to dominate.

To focus the mass character of the Parathavar conversion does not altogether reject the elements in models of 'individual conversion.' In fact, after adopting a religion mere superficial exercise of faith is quite possible as 'secret disciples' exist for a religion in other faiths. At one point of time – possibly even after the passage of a few generations – the reorientation of the soul to the same religion within which the individual is born may occur as A.D. Knock points out in the case of individual conversion. This also fits the psychological view postulated by W.H. Clarke. Nevertheless, the ideas of Robin Horton based on changes in cosmology when reduced to the individual level enriches the understanding of the process of conversion. It necessitates an understanding of the people's life from their origin to capture the comprehensiveness of religious conversion.

Endnotes

1   G.A. Oddie (ed.), *Religion in South Asia,* (New Delhi: Manohar, 1991), pp.5–6.

2   On the 175th anniversary of the French Revolution, Mao Tse Tung said it is too early to comment upon such a historical event. The same view is applicable to the religious conversion of the Parathavars. Because events like Tsunami and Koodankulam protest bring out new insights in understanding the dimensions of conversion.

3   G.A. Oddie (ed.), Op. Cit., p. 6.

4   M. Harlambos and R.M. Heald, *Sociology: Themes and Perspectives,* (New Delhi; Oxford University Press, 1999) p. 101; the contextual meaning employed here denotes that 'the source of power lies in the economic infrastructure.' The present researcher intends to stress on the idea of 'access to power as access to economic infrastructure.'

5   G. Duncan Mitchell (ed.), *A New Dictionary of Sociology,* (London: Routledge, 1999) p. 36; that what arises men's differential relations in access in terms of power is understood as a conflict in the said context.

6   Ibid. P. 1; the explicit meaning is 'adjustment to a conflict situation in which overt expressions of hostility are avoided… while leaving the source of the conflict unresolved.'

7   Ibid; the meaning is 'the process whereby an individual or a group acquires the cultural characteristics of another through direct contact and interaction.'

8   Ibid; the meaning is 'a process of becoming similar and the end state of such a process.'

9   Pralay Kanungo, *A History of Conversions* (Review Article), Frontline Vol. 21, Issue – 04, Feb 14–27, 2004, p._; the article reviews the work of Biswamoy Pati entitled 'Identity, Hegemony, Resistance: Towards a Social History of Conversions in Orissa 1800–1200. The critic of the book is of the opinion that, just explaining trends of two hundred years does not render justice to the issue under focus. The present researcher shares that opinion and has tried to provide a broader framework.

10   Noted Prof. Kunal Chakraborty delivered a lecture on the character of Hinduism in a Refresher Course conducted at UGC – ASC, Jawaharlal Nehru University, New Delhi between 24/08/2009 and 18/09/2009 in which he put forth this view. He was the author of the book 'The Making of the Bengal Purana.'

11   G.A. Oddie (ed.), Op. Cit., p.6.

12   Lecture of Kunal Chakraborty.

13   The rulers compelled their subjects to adopt their faith failing which the latter were subjected to persecution. A Saiva ruler could not tolerate Vaishnava faith within his territory.

14   S.A.A. Rizvi in G.A. Oddie (ed.), Op. Cit., p. 26.

15 Ibid; the scholar discusses an elaborate process of undergoing 'fast by way of expiation, and then they were buried in dung, stale (sic) and milk of cow for a certain number of days. When the fermentation occurred, they were dragged out of the dirt and given similar dirt to eat.'

16 George Mathew, *Politicisation of Religion: Conversions to Islam in Tamil Nadu,* Vol. 17, No. 25 (Jun 19, 1982), p. 1027; the scholar distinguishes proselytization from conversion through definition coming from data of the National Christian Council of India. Social, political and economic inducements are regarded important than spiritual realization in the case of proselytization whereas the opposite idea to an extent explains conversion.

17 G.A. Oddie (ed.), Op.Cit., p. 11.

18 Unlike the rulers of early medieval Tamil Nadu, the Muslim rulers did not resort to compulsion on a large scale. In fact, if they had attempted to convert this land into an Islamic state with the strength of their sword possibly this would have become so long back.

19 V. Sridhar, Op. Cit., P._; It is inferred from the author's statement that this perception is shared by noted historians Richard Eaton and Sumit Sarkar.

20 In a Refresher Course conducted by UGC – ASC, Jawaharlal Nehru University, New Delhi between 24/08/2009 and 18/09/2009, Prof. Najaf Haider – basically from Aligarh and presently employed with JNU – narrated this event. These are not his exact words of the scholar but the meaning is the same.

21 Thirupudaimarudhur temple murals depict the arrival of Arab traders with horses in boats. This is an evidence to depict thriving trade not only through sea but also by land. Because Thirupudaimarudhur is located on the banks of river Tamiraparani.

22 T.S. Subramanian, Tamil Nadu temple murals portray Tamiraparani battle? *The Hindu* (Madurai edition) dated 10/09/2011.

23 Britto Vincent (ed.), *Thooya Saveriar Kadithangal* (Palayamkottai: FRRC, 2002), Letter of Francis Xavier from Tuticorin dated 28/10/1542.

24 G.A. Oddie (ed.), Op. Cit., p. 11; making use of force, discriminatory laws, threats and inducements came to characterize their mode of religious conversion also. *See also* Rowena Robinson, The Cross: Contestation and Transformation of a Religious Symbol in Southern Goa, *Economic and Political Weekly,* Vol. 29, No.3, (Jan.15, 1994) pp. 94–98; for further discussions on the dimensions of Portuguese model of conversion.

25 D.P. Chattopadyaya, *Madhamum, Samugamum* (Tamil), (Chennai: New Century Book House, 2009) p.2.

26 Ibid, p.20.

27 L.F. Benedetto (ed.), *The Travels of Marco Polo,* (New Delhi: Asian Educational Services, 1994) p. 293.

28 Ibid.

29 The converted Muslims and Christian Parathavars denote each other as Chacha meaning fraternal uncle suggestive of the kinship prior to the conversion of the former.

30 Information collected through field visit conducted at Meenakshipuram of Shencottai taluk, Tirunelveli district on 24/02/2010. In 1981 reacting to a local dispute Hindu Dalits of Meenakshipuram en masse converted to Islam. Field visit here informed that at the least a generation passed before the new converts adopted practices like parallel-cousin marriage. In general, the Tamil society has the only practice of cross-cousin marriage.

31 Eve-teasing by Muslims was said to have caused communal riots. The followers of Hinduism and other local cults motivated by the offerings of the Muslims killed the Parathavars in large numbers.

32 R.N. Joe d'Cruz, *Aazhi Sul Ulagu* (Tamil), (Chennai: Tamizhini, 2004) & *Korkai* (Tamil), (Chennai: Kalachuvadu Pathipagam, 2009) pp._; Mainly practices like parallel cousin marriage contributed for the aversion among other communities although incest was not uncommon among the community as recorded by the said scholar.

33 Anonymous Author (ed.) Besse, *The Chronicles of the Pearl Fishery Coast,* ________,

34 T.S. Subramanian, *Tamil Nadu temple murals portray Tamiraparani battle?*

35 S.B. Kaufmann, Op. Cit., p. 208; according to the scholar, the original delegation was led by Vikrama Aditha Pandya, the Pandyapathy of contemporary times. In spite of migration of the Parathavar people from the Pearl Fishery Coast, the Pandyapathy's control over them pervaded.

36 V. Sridhar, Op. Cit., p._; the scholar argues more on modern terms and states that the Christians had better access to health care and education. An introspection of this kind of an argument after Tsunami has made it clear that it is not valid as far as the Pearl Fishery Coast is concerned. Seasonal famine and cholera wrecked untold miseries in the life of the Parathavars for which the Church did not take serious efforts for remedy. The earliest educational institutions remained away from their accessibility.

37 Ibid.

38 Letter of Francis Xavier from Manapad dated 1/08/1544.

39 Letter of Francis Xavier from Manapad dated 10/11/1544; in this letter, Francis Xavier had stated that the undisciplined Christians shall not have the benefits of their ocean. Such perceptions of the missionaries reflect the fact that they were very much part and parcel of colonialism.

40 Letter of Francis Xavier from Manapad dated 27/03/1544; the differential attitude towards practice like consumption can be understood through the writings of post-modern thinker Rolland Barthes. Consumption of wine by an Englishman was considered a malady whereas the same practice by a Frenchman was given a meaning with his socio-cultural context. Francis Xavier seemed to have suffered the same kind of problem. Consumption was not stated as one of the ten cardinal sins and even Jesus Christ had the habit. Consumption had been and still continue to be part and parcel of the Parathavar life.

41 Caesar Frederic in N. Athiyaman (ed.), *Pearl and Chank Diving of South Indian Coast (A Historical and Ethnographical Perspective)* (Thanjavur: Tamil University, 2000) p. 115.

42 A practice is known as 'Therippu' in which the produce of the entire village was attributed to a public cause.

43 In a national workshop entitled Towards a Theoretical Understanding on Tamil Society: Text/Praxis/Memories conducted at St. Xavier's College, Palayamkottai, between 10-11-2008 and 16-11-2008 Mr. A. Sivasubramanian delivered a lecture in which he shared these views.

44 Ibid.

45 A kind of forced labour that required the coastal people to deliver salt chiefly to temples ceased with the conversion. Particularly in the state of Travancore, the rulers sought the support of the colonial power in maritime activities which subsequently engulfed other spheres of economy. When the question of conversion came, the rulers allowed it among the coastal people probably since they were out of the geographical reach of the caste people. The missionaries convinced the rulers on the rules of Sabbath and the need for absolute loyalty to the church and won certain benefits for the Christians.

46 A. Sivasubramanian's lecture.

47 Ibid.

48 Rowena Robinson, *The Cross: Contestation and Transformation of a Religious Symbol in Southern Goa,* Economic and Political Weekly, Vol. 29, No. 3, Jan. 15, 1994, p. 94.

49 S. Viswanathan, Tamilology and a German Quest, *Frontline,*_______ ;it was only from the time of Bartholomaeus Ziegenbalg (1683–1719) and after a recognition of the native knowledge was made. Ziegenbalg observed that the natives discussed the same philosophical themes as the savants of Europe.

50 T.K. Oommen and Hunter P. Mabry, *The Christian Clergy in India Vol. I, Social Structure and Social Roles,* (New Delhi: Sage Publications, 2000) pp. 38–42.

51 Ibid.

52 Letter of Francis Xavier from Tuticorin dated 28/10/1542.

53 Rowena Robinson, Op. Cit., p. 94.

54 Teotonio R. de. Souza in K.S. Mathew, Teotonio R. de. Souza and Pius Malekandathil (eds.), *The Portuguese and the Socio-Cultural Changes in India,* (Tellicherry: Fundacao Oriente, 2001) p.437.

55 Letter of Francis Xavier from Cochin dated 15/01/1544; St. Augustine is instrumental in introducing such a historic and philosophic insight among the Christians. The present researcher is of the opinion that the missionaries were not liberated from this psychic paradigm while the spirit of the renaissance was making great alterations in the minds of other people.

56 Karl Marx was highly critical of these kinds of teachings of Christianity and brands it as 'the opium of the masses' for the abstract concept of heaven what cannot be perceived by naked eyes cannot be a justification to the exploitation in the real world.

57 In a lecture delivered by Prof. ____, during a refresher course conducted between 30-11-2010 and 20-12-2010 at the UGC – Academic Staff College, Panjab University, Chandigarh he

attempted to distinguish between chaos and order. In his opinion chaos was part of the world of nature, and hence, very powerful. The *Parathavars* who lived life as part of nature were now introduced with the order.

58 Letter of Francis Xavier from Manapad dated 8-08-1544.

59 Ibid.

60 A. Patrick Roche, *Fishermen of the Coromandel-A Social Study of the Paravas of the Coromandel*, (New Delhi,: Manohar, 1984) p. 52.

61 There were about sixty-nine family names with Portuguese titles suggesting cross-cultural interaction and possible chance of god-fathers having European origin.

62 With their pivotal position in the Christian society, the priests had details of brides and bridegrooms not only within the hamlet but even outside. However, in his capacity as the match-maker, his services were naturally available only for those who impressed him through loyalty to the church.

63 Letter of Francis Xavier from Tiruchendur dated 7-09-1544.

64 Interview with Mr. Parabaran (22), Fisherman, Manapad on 8-01-10; he said even today if affected by Chickenpox the residents secretly attribute some rituals for the mother goddess located at Kulasekharapattinam.

65 A. Patrick Roche, Op. Cit., p. 52.

66 It was believed that the Parathavar population that lived widely spreading was accommodated in the seven important settlements namely Vembar, Vaippar, Tuticorin, Punnaikayal, Veerapandyanpatnam, Alandalai and Manapad. But internal feuds and turmoil easily caused the birth of a new settlement by the splinter group.

67 Letter of Francis Xavier from Manapad dated 14-03-1544; in this letter, he commands his fellow priest Francis Manzilas to take stern steps to stop image worship. In yet another letter, he appreciates the people for having given up image worship.

68 Interview with Capt. Berchmans Mota (78), Grandson and Successor of Parathar Jati Thalaivanmor, Tuticorin on 21/04/2010; in the long absence of the priests – when the ban was imposed on the Jesuits – it was the Parathavar caste head titled Jati Thalaivanmor who maintained the people within the Catholic fold. But the priests rarely supported the cause of these leaders.

69 Letters of Francis Xavier from Manapad dated 23-02-1544, 08-04-1544 and 16-06-1544.

70 Ines G. Zupanov in Sanjay Subrahmanyam (ed.), *Sinners and Saints The Successors of Vasco Da Gama,* (New Delhi: Oxford University Press, 2000) p. 135.

71 Letter of Francis Xavier from Manapad dated 20-03-1544, 27-03-1544 and 03-08-1544.

72 Letter of Francis Xavier from Tuticorin dated 28-10-1542.

73 C. Veeramuthu in K.A. Manikumar and Vinod Vincent Rajesh (eds.), *Southern Tamil Nadu through the Ages,* (Tirunelveli: Dept. of History, M.S. University, 2011) p. 101.

74 David Mosse, *Catholic Saints and the Hindu Village Pantheon in Rural Tamil Nadu, India,* Man, New Series, Vol. 29, No. 2, (Jun. 1994) p.304; in the case of the Parathavars the caste organization and the village organization are one and the same.

75   G.A. Oddie (ed.), Op. cit., p.7.

76   The priests of the folk faith came from within the community. But in temples located in places of economic importance such as Kanyakumari both non-Brahmin and Brahmin priests tend to perform rituals.

77   A. Sivasubramanian, *Kirittavamum Tamizccuzalum,*, p. 56; the author quotes from Ambedkar and asserts that the service for the cause of humanity was strange to Hinduism. In the present researcher's opinion, the caste Hindus must have realized this and other strength of Christianity for the foreign missionaries viewed all natives as equals and did not hesitate to enter the living space of the lowest of the low.

78   Tradition maintains that they performed such services at Tiruchendur and Kanyakumari temples before conversion. That was considered prestigious within the community.

79   Letter of Francis Xavier from Manapad dated 03-08-1544.

80   Since any contact with the outside world was made first through the coast, it stood a greater chance of getting in touch with the changes occurring in the broader world.

81   Richard M. Eaton, Comparative History as World History: Religious Conversion in Modern India, *Journal of World History*, Vol. 8, No. 2 (Fall 1997), p. 244.

82   Rowena Robinson, Op. Cit.; she relates Christianity practiced by the Portuguese with feudal ethos. However, she explores it through the use of Holy-Cross by the Portuguese.

83   Letter of Francis Xavier from Cochin dated 15-01-1544.

84   Notice board information from St. Joseph's Church of Veerapandyanpattinam, Sacred Heart Church of Manapad.and Our Lady of Ransom Church of Kanyakumari.

85   Churches in Vembar, Manapad, etc.

86   A. Sivasubramanian, *Kirittavamum Tamizccuzalum,* p.20; Fr. Henriquez started service in a period contemporaneous to Fr. Francis Xavier. He worked as a priest in places like Kanyakumari and Punnaikayal. He published works such as Thambiran Vanakkam, Christiany Vanakkam and Adiyar Varalaru. The contents of this works were mainly translations from European religious literature.

87   Ibid, pp. 95–112.

88   Edgar Thurston, Op. Cit., p._.

89   R.N. Joe d'Cruz, *Aazhi Sul Ulagu*, p. _.

90   ____, *Korkai,* (Chennai: Kalachuvadu, 2009) p. 54.

91   R.N. Joe d'Cruz, *Aazhi Sul Ulagu*, pp. 100–103.

92   A. Sivasubramanian's lecture.

93   Interview with Capt. Berchmans Mota (78) of Tuticorin on 21/04/2010; the Pandyapathy was recognized as the chief of the caste and he represented the Portuguese king in Tuticorin. He was given the exalted titles of Senhore de Senhore and Soldier of the cross. He was the only person allowed to wear a gold chain with a cross. During the absence of the Jesuits, he completely took over the responsibility of protecting the church.

94 Ibid; the chief leader of the caste Pandyapathy regulated the caste affairs and punished the defectors. When the Dutch attacked the Catholic sacred places, the Pandyapathy safeguarded the image of 'Our Lady of Snow' in his residence. He also shot and killed a Parathavar man for having embraced the protestant faith under the aegis of the Dutch.

95 G.A. Oddie (ed.), Op. Cit., p. 5.

II

Historiography on Origin:
The Aborigine Vs Foreign Debate in the History of the Parathavars

Introduction

The history of the Tamil country during the Sangam period as depicted by contemporary literature is shrouded with mysteries that are yet unresolved. The geographical regions or the *tinais* as portrayed in the literature appear to be independent of each other and the sole link that unites all of them was the Tamil language. The spoken language – as we see today – was also marked by regional variations suggesting greater autonomy of the *tinais*. Moreover, everyday lifestyle, occupational specialization, worship pattern etc reflected the independent nature of the *tinais*. Assumptions based on the idea of *tinai* to two main generalizations. One stands on the premise of the evolution of Tamil civilization as any other civilization gradually from hunter-gatherer stage to that of agricultural surplus production stage within the geographical boundary as we understand today was in the past. The other is that the inhabitants of every *tinai* came from elsewhere as civilized people in the advanced stage of civilization. In this chapter, the said two generalizations as such are reviewed in the historiographic background while taking into view only the 'Parathavar folk' of the *Neydal Tinai*.

The problem in Tamil historiography chiefly owed to the attachment of unwarranted importance to the concept of *tinai*. Historians like K.A. Nilakanta Sastri in his works carefully did not allow it to overweight. One fails to notice the intra-regional variations within the *tinais* when considering each *tinai* as an autonomous zone marked with greater cultural uniformity.[1] Similarly, fishing community and profession was never marked by a universal pattern in terms of tools and lifestyle. The Sangam literature mentions about Valayar,[2] Panars[3] and Nulaiyars[4] who were engaged in fishing. A fisherman may migrate into fertile land for better livelihood. But then migration from fertile land to coastal land was rarely heard of.

The historians who dealt in some depth on coastal history of the Tamil country while examining the relationship of the Tamil people with the sea in a time earlier than the commencement of the Sangam period have not been successful in resolving the mysteries on the origin and roots of the coastal people. As early as 1984, Patrick Roche in his anthropological study on the Parathavars had recorded three major beliefs prevalent among the elitist section of the said community namely, *Aryan Sanskrit,*

Autochthonous and *Foreign.*[5] Notable in his discussion apart from the debate on origin is the historical sense of the – people rooted in the inherited memory – and consciousness on identity which is significant and foundational for the economic and socio-political assertion. The relevance of the research stems from the ongoing issues related to it in the present. Since the factors of economy are found by the present researcher to have determined the ongoing process Marxist method is being employed for analyzing the issues under focus. Hence, the present article seeks to investigate the issue by forming the hypothesis that 'the Parathavars are aborigines and early inhabitants of the Coastal Tamil country' and an attempt has been made in this article to reinterpret the views of historians like P.T. Srinivasa Iyengar, N. Subrahmanian, V. Kanakasabhai Pillai, X.S. Thaninayagam, M. Srinivasa Iyengar and Clarence Maloney – pertaining to the Parathavar community – in the light of new perspectives[6] on understanding the early Tamil society. A venture has also been made in this research to explore the subject matter through conducting of field visits, using unconventional modern literary sources and collecting oral traditions.

Independent of North: Aboriginal

P.T. Srinivasa Iyengar was one among the pioneers to write on the history of the Tamil country. He believed that the culture and history of the Tamils were far earlier than what had been proposed by historians of Northern India. In fact, he was of the opinion that the Tamil country was the original home of the human beings and it was the first cradle of civilization. His argument was sought to be strengthened by three primary observations he made each of the age, trade and the social system. His first argument took its support from archaeology. Particularly, when speaking about the Iron Age, he stated that it followed the Stone Age leaving no space for Copper Age. P. T. Srinivasa Iyengar concluded that the Iron Age began when Tamils had not come in any kind of contact with Sanskrit.[7] He even stated that the Iron Age is about two thousand years earlier to Rig Vedic period of the North.[8] In his second argument, he was influenced by W.H. Schoff who said "there was an active trade between Egypt and India in the Third Millennium B.C. They had their center of exchange at the head of the Persian Gulf. Various Arab Tribes and the mysterious Red Men (probably ancestors of Phoenicians) were the intermediaries in promoting the trade relationship. With progress of civilization they could directly go to Africa. Articles such as precious stones, spices, incenses and muslin were valued more in Egypt and it was the south Indian Paradavar[9] who took the articles in their boats to Aden and East African coast."[10]

In the third, Iyengar utilized the inferences made by Anthrop-geographers. To quote his words, "it is remarkable that the Tamils reached this idea in remote ages and defined the five natural regions, and classified races as five, each of whom followed professions suited to the region inhabited by them."[11] He saw a scientific basis and logical thinking in this classification. In his Anthrop-geographic approach P.T. Srinivasa Iyengar had borrowed heavily from the 'Evolutionary theory.' The five natural regions of habitat pertaining to the Tamils were classified into Palai, Kurinji, Mullai, Marudam and Neydal. Iyengar went on to state that "in Palai grew the nomad stage, in Kurinji the hunter stage, in Mullai the pastoral stage, in Marudam the agricultural stage and in Neydal the fishing and sailing stage, of human development."[12] Thus he outlined the movement of human life from simplicity towards complexity.

Iyengar's first two observations, although speculative, provide the logical background for the third point. In short, his approach maintained that in the peninsula by 3500 B.C., there had been the usage of iron and related technology which facilitated maritime trade in greater magnitude both of which shaped the social system. Iyengar's arguments, specifically the third one, were invalidated by later historians. N. Subrahmanian, underlining the importance of the contemporary character of the groups, expressed the view that different social groups lived side by side and no hunter was ever converted into a fisherman or herdsman.[13] Iyengar also left unexplained how in Kurinji social formation remained simple, while in Neydal it was complex.

He was attempting to explain the development of tools and consequent craft specialization. But recent archaeological data pertaining to tools suggest spread of civilization from the riverside towards the hills. In the Neolithic period hunting was a joint effort and comparatively larger tools were required. But in the Mesolithic period, raw materials for producing sharper weapons were readily available in hills that resulted in the shift of habitat also.[14] The views like that of Schoff might have had limited literary evidence but need cross references provided by archaeological excavations. The 'Jatibedi Nul' that provides information about the origin of the Parathavars states that they were offspring of a clandestine relationship between a 'kurava' male and a 'chetty' female and thus ascribe their evolution to the interaction between the *tinais*.[15] Inferences, as postulated above, put the evolutionary argument that sought to identify the entire Tamil Civilization independent of North by P.T. Srinivasa Iyengar as weak although studies based on the human genetics of the recent past point that the South Indian gene variety is different and independent from that of Northern India.[16] Moreover, his argument on the possibility of contacts through the sea with foreign lands in an earlier stage holds historical validity.

Independent of North: Foreign

As early as 1735 there had been an attempt to identify the Parathavar with the Parvaims who were contemporaries of King Solomon, mentioned in the Holy Bible.[17] The place Ophir mentioned in contemporary literature was also identified with Oovari[18] located in the Pearl Fishery Coast.[19] But establishing of these assumptions as historical facts need solid pieces of evidence. Nevertheless, among the chief proponents of the theory of 'foreign origin,' N.Subrahmanian stands foremost.[20]

Writings of N. Subrahmanian clearly suggested his stand-point on two aspects. However, N. Subrahmanian's belief on the foreign origin was extended to the entire Tamil population and he linked the entire Tamil population with the sea. Second is his view on their independent nature from that of Northern India. While making his first proposition on his own, he takes the support of V.A. Smith for the second. Thus, Subramanian maintains that "the first ethnic superimpositions on this base, which can be deemed to be the earliest Tamil (Dravidian) element in Tamil society, came from the Eastern Mediterranean regions with a culture strongly Phoenician in texture. Ethnic, linguistic, archaeological and cultural probes will easily establish an Eastern Mediterranean origin for the first solid core of the Tamils. They came perhaps in many waves and usually by the sea nestling close to the coast. They generally by-passed the hinterland of north India and the Deccan and at important points touched the coast on their way like, e.g. Baluchistan, where they left a pocket of Dravidian (Brahmi) speaking group to provide a clue to this migration. Sea-faring and other strictly Phoenician characteristics, along with many cultural traits which can be traced back to early Sumerian days, mark the Tamils. This Dravidian element had little difficulty in elbowing the indigenous people out of the plain and driving them into safe and obscure recesses."[21]

The supportive evidence which prompted Subramanian to make such assumptions was probably the existence of Brahui tribe in the present Baluchistan (presently located within Pakistan) region whose language belongs clearly to the Dravidian group. But then, Subrahmanian was just taking into consideration only sea-faring and language identity of an autonomous people for his interpretation. The Tamils altogether were not linked with sea and trade alone; there were farmers and pastoralists amongst them. Also, N. Subrahmanian did not clarify why they chose to settle in south India rather than in the Indo-Gangetic plain which was far more fertile and resourceful.[22] N. Subrahmanian appears to have been influenced by the *Aryan Migration* theory. But he could not identify *philological* evidence that sought to inform the various stages of migration which formed the basement of the *Aryan Migration* theory.

P.T. Srinivasa Iyengar who believed in the aboriginality of the Tamils had made an assumption earlier than Subrahmanian. He outlined the early contact with other civilizations to the magnitude of colonizing them; invading from the Tamil country. Identifiable are some of the names of places like Ur, Nippur etc. contribute to assume such a possibility. He opined that "extensive travels by land and sea in very early times can alone have made possible the colonization of the Mesopotamian valley by the Tamils."[23] He agreed with H.R. Halls view, unlike in the method of N. Subrahmanian, which stood on the strength of evidence provided by statues and reliefs which did not suggest similarity with that of surrounding races such as Semites, Aryans or others. Iyengar also subscribed to the view of Berossus who through the legend of Oannes[24] suggested an early maritime connection with a comparatively developed civilization through the sea.[25] On the basis of these two assumptions, Iyengar concluded that this civilization must have been constituted by the Tamils.

Though Iyengar's method enabled a better understanding than N. Subrahmanian, insofar the treatment of myths and legends were concerned he failed to compare them with the then existing legends of other societies. Such a methodology alone could have helped to establish one's value judgment firmly, especially in the field of ancient history. In this, the argument of Romila Thapar seems to be tenable. According to her, the very birth of legends involving water, particularly like that of the great deluge was born in the Mesopotamian soil and later transmitted to other parts.[26] Even in the Tamil tradition people had given importance to deluge not less than any other society. As far as the Parathavar community was concerned, Simon Chitty had also recorded one of their beliefs, according to which there had been a great flood at the close of the last 'kalpa' and in order to escape from that their ancestors constructed a boat[27] (toni) and voyaged till they landed at 'Tonipuram.'[28]

Similarly, while recording the folk-tales of Tamil Nadu, eminent writer Ki Rajanarayan[29] came across a strange traditional story extant among the fishing-folk. According to the story, a brother prompted by sexual urge tries to express it to his own sister. The sister being frightened of her brother's attitude starts running. The brother ferociously chases her. The people of the coast still believe the natural process of small wave followed by a larger wave in nature as an allegorical representation of this. Although cross-cousin marriage was common among the Tamils, direct incest (sibling sex) remains largely unknown. If we are to take P.T. Srinivasa Iyengar's theory of possible link with Mesopotamia, then it can be assumed that this tradition would have entered into the Parathavar tradition in one form or other through a cross cultural influence. D.D. Kosambi quoting the story of Cambyses through Herodotus had stated that such relationship was known among the Persians.[30]

If we are to take that this legend was transmitted into Tamil society by the Mesopotamians, then we tend to acknowledge the antiquity of Tamil tradition and the aboriginality of the Tamil people in the direction set by P.T. Srinivasa Iyengar. This works as an anti-thesis to the existing modern writings on 'Ancient Tamil History' which commence from the period of Grammarian Katyayana. In the absence of path-breaking archaeological evidence, generalizations of any kind could not be arrived at. Extensive archaeological excavations if made in the Neydal land, it may radically alter the entire historical tradition and belief of the Tamil country.

Scholars like X.S. Thaninayagam have held a different view point pertaining to the origin of the Tamils, primarily influenced by the works of Sylvain Levi and Irawati Karwe. Levi, like others mentioned above, believed in an oceanic contact several centuries before the beginning of the Christian era.[31] But more significantly borrowing the inferences from Irawati Karve, Thaninayagam underlined the kinship system prevalent in Polynesia coming close with that of the South Indians.[32] On that basis, he assumed that they might have migrated from Polynesian region. But some European scholars who experimented on the behavior of rats in different countries have identified regularity and a possible link between all of them in terms of living pattern and adaptation.[33] In case of a new challenge encountered by rats in England, rats in France together develop a response. Universally man is a social animal with a far more advanced communication system. Therefore, common traits between two groups of people separated by physical distance need not necessarily explain common origin or ancestry. Nevertheless, Thaninayagam's argument leads to Racial and Tribal identity.

Off-Shoot of Native Tribes of North

Thaninayagam was attempting to explore the history of the Tamil people starting with his understanding of race which was subsumed by tribal features later. According to him, the early immigrants into the Tamil country could be categorized into pre-Dravidians, proto-Dravidians and Dravidians.[34] He places Villavar[35] (bowmen identified with Bhils) and Minavar[36] (fishermen identified with Minas) as pre-Dravidians who inhabited the region of the Tamil country along with the mysterious Nagas.[37] They were conquered by the proto-Dravidian invaders. The invaders and the subjects together formed the three kingdoms and freely mingled to evolve the Dravidian culture. The genetic study of races was long before rejected as not having any validity in view of several complications, and therefore, historians tend to keep themselves away from results derived from the anthropologic study of races. However, much researching has not been done on Bhils and Minas in a comparative perspective by historians writing the history of South India.

Considerable importance on the tribal side was discussed among others by V. Kanagasabai Pillai. In his opinion 'Naga' was a conglomeration of several tribes constituted in the Tamil country by the Maravar, Eyinar, Oliyar, Oviyar, Aruvalur, and Parathavar.[38] According to him "the Parathavar were a Naga tribe who occupied the sea coast and maintained themselves by fishing or by sea faring. They had known the art of keeping off sharks."[39] But both Kanagasabai Pillai and Thaninayagam were, unlike P.T.S. Iyengar who was able to provide a time period for the Iron Age in the present-day Tamil country, not able to make their view points strictly based on a scientific chronology. Similarly in his 'Tamil Studies,' M. Srinivasa Iyengar tried to classify the contemporary population of the Tamils into Aryan, Dravidian and Naga. To him, the Brahmins are pure Aryans and the Velalas are pure Dravidians. Others such as Valayars,[40] Pallar, Shanar,[41] Idayar, Maravar, Agambadiyar, Paraiyar,[42] Kaikkolar, Kammalar, Vanniyar[43] (Palli), Kallar, Ambalakarar are pure Nagas.[44]

As the study does not spin around the Aryan-Dravidian linguistic identity, M.S. Iyengar's stratification can be ignored in the present context. But what has to be noted is the importance attached to the Naga tribal identity. There could be two possibilities for the idea of Nagas to have penetrated into the South. One is through the spread of Buddhism.[45] The Koliyans were a tribe engaged in the fishing profession. They were neighbours of the Sakyans and listened to the Buddha and claimed a share of his ashes after his cremation. Many of them were in a primitive stage and were worshippers of totemic icons (Kol tree). The Koliyans as a whole were, therefore, often counted among the aboriginals with the generic label Nagas.[46] Unlike the harmonious relationship that the Nagas had with the forest residing Brahmins, confrontations ensued between Koliyans and the Sakyas. Particularly, there was a dispute among them in sharing the water of river Rohini.[47] The image of the Nagas, which entered into the Buddhist legends through the above-cited experiences, might have been transmitted in the South.

The other possibility was through the legend of Parasurama[48] with which the cult of the Nagas might have entered into the South. According to a popular legend, Parasurama after concluding 21 expeditions against Kshatryas presented the whole of the world to the Brahmanas. After that, he was said to have left with no land for his living. Then with the assistance of Subramanya,[49] a Tamil deity, he identified the present Kerala region as his permanent abode. He brought Brahmins to disseminate Vedic thoughts and ideas in the region and settled them in sixty-four villages. Although this could be treated as a legend, every single aspect of religion in later days came to be associated with the name of Parasurama.[50] P.P. Narayanan Nambudri believed that the consecration of Nagaraja[51] and Naga Yaksi at the Ambeda Temple that stands on the Eastern Coast of Kaitappuzha was the deed of Parasurama.[52] Otherwise, the theory that Parathavars were part of the Naga tribe was not well substantiated by scholars like Kanakasabhai, M.S. Iyengar and Thaninayagam.

The Aryans and the Parathavars

Assumptions suggesting 'Aryan Origin' was also made chiefly because of certain aspects of identical nature, particularly names, found during Vedic period. The idea of navigation was known to the Aryans. Rig Veda mentions boats with hundred oars.[53] Evidence point to an important tribe of this period settled in the Jaipur-Bharatpur region of Rajasthan. This Vedic tribe was known as 'Matshya.' They were believed to be 'totemic' clans[54] and their totem being fish. But within the varna system what is fundamental to the Vedic period, a separate class of people involved maritime activities including fishing was not known.[55] Therefore, Colebrooke in his classification based on 'Dharma Sastras' brought the Parathavars under the category of 'Nishadhas' who were outcastes and said to have born out of the wedlock between a 'Brahmin' male and a 'Sudra' female.[56]

The Parathavars were also said to have claimed 'Kshathrya' status.[57] Even today we find categories of 'Suryavamsam' and 'Chandravamsam'[58] present among a section of Parathavars of the Pearl Fishery Coast. The Chandravamsis trace their root from the Mahabharatha and the Suryavamsis from the progenitors of the protagonists of Ramayana. But in both the epics, there is also evidence that suggests those who were involved in fishing and sailing were independent forest tribes. Mahabharatha narrates the story of Satyavati, originally born out of a fish, and later adopted daughter of the king of fishermen and was first impregnated by Sage Parasara. Later she became the mistress of King Shantanu of the moon clan and from their line emerged the Pandavas and Kauravas in the fourth generation.[59] Similarly in the line founded by Manu at Ayodhya[60] was born a great king named as 'Para.' When the Kosalan kingdom was dissolved, Para's successors were believed to have migrated from North and settled on the Southern Coast. One of the tribes involved in driving Bahu, the eighth successor of Harichandra was 'Paradas.'[61] However, Guhan, the chief of the boatmen, depicted in the Ramayana at par with Satyavati's father in Mahabharatha, was only a tribal chief outside the Aryan fold. The tribal identity was under played and making use of the evidence of sun and moon clans in the Ramayana and Mahabharata respectively, the Parathavars could have identified themselves with the Aryans.

This can at the most be explained 'Mythologisation of Origin' – an aspect in which every community indulged during the late ancient and early medieval periods. Particularly, the Pandyan kings from who the 'Chandravamsis' of the Parathavars claim succession traced their origin from the Mahabharata narratives. But noticeable in actual history was the ability of the Parathavars to get the service of the Brahmin priests and the Visvakarmas – both associated with the wearing of sacred thread. The Brahmin priests served in the temples[62] and other rituals whereas the latter found good employment as boat makers[63].

Linguistic and Etymological Analysis

The real basis of the Parathavar origin was sought to be examined by linguistic research also. M.A. Dorai Rangasamy had traced the root of the word "Parathavar." According to him, "the word Parathavar or Paratar, a variant form found in Pinkalantai and Kampa Ramayanam, and approved by Naccinarkkiniar as meaning of the people of the sea is connected with paravai, the sea coming from the root "para" to expand. Paravai and Parappu mean an expanse. If the formative tu is added on to the root para (பர) parathu (பரது) will result. Probably to this word the honorific suffix ar (அர்) has been added."[64] This view of Dorai Rangasamy was rejected by S.N. Sadasivan and Clarence Maloney. Sadasivan made his interpretation assuming that the word was of Sanskrit origin. He sought to explore the term 'Parava.' Here Sadasivan's theory went flaw chiefly because the name of the community as such is not Parava. It is a later day corruption under the Portuguese pronunciation. The original word used to denote the community was Parathar[65] or Parathavar and not Paravar.

Clarence Maloney, rejecting Sadasivan's view had explained that the term 'Parata' itself was a Tamil rendering of Sanskrit 'Bharata' and Prakrit or Sinhalese 'Barata.'[66] His assumption derived its strength from Sri Lankan epigraphic sources and in the light of Indian Great Tradition. No doubt, the people of the Parathavar community had early links with Sri Lanka and available evidence from there points to their prosperous life. The wealthy Parathavars of Sri Lanka might have even taken to Buddhism. Their language, however, remained Tamil despite the influence of the Sinhala Great Tradition. But then, there is no way by which we could trace the genesis of the community, mainly constituted by the non-migrant fishing groups that inhabited in the Neydal land, from Sanskrit or Prakrit or Sinhalese languages.

Conclusion

The variation in the historical consciousness of the community as pointed by Patrick Roche has had been a fluctuating phenomenon in response to economic opportunity. Recent Studies on the genetic features of the Indian population have categorized the people of Northern India and Southern India as distinct from each other. Geographically Northern India comparatively was known for the wealth of natural resources than that of Southern India. There was no clue as to why they should invade and physically superimpose themselves through invasion and settle in a drier area. Migration has been a constant phenomenon. Scholars agree on the possibility of continental migration of an entire civilization. The Tamil people have had always traced their origin from an indefinite period from Lemuria continent which has been now concluded as merely a myth.[67] Similar myth shared by the Parathavar community stand testimony to the idea of their being early inhabitants of the Coastal Tamil Country.[68] But the migration of Northern elite in the historical period was ascribable to the patronage of scholarship and the receptive nature of South India through which cultural interaction took place that led literature and folklore of the North to find their way into the South, and consequently, the people trace their identity from a common past. As far as the food distribution pattern, production relations, decision making, and etc of the Parathavars were concerned the tribal characteristics tend to project more. But this is not sufficient evidence to claim origin from the Aryan tribal grouping such as the Matsyas though provides scope for the communal reservation based claim of the community.

Social isolation and exclusion that marked the lives of forest or hill based tribes could not be applied to sea-tribes. By virtue of being inhabitants of the coast, the economic need that occurred in other civilizations exposed them to foreign elements. Moreover, the inner urge of any group of people settled on the coast to explore the sea to the maximum. Sea is more complex in geographical traits than land. Exploring it needs masterly skills. Such skills received recognition among the Parathavar people who prefer to be called as *Kadalodis* than *Meenava Makkal*[69] regardless of their identity based on appearance or language or any other aspect. However, the major clue that pertained to the Parathavar origin comes to us from the kinship pattern which is classifiable only with Tamil-speaking South as inferred from Ki. Rajanarayan's work. Of course, as said already, there had been the influence of foreign cultures among these people and vice-versa as well as the impact of the Aryan life, certain tribal traits in modes of economic life underlined by uniqueness in terms of exchange and sharing as postulated by historians and other social scientists. But the cultural-core is one of South Indian as evident from the studies on genetics and kinship pattern. This found its reflection in the literary concept named 'tinai' which was only an ideal and the real based on material being different. Hence, the hypothesis 'the Parathavars are aborigines and early inhabitants of the Coastal Tamil country' is proved.

Endnotes

1. Interview with Mr. Parabaran(22), Fisherman, Manapad on 08/01/10; Oovari and Manapad are separated by a few kilometers. But marked variation is found in their spoken language and ideas of livelihood.

2. Maduraikanchi: 256; it speaks in the meaning that they are 'fishermen having nets with knots.'

3. Ibid: 269.

4. Sirupanattrupadai: 158.

5. A. Patrick Roche, *Fishermen of the Coromandel-A Social Study of the Paravas of the Coromandel,* (New Delhi,: Manohar, 1984) pp. 13–16.

6. R. Krishnakumar, Muziris, At Last, *Frontline* dated April 23, 2010; until the vast excavations at the site many thought, particularly in Kerala, that Muziris was only a legend. But the scales in which artifacts have been traced provide scope for fresh writings. In the article, the author informs about the various findings. But what is significant is to relate that with the actual people living in the region as underlined in ethnoarchaeology. For instance, there is a place called Paravur located near the site of excavation. But the significance of the place with details of its inhabitants is very important in view of categories of people have 'Para' suffix in their castes.

7. David Shulman's interview by A.S. Panneerselvan in *Frontline* dated 29 September 2017; he states that the early Brahmi scripts dating back to second century B.C. are saturated with Sanskrit and Prakrit words.

8   P.T. Srinivasa Iyengar, *Pre-Aryan Tamil Culture* (New Delhi: Asian Educational Services, 1995) p. 4–5.

9   The noun Parathavar is variously spelled by Historians. P.T. Srinivasa Iyengar spells it as Paradavar. Many other historians spell it as Paratavar. The word Parathavar as used by the present researcher is the standard spelling followed by eminent historian R. Champakalakshmi.

10   P.T. Srinivasa Iyengar, *History of the Tamils: From the Earliest Times to 600 A.D.* (Madras: Asian Educational Services, 1995) p. 39.

11   P.T. Srinivasa Iyengar, *Pre-Aryan Tamil Culture*, p.19.

12   Ibid.

13   N. Subrahmanian, *Sangam Polity: The Administration and Social Life of the Sangam Tamils* (Madras: Asia Publishing House, 1966), pp. 248–249.

14   Romila Thapar, *The Penguin History of Early India: From the Origins to A.D. 1300* (New Delhi: Penguin Books India (P) Ltd, 2002), pp. 72–73.

15   Simon Casie Chitty, Remarks on the Origin and History of the Parawas, *Journal of the Royal Asiatic Society of Great Britain and Ireland*, Vol. 4, No. 1 (1837), p. 130.

16   Tony Joseph, How Genetics is Settling the Aryan Migration Debate, *The Hindu* dated 17 June 2017.

17   Simon Casie Chitty, Remarks on the Origin, p.130.

18   The present researcher in his field visit conducted at Manapad, a place not much far from Oovari, remains of an ancient port probably contemporary to King Solomon's period was identified. Therefore, a possible contact at the least indirectly could not be altogether ruled out.

19   S. Decla, *Muthukulithuraiyil Porchukeesiyar* (Tamil), (Chennai: New Century Book House, 2009), p. 2.

20   S.N. Sadasivan, *A Social History of India* (New Delhi: A.P. H. Publishing Corporation, 2007), p. 357; He argued that the word 'Parava' derived from the Sanskrit word 'Para' gives the meaning 'other' or 'foreign.'

21   N. Subramanian, *Sangam Polity*, pp. 253–254.

22   K.A. Nilakanta Sastri also postulates such a question in his book *Cultural Contacts between Aryans and Dravidians*.

23   P. T. Srinivasa Iyengar, *History of the Tamils*, p. 36.

24   Oannes is a man-fish. According to legend, he swam up to the Sumerian cities via Persian Gulf.

25   P.T. Srinivasa Iyengar, *History of the Tamils*, p. 36.

26   Romila Thapar, *The Penguin History of India*, p.100.

27   *Toni* is a vessel bigger than a boat and smaller than a ship, which was extensively used from the Pearl Fishery Coast for maritime trade in the Peninsula and Sri Lanka. It was also used for passenger traffic. Ambitious captains of the *tonis* aspired to reach the Arabian Gulf. But it rarely happened.

28   Simon Casie Chitty, Op. Cit., pp. 130–131.

29 Ki. Rajanarayan is a famous writer in Tamil. He records such a story in his book *Vayadhukku Vandhavargalukku Mattum.* See also R.N. Joe d'cruz, *Korkai,* (Chennai: Kalachuvadu Pathipagam, 2009) p. 756; in this fiction, the author records a similar incident.

30 D.D. Kosambi, *Myth and Reality* (Bombay: Popular Prakashan Pvt Ltd, 1992), p. 108.

31 X.S. Thaninayagam, *The Tamil Culture and Civilization, Readings: The Classical Period* (Bombay: Asian Publishing House, 1970) p. 134.

32 Ibid; the marriage pattern is more akin to the Dravidians. A girl can marry her mother's brother as well as her cross cousins.

33 Sundara Ramasamy in *Kalachuvadu* dated _______. Although the scholar who is putting forth this contention has stated that this has not experimented with human beings one cannot entirely rule out such possibilities.

34 X.S. Thaninayagam, Op. cit., pp. 128–129.

35 There are Parathavar people with Tamil title 'Villavarayar.' Even after their conversion to Christianity, this title remains. Similar titles still in vogue are Poobalarayar, Kalingarayar, and Singarayar (the latter two titles are not as common as the first two). Arayars are generally believed to be tax collectors in coastal areas. The Pandyan kings seem to have given a similar title to their thrown.

36 Interview with Mr. Chandrasekhar, ex-president of Parathavar Welfare Association, Tuticorin on 11-03-2010; he identifies six categories of fishermen in the Tamil speaking region including the Parathavar. Others are Parathava Rajakulam, Chempadavar, Mukkuvar, Meenavar and Pattinavar. Each category is a separate endogamous group, at times ascertaining superiority over others. However, he did not include Valayar, Nulayar, etc. among the chief fishing communities.

37 X.S. Thaninayagam, Op. cit., pp. 128–129. If the term Naga is to be taken to represent snake then again it has some relevance. The devil dancer picture inserted in Edgar Thurston's *Castes and Tribes of South India Vol. VI* wears a head dress in which snake is portrayed at the top suggesting a kind of ritual importance.

38 V. Kanakasabhai, *The Tamils Eighteen Hundred Years Ago* (New Delhi: Asian Educational Services, 1989), p. 42.

39 Ibid, p. 44; Marco Polo's observations have maintained that the Brahmin Priests were involved in controlling the sharks during pearl-diving seasons for which they were given 1/20th of the total pearls collected.

40 R.N. Joe d'cruz, *Korkai,* p. 540; Valayars were wrongly believed by many as Parathavars. One of the meanings of the term *valai* was the fishing net. They are in fact not fully engaged in maritime activities. They entered into matrimonial alliance with the Ambalakarars and Mutharayars who are people of the mainland. At times they gave themselves to coastal fishing.

41 They are chiefly toddy-tapers. However, in certain places, they are also engaged in fishing. For example, in a place called Kallamozhi, near Udangudi (within the limit of the Pearl Fishery Coast) this can be witnessed. Similarly, they dominate the salt manufacturing industry in Tuticorin. At

this juncture it has to be noted that the *Sangam* literature speaks about the *Umanars* who are engaged in the selling of salt in the mainland, distinguishing them from the Parathavars. Despite it, many scholars have considered them as Parathavars.

42 In coastal towns like Veerapandianpattinam and Manapad, the presence of people of this caste is significant. They assist the fishermen in fishing but do not own boats. They collect shells and conches and prepare lime. Their important contribution would have been in building construction. When other service castes in the coastal areas preferred conversion to Christianity with the Parathavars, they did not decide in favour of it. Nevertheless, they hold a positive memory about their relationship with the Parathavars. It is doubtful whether the Parathavars would compliment with similar memory.

43 J.H. Nelson, *The Madura Country A Manual,* Part II (New Delhi: Asian Educational Services, 1989), pp. 56–74; Like the *Umanars* of the Sangam period, the *Vanniyars* of South Tamil Nadu are also a linking caste that carries sea fish to the mainland. On the basis of their settlement pattern, trade routes from the coast towards the Western Ghats can be mapped. The *Vanniyars* take *Padayachi* title. There is a sub-caste within *Vanniyar-Padayachi,* known as 'Chavalkarars.' Apart from the selling of fish also are engaged in inland fishing. These 'Chavalkarars' mix freely with the Parathavars in areas around Nagerkoil and even enter into matrimonial alliances. But J.H. Nelson while surveying the population of Madurai identified and enumerated all of them separately. He also finds *'Chavalkarars'* directly engaged in coastal fishing.

44 N. Subrahmanian, *Sangam Polity,* p. 250.

45 The Tamil epics Silapathigaram and Manimekalai, provide information about the spread of Buddism in the Coastal areas. A place like Nagapattinam still carries several pieces of evidence in this connection.

46 D.D. Kosambi, *The Culture and Civilization of Ancient India in Historical Outlines* (New Delhi: Vikas Publishing House Pvt Ltd, 1999), p. 109.

47 Ibid.

48 The icon of Parasurama is significant in the context of the Pearl Fishery Coast. He is associated with the reclamation of land. When the entire history of the Tamils focuses on the Lemuria Continent that was swallowed by the sea, ancient archaeological sites like Korkai provide evidence for the receding of the sea. Similarly, Parasurama is considered to be an avatar of Vishnu but himself a devotee of Siva. The Pearl Fishery Coast carries evidence of the interaction between Saivism and Vaishnavism.

49 He is one of the very important deities seated at six important centers which are normally hill tracts except *Tiruchendur,* which is a located on the sea shore. At *Tiruchendur,* he is the guardian deity of the Parathavar. This again greatly outlines the interaction between the *Kurinji* and *Neydal.*

50 K.A. Nilakanta Sastri, *A History of South India: From Prehistoric Times to the Fall of Vijayanagar* (New Delhi: Oxford University, 1958), p. 66.

51 The cult of Nagaraja also spread into the Travancore region (present day Kanyakumari district was part of it) wherein a considerable population of Parathavars lived and still live.

52 P.P. Narayanan Nambudiri, *Aryans in South India,* (New Delhi: Inter-India Publications, 1992), p. 214.

53 D.D. Kosambi, *The Culture and Civilization of Ancient India,* p. 90.

54 Ibid., p.81.

55 Strangely in later times crossing of the sea was barred for the twice born varnas, including the Vaisya traders. But the impurity that was attached to other non-vegetarian foods was not attached to fish at the least in equal degree. The Brahmins of Bengal include fish in their food.

56 Simon Casie Chitty, Op. Cit., p. 130.

57 Edgar Thurston, Op. Cit., pp. 140–146; he also records a tradition that states that they are Kshathryas and will only eat in the house of Brahmins. The evidence that comes through Sangam literature identifies them as traders at the largest numerical level than warriors. It is strange that they did not prefer to take Vaisya status. Marco Polo in his observations of the Pearl Fishery Coast eulogized their wealthy status and at the same time pointed to their weakness in chivalry. Even their security at the village level seemed to have been undertaken by the Maravas. When Lord Roberts in the second half of the 19th century identified certain castes and tribes as martial on the grounds of discipline and loyalty, he did offer martial status to the Parathavars. Probably owing to that reason the caste leadership of Pandyapathy also vanished. Even now the caste men prefer a carreer in merchant navy to navy under the Defence Ministry. See also R.N. Joe d'cruz, Korkai, pp. 325–326.

58 Interview with Capt. Berchmans Motha; the Capt. stated that they belong to Chandravamsam.

59 Simon Casie Chitty, Op. Cit., pp. 131–132.

60 R.N. Joe d' ruz, *Korkai,* p.209; the Parathavar Jati leaders known as Pandyapathys trace their origin from Ayodhya which is more associated with the sun clan. But they call themselves as belonging to moon clan.

61 G.P. Singh, *Early Indian Historical Tradition and Archaeology* (New Delhi: D.K. Print World Pvt Ltd, 1994), p. 39.

62 Interview with Mr. Sukumaran (47), Resident of Kottar on 27/03/2010; he stated that at first the Meenakshi temple at Madurai was in early times the rallying point for the Parathavar pilgrims which after the fall of the Pandyan kings was replaced with Uttarakosamangai, located near Ramnad. In both these temples, Brahmins served as chief priests. This is also noticeable in the temples of Kanyakumari and Tiruchendur.

63 Small size boats and catamarans were built by the members of the Parathavar community itself who normally were found in every coastal village and called 'odavis.' But bigger boats were constructed in the trading center like present day Tuticorin by Visvakarmas, popularly known as Aasaris.

64 M.A. Durai Rangasamy, *The Surnames of the Cankam Age: Literary and Tribal* (Madras: Manorama Press, 1968), p. 130.

65 Maduraikanchi:144, Perumpanattrupadai:333.

66 Clarence Thomas Maloney, *The Effect of Early Coastal Sea Traffic on the Development of Civilization in South India,* Unpublished Ph. D. thesis submitted to the Dept. of Anthropology, University of Pennsylvania in 1968, pp. 112–115.

67 S. Christopher Jayakaran, The Lemuria Myth, *Frontline,* Vol. 28 – Issue 08, Apr. 09–22, 2011, pp._; the scholar explores all the existing views on Lemuria including those from the Sangam literature and concludes it as mere myth. Surprisingly this writing was not challenged by scholars of Tamil language and history.

68 S. Padmanabhan in K.A. Manikumar and Vinod Vincent Rajesh (eds.), *Southern Tamil Nadu through the Ages,* (Tirunelveli: Dept. of History, M.S. University, 2011) pp. 34–38.

69 Interview with Mr. Parabaran of Manapad on 08/01/10 and Interview with Mr. Chandrasekhar of Tuticorin on 11-03-2010; The term Kadalodi includes all activities pertaining to the sea whereas Meenava Makkal reduced them to the level of mere fishing folk.

III

Time, Space and Life:
Early Parathavars of the Pearl Fishery Coast

Introduction

The skill of adaptation and negotiation with respective domains of the environment was responsible for the evolution of varied human categories associated with particular regions such as people of the coast, of the fertile valley or plain and of the desert.[1] Comprehension of the secrets of nature was one of the chief causes that determined the pattern of adaptation and negotiation. In consequence emerged a remarkable regularity characterized by advancement in human life what arrested restless migration and provided space for settled life.[2] People such as Kuravar, Idayar, Vellalar, Maravar and Parathavar were classical expressions of such human categories in the historical context of the Tamil country since they were chiefly associated with one or another landform at the least from a definite period of time.[3]

Among others, the aim of the present article is to study certain issues[4] on historical geography pertaining to the Parathavar community. Though historical geography has potential to accommodate a spectrum of issues, in the present context indicators such as time, space and everyday activities of the Parathavars have been taken into primary account in a mode of each succeeding the other. Conventionally the study of historical geography continues to remain more a part of geography than history as it stresses more on details about space relegating to the background the importance that has to be essentially attributed to time.[5] Since the present study is part of history, departing from that convention attempt has been made to create a framework based on time through which issues on space followed by the description of the regularity in human activities have been discussed.

In the historiography that pertained to the ancient Tamil country complexity characterized the treatment of both time and space. In the first case i.e. time, history was more often than not was shadowed by myths. Yet some of the myths associated with human activities conformed to the reality of space. Therefore, not only the second case i.e. space but also the activities of the people through time and space attained importance, for the very historical nature of space in itself was qualified through the activities of the people. In the history of the Parathavar community, the negotiation between time and space underlined certain unique characteristics.

The present study is a manifestation of the realization of time and space discourse in informing people's history. The method of inquiry takes the cue from Frank Kermode's view that stands on the premise of 'myths are the agents of stability whereas fictions are agents of change.'[6] For the sake of this article, the meaning of the term 'stability' is inferred as stagnation since it is placed in opposition to change. Thus hypothetically approaching Frank Kermode means, orally transmitted traditions or the Sruti literatures such as the Rig Veda, the Ithihasas like Ramayana and Mahabharata and the Puranas like Kandapuranam, Periyapuranam etc and some traditions of Christianity contain innumerable myths within them suggestive of stability of social life whereas native classical literature like Silapadhigaram and after a long gap Aazhi Sul Ulagu and Korkai represent change.

The sources of mythic information are distinguishable from other literature with their potential to create larger than life images.[7] Of course, within Silapadhigaram and Aazhi Sul Ulagu also there are similar elements. But the lives under focus in these sources are predominantly observable in everyday life. Being the latest in the line as well as in his capacity as an insider, scholarly contributions of Joe d'Cruz attain significance. His memory shaped through internalizing of self and shared experiences informs the details of various issues with the mix of imagination. In an attempt wherein historical geography of specific communities is made, an exploration into the memories of such individuals who can be considered as a representative sample is inevitable.[8]

In spite of all these, one has to essentially realize the time gap between each of the works mentioned above and thereby the limitation of bringing into purview only some of the important episodes. Since the basic tools of production – catamaran and vallam – continues over time through these episodes, it can be ascertained that effective linkages between them exist making useless sketching the details of intervals in-between. It also gives an impression that the Parathavar people appear to live in the same episteme for a longer period providing scope for accommodating ethnography in writing their history.[9]

In order to arrive at a historical framework of time scholarly ideas of noted archaeologists, Gordon Childe and K. Rajan have been borrowed. Similarly, understanding on the spatial element has been made through the writings of K.K. Pillai, R. Pavananthi Vembulu and K. Ramapandi. Insofar the writings of R. Pavananthi Vembulu and K. Ramapandi are concerned; their skill in anthropology throws light on the traditional knowledge system. Although the crux of the discussion is inspired by the ideas on discoveries by D.P. Chattopadyaya, in order to avoid repeating the details of the subject matter by Vembulu and Ramapandi, brief notes on the knowledge system are made only in the footnotes. The remaining part of the article is shaped by inputs from S.B. Kauffman, A. Sivasubramanian and S. Lazarus. Other scholars of importance include H.R. Pate, T.S. Subramanian and C.T. Maloney. The writings of these scholars have been substantiated with several seasons of field visits in the areas chiefly where religious conversion of Parathavars to Christianity took place. Thus the study is an attempt to capture some current from the prehistoric period to the point of conversion through anthropological insights.

Time

The pre-history of the Tamil people was chiefly characterized by the dialectics of land and sea.[10] Particularly while discussing the historical dynamics of the coast, the great hypothesis on Lemuria – a great land mass believed to have submerged in sea – had remained central.[11] More specifically, this hypothesis became inevitable for historical research pertaining to the southern Tamil country that was politically under the rule of Pandyan kings since their capitals were said to have been swallowed by the sea with some time gap in-between. The uniqueness about the History of the Pandyans was the involvement of a comparatively wider landmass that made historical analysis complex. Historians have traced islands named Madurai near northern Java and Coast of Borneo.[12] In contrast, Kaveripattinam, ruled by the Cholas was also destroyed by the sea albeit the physical distance between the historic underwater site and the modern place that carried the same name was only a few kilometers. Though some scholars altogether rejected the Lemuria hypothesis as a myth,[13] an answer was needed for the logical question of 'why some regions in deep sea bore the names of forests and hills?'[14] Therefore destruction of Ten Madurai and Kapatapuram by sea became an adjunct hypothesis to the great hypothesis and remained a matter for further exploration.

If Lemuria was the manifestation of wider geographical knowledge, there remained other regions beyond sea conceived to be located in a comparatively shorter distance. According to tradition, it was maintained that beautiful places ruled by evil rulers existed beyond the sea. Sri Lanka and Mahendragiri were such places, the former geographically historic and mythic in other details whereas the later was purely mythical. As far as Sri Lanka was concerned, it was believed as the country ruled by Ravana. He was killed by Rama who as a warlord was deified at Rameshwaram. In the case of Mahendragiri, it was ruled by a demon by name Surapadman later killed by Lord Murugan the success of which was symbolized by the establishment of Tiruchendur temple.

In the case of Sri Lanka reasons that owed chiefly to the short distance with India made the contact historical. In the earlier period known as Tamiraparani – either after the name of the river or vice versa – it was known for physical prosperity.[15] It had the natural attraction on people and contributed to the smooth movement of people from both sides. It was argued by scholars that since the pearl fishing areas[16] in the Sri Lankan side were frequently invaded by the Tamil rulers, the influx of the Tamil people was common.[17] It also seemed that coastal people's settlements in Sri Lanka paralleled that of Indian settlements and the commonality that ensued in result eroded the differences made on the grounds of location.[18] Apart from Sri Lanka, there were tiny islands such as the Pandyan Island[19] chiefly utilized by the rulers for safeguarding precious materials. Such islands together with the image of Sri Lanka and conditioned by challenges like severe storms and sea ravages shaped the imagination on myths about places like Mahendragiri.[20] However other information pertaining to Sri Lanka and Mahendragiri tended to remain hypothetical and needed proof.

Similarly hypothetical were the arguments that trace the roots of Tamil civilization from the Indus Valley. Noted archaeologist Gordon Childe linked urban developments that occurred in the world with anyone of the civilizations that included only Egyptian or Mesopotamian or

Indus Valley.[21] Apart from several polemical debates with political undercurrent on the subject, archaeological evidence that came from villages in the Coramandal Coast such as Sembiyankandiyur and Melaperumpallam testify the material proximity of the region to the Indus Valley civilization.[22] Importantly, in a megalithic pottery that belonged to the period between 300 B.C. and A.D. 100 was found arrow–mark graffiti twice incised similar to the Indus Script.[23] Similarly, other evidence from Sembiyankandiyur included ceramics such as black-and-red ware, black ware and red ware with graffiti marks and geometrical designs that depict fish among other things.[24] Though there was a time difference of at the least 1600 years, the range of evidence were not only pointing to the smooth travel into chronological cultural phases of Tamil Nadu that started from Black and Red Ware, Megalithic, Early historic and Historic[25] but also the link with Indus Valley for the historic period was characterized by attainment of linguistic standardization.[26]

The prehistoric cultural developments as stated above found expression in Adichchanallur, a site of importance from the first half of I millennium B.C. known for the complex assemblage of artifacts and monuments. The site spread in an area of more than one hundred acres was urban in nature by virtue of the presence of planned life, granaries and port suggestive of links with the Indus Civilization. Though ideas and materials from Indus Valley found their way much earlier, probably the circulation of Indus Script was coterminous with the linguistic cohesiveness that was arrived in Tamil Nadu by the 5th century B.C. By this logic, the hypothesis based on Gordon Childe's historical view attains greater chance of validity.

Since Adichchanallur met with decay – most possibly because of the silt caused by the river Tamiraparani – the urban character was soon taken over by Korkai. The common current that underlined the difference in time and place was traceable from the worship of Murugan[27] what provided the philosophical justification for the process of collection of surplus and distribution.[28] Moreover, Korkai was landlocked and better secured, unlike Tondi and Dhanuskodi ports which were located near the border of the Chola territory frequented by invasions.[29]

The historic town Korkai contributed its share to the myth that was also of good use to understand the entry into the historical period marked by improvement in the domain of ideas. While on the one hand it was associated with the origin of the three native monarch's namely the Cheras, the Cholas and the Pandyas with whom the historic period or the Sangam Age was politically identified,[30] on the other hand, it was also linked with narratives that pertained to the origin of Sage Agastya who was stated to have come from Tibet to organize the Sangams[31] suggestive of the harmonious blend of both localization and borderless trends in mythical aspects.

Moreover, the female divinity worship that was present in Korkai provided a hint to the knowledge about the Himalayas.[32] The virgin god with martial features was eternally engaged in meditation like the Pasupathi Mahadeva of the Indus Valley only to reach her supposed spouse in the Himalayas. Subsequently, the status of chief abode of the goddess was attributed to Madurai[33] – headquarters of the Pandyans – wherein she took the title Meenakshi or 'female ruler with fish like eyes.' Another important spot where their love exploits took place also during the Saivite Bhakthi Movement was

Uttarakosamangay.[34] After their marriage, the couple was recognized as parents to Lord Murugan seated at Tiruchendur.

These myths were not only suggestive of localization of indigenous elements and information on the geographical area beyond tangibility but also evidence for standardization attained in the sphere of religion guided by the appearance of the script, usage of coins, the formation of trade routes, migration of people, formulation of various clan groups and the emergence of state.[35] Also, the key points of the region under Pandyan rule was marked with the icons of Rama, Siva, Murugan and Virgin Goddess located respectively in Rameshwaram, Uttarakosamangay, Tiruchendur and Kanyakumari.[36]

Space

Independent of the hypothesis of Gordon Childe, the conventional understanding of Tamil Civilization what marked the peak time of Korkai was made on the grounds of the concept of Tinai which sought to divide the entire landscape of the Tamil country into five environmental zones, namely, Kurinchi, Mullai, Marudham, Neydal and Palai. Although these were concepts of literature, for a historian they provided the clue for broadening the understanding of the socio-cultural life of the ancient people. Though the three chief kingdoms and other chieftaincies of the Sangam period were built over and above these zones, in every kingdom was found all the five environmental zones but not in the same mixture of proportions. In certain regions, there were overlaps of several zones whereas in some other the spread of people in a wider geographical space was observable than what was usually understood.

Korkai was a culmination of all these by which it assumed the status of a city and probably the status of second capital. It was situated near the bank of river Tamiraparani which was well known for its mineral wealth. The pearls harvested from this region – probably reasons that owed to the impact of the minerals – showed the colours of rainbow within them unlike pearls of other regions in the world. The perennial character of the river, its broader width that suited transportation to some extent,[37] the potential to deposit alluvial soil and ability as the water source for several channels[38] added to the wealth of Korkai. These along with the number of Chank industries[39] and the vegetation contributed to the occupational diversity that reflected in the population. Therefore, alongside Parathavar linked with the Neydal (coast), also were found Nalkudi Velallar and Konars, the people of Marutham (fertile plain) and Mullai (forest) respectively.[40]

A contemporary coastal town of prominence to Korkai was Kaveripattinam which was believed to have submerged under the sea as said already. To its contrast, the changes that occurred in the course of river Tamiraparani compounded with continuous silt depositions caused the sea to recede back.[41] Thus the distance between sea and land became wider to the tune of near about 6 to 7 kilometers. However, since Korkai was associated with trade activities till 13th century as depicted by Marco Polo and concurred by numismatic evidence these developments were attributable only to post 13th century A.D. Possibly with the decline of Korkai, Pazhyakayal emerged as a significant port.

It also met with the same fate like Korkai that also owed chiefly to river silt.[42] Therefore, by the time of the arrival of the Portuguese, Punnaikayal became an important port. It was in turn relegated to the background in favour of Tuticorin during the political dominance of the Dutch after 1658. Since the Dutch were known for trade in cotton, the inadequacy of water supply in Tuticorin[43] did not affect the port environment to a great extent.

Thus the drainage system was an important factor at one point of time in determining the importance of a port. Apart from river Tamiraparani, rivers Chittar and Nambiyar formed part of the drainage system in the Pearl Fishery Coast.[44] Since river Vaigai met the sea near Rameshwaram, to some extent it can also be considered as part of the drainage system. At land, they contributed for the fertility[45] while in the delta they attracted not only fish culture but also shaped the coastal ecosystem. Particularly the perennial Tamiraparani River gave birth to mangroves which helped them in several ways.[46] The estuaries formed at the mouth of the rivers – mentioned locally as Kayal – were responsible for the richness of not only fish but also other resources. Importantly from north to south Kayals were located at Vaippar, Pazhyakayal, Punnaikayal and Manapad. While Kayal in Vaippar was formed by Chittar, Kayals in Pazhyakayal and Punnaikayal were formed by Tamiraparani and in Manapad by Karumanaiyar that was part of Nambiyar drainage.[47]

The coastal spots linked by the river were comparatively more important for they had the possibility to carry out navigation.[48] Particularly, important was Manapad where the present researcher observed the remains of a very ancient port of greater magnitude.[49] There was a broad platform made of dressed stones stretching more than 150 meters in length. The width could have been around 20 to 25 meters but eroded by the sea. It was located at the bottom of a hillock. The hillock formed a natural wall perpendicular to the platform and had been severely damaged due to wear and tear activity of the wind and air for several years. At the place where the width possibly ended was deeper and boats plied on a straight line without interception of any rocky structure. The linkage between land and sea envisaged by the river was most possibly responsible for the development of the port. Though the potential of Manapad as a major port or not was subjected to debate, during the medieval period Kulasekharapatnam located just 3 kilometers away from Manapad emerged as a significant port.[50] Possibly the proximity to Manapad was an important factor that guided the growth of Kulasekharapatnam.

Freshwater was the major requirement to sustain life in the coast.[51] It was well reflected in their selection of residential settlements for which availability of drinking water, physical safety, nature of the sea and connectivity with land were considered as major preconditions. Apart from running water bodies, wells were the common source of drinking water. The underground water was not necessarily saline.[52] The indigenous knowledge system possibly had the ability to identify the nature of underground water. At the sea, they needed shoals for anchoring the vessels.[53] It was the combination of both which qualified a settlement site.

It also seemed that the coastal people possessed the intelligence as to predict the fury of the sea by the symptoms given by the sea-water. Though nature did not provide experience on a regular basis through collective memory inherited from ancestors that shaped their knowledge system, they chose their place of settlement either in elevated grounds or in curved beaches. As said already, in Pazhyakayal the sea was near about 3 kilometers away from the settlement and they reach the sea by boats through the Kayal. In Vembar the very nature of sea was always ferocious at the coast. Such sea was identified as male and usually confined in the shore. In Vaippar and Punnaikayal grooves of coastal plants form natural defence line which was protected by the local people for such a value.[54] In Veerapandianpattinam, Alandalai and Manapad their settlements were in an elevated location. Places between Manapad and Kuthanthurai were located in an inner curve that prevented excessive wave motion and thereby kept the region safe.[55] There was always a reasonable distance between one village and another. Sometimes people of other communities settled between two villages.[56] These were the reasons why the area was able to escape the wrath of Tsunami that ravaged the region.[57]

In the sea, the movement of the fishermen was not restricted.[58] On the basis of simple logic what can be stated was the point that the fishermen were primarily dependent upon the environment in the sea observable from land. Therefore, knowledge on the nature of formations in the sea-line parallel to their settlements was inevitable.[59] Though a definite regularity cannot be traced on that count for the entire Parathavar community, as far as the knowledge on the effect of sun and moon was concerned there evolved a said pattern. During sunrise and sunset the sea water expanded into the land and at day peak it withdrew.[60] The synchronization of the sea water with the gravitational pull was another matter internalized.[61]

Usually, in the Pearl Fishery Coast, rocks and coral reefs prevented the immediate formation of depth near the shore.[62] There were spots known locally as madai in the sea the width of which determined the quantum of catch.[63] The rocks and reefs led towards another water formation mentioned as Aazhi, a spot within the ocean, where wave motion tended to be severe classified into single surf beating and double surf beating.[64] Apart from that, astronomy,[65] ocean currents[66] – in general, known as Neevadu – and wind motion[67] occupied an important place in the local knowledge. It was important both to ensure the safety of their settlements and also in their sea ventures. Thus, if a fisherman did not return from the sea, the rescue team formed by his fellow fisherman never searched him in the same direction.[68] They made a calculation on the basis of the place of his disappearance and ocean current and searched accordingly. Likewise, in the Northern edge of the Pearl Fishery Coast (particularly near Rameshwaram) woods for building boats were bought at Sri Lanka and pushed into the sea and they reached the shore in the other side safe. Though there were many kinds of wood the ordinary catamarans that enabled to cross dangerous points like the Aazhi was made of Alpecia.[69]

Apart from their activities in the sea, their movement on land was equally important. The myths outlined in another section of the present article possibly were notions of migration that pertained to the Parathavar community in particular. The general impression arrived through the observation of the trends in migration was the role of wealth that determined it. The precursor to that was the discovery of the use of salt with food. Salt was a perfect manifestation of the dialectics of land and sea.

By virtue of its durability as well as unavailability in non-coastal areas, it was valued at par with other food grains in the barter system. Thereby coast pulled towards its direction either the produce or the proceeds of other regions. Wealth thus generated at the coast had caused migration from one city to another better one.

Trade routes via land were inevitable that owed also to the rough nature of the sea with seasonal winds that made the circumnavigation of Cape Comerin to reach Malabar difficult and time-consuming. Therefore, the land route was equally important and the traders moved along the bank of river Tamiraparani to reach Kerala via Achankoil Pass in the Western Ghats.[70] There emerged quite a number of settlements that belonged to the coastal communities in the route at Alwarthirunagari[71], Karungulam, Kaliavur, Palayamkottai, Pettai,[72] Nochikulam, and Shencottah.[73] Similarly in the areas south of Kerala, one could find a considerable number of Parathavar settlements.[74] The areas beyond the coast were significant for their supply of wood. Along with salt gradually, other articles produced in the coast as also imported from foreign countries reached inland. Despite scattered population in a wider geographical zone, there had been a powerful control mechanism sphere headed by the caste-headman known as Pandyapathy.[75] The loyalty of the Parathavar was not with the land but with the community at large as found in any tribe. Therefore certain scholars preferred to call them as a separate nation than merely a caste.[76]

Everyday Life

In spite of constant expansion, the Parathavar people traced their roots chiefly from any one of the coastal villages. However, they were linked with the capital wherein the density of maritime trade tended to be greater. As said already, the location of the capital changed with time. It was Adhichchanallur in the beginning and later replaced by Korkai and subsequently by Tuticorin. But the entire coastal community was linked to the traffic of the Toni[77] and someone in the joint family was involved in overseas trade activity. But these were only minorities in the coastal context and the overarching population was composed of ordinary fishermen who toiled in the sea for a livelihood.

The life pattern of the fishermen was determined by the tools used by them that included the boats. Possibly in the early times with simple tools fishing was carried out in parts of the sea not far away from the coast. The tools known as ethanam chiefly denoted various kinds of nets.[78] One of the earliest learning that pertained to the nature of the sea was the movement of fish to particular spots on a daily basis.[79] That particular place was identified and explored. The technique used for catching was so primitive that only a limited catch was possible and did not necessitate the involvement of more human labour. Two persons were sufficient to undertake the enterprise in a boat. In a day many such pairs entered the sea to bring an adequate catch to meet out the needs of a tribe.

With the advancement of tools, the secrets of the sea were further explored and movement was made towards spots of availability.[80] It necessitated a crew for which societies with tribal nature provided support. The advanced tools were also used for the earlier fishing technique of going to the place where fish arrived. Also, the fishing venture carried out by two persons continued. Gradually the advanced technology altered the social life and contributed for attaining economic self-sufficiency.

In the case of large-scale fishing, the person who planned the venture formed a crew. By virtue of forming a team, he did not claim the headship of the crew. Persons with work experience and comparatively better knowledge on oceanic geography became the natural leader of the crew.[81] Kinsmen belonging to the same tribe or large joint family made a joint venture. In that case, the paterfamilias or the father or the eldest brother took the responsibility of leading. When it was formed out of the family, skills of the individual and personal relationship determined the membership and position in the crew. The person who planned the venture had to decide on the spot to be explored and the kind of fish he wanted to catch. Usually, he consulted the experienced member in the crew. He also brought the tools according to requirement – particularly nets. The profit and loss were shared equally. For example, a boat with a crew of six men divided the catch into eleven equal shares and the boat got 5 shares which were taken by the owner of the boat.[82] During seasons of labour shortage, the non-family members of the crew were allowed to bring a limited number of nets along with them.[83] The fish that fell in these nets belonged to them alone.

With the arrival of market and property consciousness among the people the tribal nature of life underwent certain changes, matrilineal forms subsided, families with patriarchal values were evolved and paterfamilias emerged as the central figure in families.[84] Thereafter, every family aimed to own a boat or more and tools of fishing, for the highest aspiration to attain an economic status at par with the middlemen or traders who took the catch in an auction.[85] Ownership of a boat did not mean that the members would not join other crews at a time of need.

It was the surplus catch which created a class of middlemen.[86] These middlemen developed clear symbols of status reflective of their external contacts and with that, they distinguished themselves from the ordinary fishermen. They bore the risk of marketing the catch.[87] Since fish was a quickly perishable material their role became inevitable. Even in the basic aspects of everyday life such as food, clothing, housing pattern and interpersonal relationship sharp differences emerged between the two classes.[88] The elevation of status meant an adoption of a lifestyle at par with the traders. The possible chance was through diversification of the professional activities and establishment of command in the market. It involved migration of people with entrepreneurial skills to business centers. Therefore, in cases of families with numerically large male members, any one or more persons who did not participate in fishing took the responsibility of directly marketing the catch in the nearby places. Since the status of families came to be viewed parallel with the seclusion of women at a point of time, few young girls were involved in the marketing process.[89] It was doubtful whether even elderly married women traveled as far as their male counterparts for that purpose.

Over and above all these, owning of boats by families had its own limitation. There was always a limit to invest on boats and tools of fishing. In a small coastal village, a family cannot hope to own several boats and too many nets though there was present scope for an incentive that came via rent for owners of boats and other fishing tools. In the early periods, it was repaid in kind. In the money economy, it was either repaid in cash or kind. Money became important to adopt a social image in the shade of the dominant class.[90] Money was also extended in the name of a loan by individuals. At times, the owner of a boat took the loan in the mode of a lease and repaid by way of a share in the catch.[91]

The tribal nature of life continued to exist in certain fronts cutting across economic value attached to the produce. The residents of the village collected fish from the nets without seeking permission or offering objects of value on the basis of kinship affinity. Unlike agriculture, fishing had been a short duration enterprise and cannot be performed individually. As said already, nobody can claim ownership over sea water and its resources. Anybody can explore any spot in the sea and the general rule that had to be adopted was that no one shall embark upon another person's labor. A person irrespective of the place to which he belonged could move along the coast in boat parallel to another village and spread his net anywhere as he wished. Normally he moved three to four kilometers parallel to the coastal line and ambitious fisherman went further deeper even near Sri Lanka. Conventionally, in the case of heavy catch to the extent of unable to move, they requested the service of fishermen who worked nearby and offered them a share.[92]

The tribal nature of the society encountered severe challenges with the changes that occurred in the sphere of economy. Though families with patriarchal undercurrent and paterfamilias at the center emerged, by all means, it was not sufficient enough to totally replace the tribal way of life. Neither the correspondence with the non-coastal regions and foreign lands, nor the emergence of internal divisions altered the fundamental premise of it.

Conclusion

Though Sangam literature depicted the life of people in geographically autonomous environments, the mythical ideas pertaining to time and space were shared by all the people by virtue of common language and also for reasons that owed to the poor interval between the coast and the mainland.[93] Despite the seeds of myth found in the Sangam literature, it was the Bhakthi Movement that started in the region during the medieval period which ingrained mythical ideas in the minds of the people. However, when myths appeared to pass through different periods of time, they did not correspond with changes in the economic sphere more specifically in matters of tools. Therefore Frank Kermode's view modified for the present study as 'myths point to stagnation' was proved.

Stagnation engulfed the region for a longer duration since the end of the Sangam period. During the Sangam period, the volume of the Indo-Roman Trade infused the spirit of fiction that culminated in the production of Silapadhigaram. After the Sangam period until the Indo-Norwegian Project of the 1950s and subsequent developments caused definite changes what found expression in the production of fiction by Joe d'Cruz. The period in between might have remained prosperous in the economic front. But as Marco Polo observed, it was characterized by degeneration in the socio-cultural front. At that juncture again time and space were viewed in relation to myth and superstition marked their everyday life probably during which Parathavapuranam and Valaiveesupuranam were authored.[94]

In the dialectics between land and sea, the adaptation of the Parathavar remained compatible with the spirit of nature until the introduction of the Indo-Norwegian Project in the 1950s. Within that, they were able to develop active trade corresponded with extensive migration. Although the Parathavar population was widely spread, with conversion into Christianity importance was attributed to seven coastal towns popularly known as Yelu Ur. Nevertheless, since conversion did not bring about tangible changes in the tools of production their mode of negotiation with nature continued as before.

In spite of the emergence of local variation in the dialectics between land and sea, the knowledge system evolved over a period of time, based on the effect of sun and moon united the Parathavar people which probably culminated in the formation of Suryavamsam and Chandravamsam clans. But the lifestyle of the Parathavar people on an average had several compatible elements with other people in terms of food consumption,[95] mode of dressing,[96] kinship pattern, etc. Their engagement with the sea was for a brief time in a day what provided scope for other activities that included even agriculture. On such grounds, it can be asserted that they were not only part and parcel of the Dravidian stock but also not much distinguishable from the people of the plains. In such a context, the Indo-Norwegian Project of the 1950s was a breakthrough in aspects of tools which definitely altered the lives of the Parathavars symbolized by the production of a fiction by Joe d'Cruz.

Endnotes

1   According to the 'Biological-evolutionary Theory' of scholars like Darwin constructed mainly on the idea of 'survival of the fittest,' adaptation required definitive skills generated by the demand of time. Though not directly felt by the lives in the earth themselves, in actuality it was true.

2   D.P. Chattopadyaya, *Madhamum, Samugamum* (Tamil), (Chennai: New Century Book House, 2009), p. 30.

3   The expression 'Tamil country' is preferred because the language based geographical boundary is only a later period evolution. Likewise, definite period denotes the 'Sangam Period' the beginning and end of which is a controversial topic. The present researcher's opinion concurs with the historians for who the period is between 1st and 3rd centuries A.D.

4   Though the fundamental framework of the present study is attributable to Marxist style of history writing, in line with the Annales historians, the focus is on issues over events.

5   Robin A. Butlin, *Historical Geography: Through the Gates of time and Space,* (New York: Edward Arnold, 1993) pp. 51–54.

6   S. Manickam, *Facets of History: A Spectrum of Thought,* (Madurai: Madurai Kamaraj University, 1998) p. 31; Frank Kermode (1919–2010) is a British literary critic inspired by Annales' school of historical thought. His famous scholarly works include 'The Sense of an Ending: Studies in the Theory of Fiction wherein he has made the said observation.

7   Akshaya Kumar, Professor of English Literature, Panjab University, in a lecture during a refresher

course in social sciences conducted at the UGC-ASC of the same university conducted between 30-11-2010 and 20-12-2010 expressed these views.

8   Nonica Datta, a scholar from Delhi University successfully brought out a historical research work entitled 'Violence, Martyrdom and Partition: A Daughter's Testimony' in 2009 through Oxford University Press in which she has followed the method of using memory as the chief source of history.

9   The concept of episteme that denotes a 'time-period' flows from the ideas of Mitchell Foucault, a noted post-modern historian. According to him, every episteme gives birth to certain ideas which attain maturity and dies in that particular epistemic period itself. Therefore, it is not possible to understand the occurrences of another episteme by virtue of living in the present episteme. This is a limitation of the discipline of history. Since people at the margins live in the same episteme for a longer period their social history can be sketched by way of mere observation. Under this pretext, subaltern historiography takes its justification. The present study has methodological parallels with that.

10   R. Pavananthi Vembulu and R. John Suresh Kumar, *Circling the Triangle: Vulnerability, Social Exclusion and the Making of Disaster*, Research Paper Series, (Tirunelveli: Centre for the Study of Social Exclusion and Inclusive Policy, Manonmaniam Sundaranar University, 2010) **p._.**

11   Romila Thapar, *The Penguin History of Early India*, p. 100; according to her the 'deluge myth' was authored at Mesopotamia during the Indo-European lingual period and found the way into almost every ancient literature from there.

12   K.K. Pillay, *Historical Heritage of the Tamils*, (Chennai: MJP Publishers, 2008) p. 11.

13   S. Christopher Jayakaran, The Lemuria Myth, *Frontline*, Vol. 28 – Issue 08, Apr. 09–22, 2011, pp._; the scholar explores all the existing views on Lemuria including those from the Sangam literature and concludes it as mere myth.

14   R.N. Joe d'Cruz, *Aazhi Sul Ulagu* (Tamil), (Chennai: Tamizhini, 2004) p. 380; some of the points in the sea are named Chinnauchankadu, Periyauchankadu, Periyamalaipaaru, Usimalaipaaru, Sozhathamalai etc. Notable is the meaning of the terms kadu and malai which denote forest and hill respectively.

15   Romila Thapar, Where Fusion Cannot Work, *The Hindu*, 28 Sept. 2007.

16   R. Pavananthi Vembulu and R. John Suresh Kumar, *Circling the Triangle;* The location of the *Pearl Fishery Coast* falls in the coastline between South of *Rameshwaram* and *Kanyakumari* (Cape Comerin). In the sea, the *Pearl Fishing Zone* is about 330 kilometers in the *Gulf of Mannar* from *Pamban* to *Cape Comerin* though the *Coramandal Coast and Palk Strait* together with the gulf constitutes the Coast of Tamil country.

17   Clarence Thomas Maloney, *The Effect of Early Coastal Sea Traffic on the Development of Civilization in South India,* Unpublished Ph. D. thesis submitted to the Dept. of Anthropology, University of Pennsylvania in 1968, pp. 130–131.

18   Ibid. p. 115; it can be inferred from the writing of the scholar that though the Sinhalese people treated Tamils with indifference they did not distinguish between them and the Parathavars.

19 R.N. Joe d'Cruz, *Korkai* (Tamil), (Chennai: Kalachuvadu Pathipagam, 2009) pp. 274–275; according to the scholar, in 1603 when the Pandyan kings were attacked by the Nayakka rulers of Madurai, they took refuge in these Islands to safeguard their material wealth.)

20 _________, *Aazhi Sul Ulagu* , pp. 214–217; one such island that was ravaged in 1964 was Dhanuskodi.

21 D.P. Chattopadyaya, Op. Cit., p. 27.

22 T.S. Subramanian, From Indus Valley to Coastal Tamil Nadu, *The Hindu* (Madurai edition), dated 3rd May 2008.

23 Ibid.; the marking belonged to the mature Harappan period that fell between 2600 – 1900 B.C. In the case of the Tamil country, the same marking was found during the period between 300 B.C. and A.D. 300.

24 ______, Megalithic Period Pottery Found, *The Hindu* (Madurai edition), dated 27 April 2008.

25 *Situating the Beginning of Early Historic Times in Tamil Nadu: Some Issues and Reflections*, Social Scientist, (_______) p. 47.

26 Ibid., p. 41.

27 K.K. Pillay, O. Cit., pp. 189–190.

28 D.P. Chattopadyaya, Op. Cit., pp. 31–32; according to the scholar, gods with human attributes becoming central to religion was a need generated by the changes that occur in the sphere of economy evoked by discoveries in the third millennium B.C. If this criterion was applied for civilizations then the basic character of religion did not change once urban life was established.

29 Clarence Thomas Maloney, Op. Cit., pp. 123–124.

30 H.R. Pate, *Tinnevelly District Gazetteer (1916),* (Tirunelveli: Manonmaniam Sundaranar University, 1993) p. 40; in a folklore pertained to Mukkani – a place located near Korkai – it was maintained that in the town the three monarchs divided among them the revenues of the Pearl Fisheries.

31 Ibid.; the author has inferred this myth with the support of a Siva temple located at Manapadaiveedu near Korkai. He also sought to establish the Saiva connection of Korkai through the tradition wherein sacred sand was sent from here to Nellaiappar temple in Tirunelveli during festival occasions. The author also discusses Mukkani Brahmins who trace their origin from the birth of Tiruchendur temple. Probably these are the shark-charmers mentioned by Marco Polo who took a voluminous share in the proceeds of the Pearl Fishery.

32 S. Ramachandran, *Korkai Varalatril Sila Pudhiya Seidhigal* (Tamil), Archaeological Report of Curator, Korkai in a manuscript dated 13-06-2000 sent to headquarters, p. 1; in the report, the curator has mentioned about a thirteenth-century temple attributed to Goddess Vetriver Chezhiyanangai cast in the usual mould of Parvathi. Since worshipping of deities pre-existed temples, what can be inferred was the point that the worship of Siva's spouse was present in the region long before.

33 J.H. Nelson, *The Madura Country A Manual,* Part II (New Delhi: Asian Educational Services, 1989), p_; surprisingly there were comparable parallels in terms of living standards between the Parathavar residents of the non-coastal city of Madurai and the coastal city of Kaveripattinam as depicted in Maduraikanci and Pattinapalai respectively. However, in the nineteenth-century observations of J.H. Nelson, there were hardly less than hundred people in Madurai town.

34 The place is located in the Ramnad district, not much far from Rameshwaram. It was also believed to have been the head quarters of the Parathavars since at one point of time their caste leader was stationed here.

35 K. Rajan, Op. Cit., p. 42.

36 Interview with Mr. Sukumaran (47) of Kottar on 27/03/2010 and also field visit conducted at Kanyakumari; the temple pillars and monuments around the temple bear symbols of boats and fish respectively suggesting their Pandyan connection. Kanyakumari. The interviewee was of the opinion that there was a planned effort to project them as belonging to Kerala.

37 Step like structures has been unearthed about 250 mts west of the river just 50 mts near railway lines in Tirunelveli Junction. It's real width to a substantial level can be seen at Srivaikundam not much far from Adichchanallur an important Megalithic site.

38 Slum Survey conducted for Tirunelveli Corporation between 20th April and 20th June 2010; the network of the channel system in the district belonging to the past centuries was a marvel that requires a separate study.

39 James Hornell, The Indian Chank in Folklore and Religion, *Taylor and Francis,* Vol. 53, No. 2 (Jun, 1942), pp. 113–125; the author provides vital information on the geographical details and thoroughly explains the religious importance of the chank.

40 Information collected through field visits conducted at Korkai and Maranmangalam on 10/09/2010; a few families of Parathavars who fish in the freshwater for livelihood do live in Maranmangalam. It seems that government mechanism does not recognize them as Parathavars for the reason of their dependence on freshwater.

41 Interview with K.S. Narayana Pillai of Korkai on 10/09/2010; he remembers his conversation with Clarence Maloney who during his field visits in the 1960's had said for every hundred years the ground level near rivers would rise by 1 feet. The depositing of alluvial soil by river *Tamiraparani* could have been one of the factors responsible for the rise of ground level what may have caused the receding of the sea. This would have been also the reason for instances of Chanks occurring at 5 to 7 feet depth at Korkai.

42 Field visit conducted at Pazhayakayal on 10/09/2010; the village is separated from the sea by salt-fields in between. A branch of the river passes by the side of the village in which boats are anchored. The fishermen sail through the fresh water to reach the sea water.

43 It was Curuz Fernandes in his capacity as municipal chairman who put an end to the water scarcity of Tuticorin town. Under the British administration, a project was drafted to bring Tamiraparani water from the Valanadu village.

44 H.R. Pate, Op. Cit., pp. 148–194.

45 R.N. Joe d'Cruz, *Aazhi Sul Ulagu* p. 71 & p. 352; the author gives a picture of the fertility of Athur, the location of which is between Korkai and Punnaikayal. Here in a year rice cultivation takes place in all the three seasons. Beetle leaves and banana plantations also added to the fame of Athur. Similarly, the author also speaks about the specialty of bananas and brinjals of Oovari (symbolized through the name Amanthurai in the book)

46 Staff Reporter, *The Hindu* (Madurai Edition) dated 27 April 2012; mangroves were found in Pazhyakayal to the tune of 1500 hectares. The mangroves protected them from storm and Tsunami as also provided breeding and nursing ground. Salt-fields spoil the fertility of land and reduce the total coverage of mangroves.

47 R.N. Joe d'Cruz, *Aazhi Sul Ulagu* p. 71 & p. 352.

48 H.R. Pate, Op. Cit., p. 179; since the British government accepted the navigation potential of the river they attempted to connect the paddy rich Ambasamudram with Tuticorin, Punnaikayal and Kulasekharapatnam.

49 Staff Reporter, *The Hindu* (Madurai Edition) dated 26th April 2012; the article speaks about the lighthouse that was erected to 'monitor the steering ships along the coast'. It also states that the ships bound for international trade from Tuticorin were bound to proceed through Manapad.

50 H.R. Pate, Op. Cit., pp. 19–21; he mentions Manapad as the southern arm of Kulasekharapatnam harbour. He also gives details of a series of rock shoals extending from Manapad point to Vaippar interrupted at Kulasekharapatnam by a reef front which is suitable for anchorage.

51 Interview with Mr. Amaladas, (65), Fisherman of Alandalai on 02/01/10; he was of the opinion that the place which was under the spiritual guidance of the missionaries since the sixteenth-century was not viable to start educational institutions for want of water. But for a period of time, a seminary was conducted at Manapad.

52 There were evidence for sweet water wells very close to the sea in several places including Tiruchendur, Manapad and Nadar Oovari.

53 H.R. Pate, Op. Cit., p. 20.

54 Interview with Mr. R. Michael Fernando of *Punnaikayal* on 10/09/2010.

55 R.N. Joe d'Cruz, *Aazhi Sul Ulagu,* p.60.

56 Kallamozhi is a village inhabited by the Nadars and located between Alandalai and Manapad. Here Nadars venture into sea to catch fish. Similarly at Tharuvaikulam near Vaippar, Nadars venture into sea.

57 Those who were affected by Tsunami were predominantly the Mukkuvas who were brought and settled on the Coast of South Travancore region by the native king a few centuries ago.

58 The birth of independent states of India and Sri Lanka caused the creation of marine –boundary which the fishermen of both sides find difficult to adopt.

59 R. Pavananthi Vembulu and R. John Suresh Kumar, *Circling the Triangle,* p._.

60 Ibid.

61 Ibid.

62 The rocky bottom of the sea where pearl oysters occur is known as 'pearl beds' or 'pearl banks'. For detailed information on that, *see* N. Athiyaman (ed.), *Pearl and Chank Diving of South Indian Coast (A Historical and Ethnographical Perspective)* (Thanjavur: Tamil University, 2000).

63 R.N. Joe d'Cruz, *Aazhi Sul Ulagu*, p.38.

64 R. Pavananthi Vembulu and R. John Suresh Kumar, *Circling the Triangle*, p._.; known locally as ottha madangu kadal and irettai madangu kadal. Though both were regarded as dangerous, the intensity in the latter was more.

65 K. Ramapandi, *Panpaatu Marabukal* (Tamil), (Palayamkottai: Madhumitha Pathippagam, 2010) pp. 13–24; the author discusses the traditional knowledge based on the position and movement of stars in the sky. Both natural and artificial structure of height facilitated trigonometric calculation of positioning their location in the sea.

66 Ibid., ocean current that passed towards north from South was known as Sonuvadu and that passed towards South from North was Vanuvadu, towards East from West was Aranivadu, towards West from East was Karaikanaitha Nivadu, towards Southeast from Northwest was Vanuvadu Aranivadu, towards Southwest from Northeast was Vanuvadu Karaikanaitha Nivadu, from Southeast towards Northwest was Sonuvadu Karaikanaitha Nivadu and from Southwest to Northeast it was called Sonuvadu Aranivadu.

67 R.N. Joe d'Cruz, *Korkai,* p. 1130; the wind that blew from the North was called Vadai, from South was Chozhavalam, from West was Kachaan, from East was Kondal, from Northwest it was Vadaikachaan, from Northeast was Vadaikondal, from Southeast was Chozhakondal and that from Southwest was called Chozhakachaan.

68 Interview with Mr. R. Pavananthi Vembulu, Field Worker in Tsunami Project on 14/09/2008.

69 The alpecia species suitable for making boats were found throughout the trade-route from the Pearl Fishery Coast to the Western Ghats. However, the best specimen was found on the hill. Dr. Chellathurai, author of the book Medicinal Plants in the Western Ghats in a personal discussion said that among the three specimens of alopecia, the lebbeck kind is thought to be indigenous whereas Albizia procera and Ailthanus excels are not indigenous to our country.

70 There are several *Mandapams* and *Chathrams* in the route. To cite an example, a *Mandapam* is located outside *Alwarthirunagari* in the West and a *Chathram* (V. M. Chathram) is located by the entrance of *Tirunelveli* in the East on this trade route.

71 S.B. Kaufmann, A Christian Caste in a Hindu Society: Religious Leadership and Social Conflict among the Paravas of Southern Tamil Nadu, *Modern Asian Studies*, Vol. 15, No. 2 (1981), p._

72 Ibid.

73 Significantly the settlements of the Parathavars, Muslims and Vanniars were found one after another in most of the places.

74 S.B. Kauffman, Op. Cit., p. 228; a settlement of the Parathavar caste is found in Chinnakadai of Kollam district.

75 The caste-headman was once believed to be stationed at Uttarakosamangay and subsequently shifted to Tuticorin.

76 Anonymous Author (ed.), *The Chronicles of the Pearl Fishery Coast,* p.

77 For details on toni *see* A. Sivasubramanian, *Toni* (Palayamkottai: Folklore Resource and Research Centre, _____).

78 R. Pavananthi Vembulu and R. John Suresh Kumar, *Circling the Triangle,* p._.; twines in the nets were chiefly made of fibers of cotton and hemp.

79 S. Lazarus in A.K. Perumal and G. Stephen (eds.), *Alaigalinoode,* (Chennai: United Writers, 2005) p.15.

80 Ibid.

81 A crew that started before dawn returned by sunrise. In total three to four hours of hard work was involved. At the same time, predictability and certainty were not attached to the profession. An uncertainty of life and ultimately chaos was the basic feature of their everyday professional life. These were not calculated while transferring the commodity.

82 Interview with Mr. Parabaran of Manapad on 08-01-10.

83 Interview with Charles Pachek (45) of Vaippar on 11-02-2011.

84 Paterfamilias of a family was central to its economic activities. His image as a fisherman together with his chief mistress' social image also went in the shaping of the status of families.

85 R. Pavananthi Vembulu and R. John Suresh Kumar, *Circling the Triangle,* p._.

86 Since there emerged a variety of boats in the historical period – conveniently termed as Sangam period – it can be ascertained that surplus was produced in the fishing economy.

87 These were the people who made business by distributing seafood to retailers. These middlemen fixed the value and took the total catch. Then they attached a profit margin and marketed it.

88 The influence of Sri Lanka was easily observable among the Parathavars. Importantly, lavish spending on food and clothing was an inspiration derived from the Sinhalese.

89 A. Sivasubramanian, *Uppittavarai* (Chennai: Kalachuvadu Pathipagam, 2009) p. 32; the scholar with the support of Sangam literature speaks about unmarried girls involved in the sales of salt. However, it can be asserted that in subsequent periods a family that subjected young girls to hard labor had a very poor image in the eyes of the dominant class of people. It should also be mentioned here that an easy method of improving the socio-economic status was attained through a matrimonial alliance.

90 Social expenses were higher. Usually, they spent more on food and clothing than other people. Similarly, matrimonial alliance with the dominant class was possible by offering a high rate of dowry. An ordinary man spent on all these beyond his ability through borrowings from outside.

91 R.N. Joe d'cruz, *Aazhi Sul Ulagu,* p_. A part of the catch usually went for the repayment of the loan.

92 Ibid.

93 Tiruchendur is believed to be one of the six holy-abodes of Lord Muruga. Usually, the Lord's abode is located in a hillock conforming to the Tamil phrase 'Kundrirukum idamellam Kumaran irukkum idam'. Though Tiruchendur is a sea-shore, there exist a cave and similar rocky forms as in the hills. Tradition also informs that Valli a Kurava girl belonging to hill region who married Lord Muruga hided herself in Tiruchendur for fear of an elephant. Thereby the looseness of land division can be understood.

94 L.F. Benedetto (ed.), *The Travels of Marco Polo*, (New Delhi: Asian Educational Services, 1994) pp. 290–305.

95 There was a preference for fish-curry with everyday food. Otherwise, they also consumed such food as in the mainland.

96 Simon Casie Chitty, *Remarks on the Origin and History of the Parawas,* Journal of the Royal Asiatic Society of Great Britain and Ireland, Vol. 4, No. 1 (1837), pp. 132–134.

IV

Surplus Formation and Beyond:
Understanding the Economic Life of the Parathavars before Conversion

Introduction

The economy of the early Tamil country was viewed from various angles. Specifically, from what was called the Sangam period, the interdependence of the geographical units namely the Tinai formed the chief subject matter. In such studies, the predominance of agricultural output and cattle wealth were projected. This made even the study of the Indo-Roman trade an adjunct to the agricultural economy. Thereby the actual capacity of the coastal region and its economic resources that went in the shaping of the socio-political life was relegated to the background. In the one hand, historians interpreting the past have dealt the subject in a very limited quantum. Even as great a historian as K. A. Nilakanta Sastri himself was of the view that it was the agriculture and not trade which formed the mainstay of polity and war.[1] Noburu Karasimha in his discussions on Valangai and Idangai communities related to trade – of the early medieval period –did not give any place for the Parathavars.

In the other hand, scholars of other social sciences who made observations on the contemporary life of the people chiefly through field visits generalized the economy of the coast as merely fishing enterprise. Some of them also believed that the lifestyle of the coastal people came close to primitive communism.[2] Contentions like these were made chiefly on the grounds that, since fish tended to perish quickly, it cannot be stored for longer duration and had to be essentially distributed. Such assumptions logically led towards understanding the coastal village economy as self-sufficient that depended on the outside world only for the supply of foodgrains as the vice-versa happened in the villages of the plains, hills and forests wherein isolation marked by self-sufficiency was broken by the supply of salt from the coast. However, an approach of viewing the coastal economy independently or its effects on the agrarian economy was hardly attempted. This may possibly infuse an epistemic change in the understanding of the early Tamil economy.

The present article seeks to merge the gap between the perceptions of historians and other social scientists. At the same time, it intends to place the economic life of the Parathavars within the framework of social history what can render inter-disciplinary justice. In an approach of this kind, a general outlook of the major shades could be arrived at than sketching of particular issues. Therefore the

65

interplay of political and social systems has been viewed through the prism of economic determinism. It is also an attempt to liberate the history of the Parathavars from the general understanding that the dynamic in their economic life is the product of their conversion to Christianity. Since Indo-Roman trade has been a constant subject matter at the textbook level chiefly dealt by archaeologists handling of it in the present study would violate the ethic of a researcher and may even cause the danger of attributing the achievements in that segment to the Parathavars alone. Therefore that is being ignored in favor of observations made through field visits and discussions have been used to trace the seeds responsible for causing the evolution of the coastal economy and the link among the variable units of the coast.

The approach of the study starts with the tracing of surplus formation and its impact. Further, it indirectly seeks to compare the coastal economy with the agrarian economy and tries to identify whether there was present any scope for feudal formation or class division. It also takes into purview the elements of local governance within which economic aspirations of individual are placed. An attempt has been made in the latter half of the article to write the economic history of the coastal people through ethnographic method. For the present study, evidence other than anthropological come from Sangam literature and foreign accounts such as that of Marco Polo. Supporting secondary works are those of D.P. Chattopadyaya, Edgar Thurston, Rajan Gurukkal, A. Sivasubramanian, N. Athiyaman, S. Lazarus, R.N. Joe d'cruz and others.

Formation of Surplus

The idea of self-sufficiency on the economic front was theoretically linked to social stagnation for the reason that it denuded the possible interaction with the outside world. In the case of the Tamil coast in general, if even fishing had been the only economic activity, still there was sufficiently present scope for progress. That may be explained even from a period before advancement in tool making wherein life was certainly difficult and physical might remained the order of time both in the plain and the coast. Particularly, basic life challenges unleashed by famines during summers considerably reduced the availability of fish in the sea. In such situations, the pattern of economic life necessitated plundering raids[3] modelled in the format of that existed in the plains. The plunder raids of the time were performed by big and small chieftains independently and at times by forming a confederation.[4] Movement of any kind, either from the coast towards the plain or vice-versa would have definitely disturbed the isolation of the coastal settlements. This was mooting the point that 'the isolation of the coast from other economic zones' was only a preconceived notion without adequate evidence. Possibly since the coast maintained a level of autonomy in its social life it gave rise to a suggestive notion that they had nothing to do with the overall progress of the larger Tamil society. In any case, while studying the economy of the coast the overall impact of the agrarian economy should be considered.

The question of the possibility of surplus production in the coastal context arose because; from the historic period, fish was known to be only a supportive food, the main food being grains of various kinds and paddy. The coastal stretch that included both sea and land was but another ecological sphere with its own wealth potentials with limited projections into other land forms.[5] With the gradual development of tools, the nature of land was explored and learned whereas in the case of land in the plain the potentials were always observable without special effort.

The impact of developments in the agrarian economy on the coast was indirect. The discovery of better methods of water management[6] that resulted in the improved production of food crops had its impact in the coastal life. Surplus produced in fertile lands beyond the need of local subsistence liberated a set of people from being directly involved in food production.[7] A section of such people definitely had a share in the development of the coastal economy for they contributed in the field of ship-building, transporting of imported goods from the coast to the plain, treating and taming of pack-animals and importantly shaping the understanding of the people on their beliefs on the external element.

The fishing economy that was basically characterised by uncertainty and insecurity of life entered a new phase of the economy with the advancements as mentioned above. Particularly, the discovery of buoyancy and pressure of water bodies as well as learning of other related features of sea water came to alter the socio-economic aspects of the coastal region. In turn, this culminated in the discovery of boats, the common salt and valuables like the pearl and chank. The discovery of boats by 3rd millennium B.C.[8] as postulated by D.P. Chattopadyaya for the general history of the world would have entered the Tamil Society much later.[9]

By the beginning of the Sangam period, we find reference to boats of several kinds including that usable in fresh water.[10] The common varieties of the boat are categorised into Ambi, Pahri, Odam, Padagu and Timil.[11] N. Subrahmanian says Ambi and Padagu were ferry boats for crossing streams and rivers and Timil was a fishing boat.[12] In the harbour of Puhar there were rows of large boats, Pahri which had returned laden with grain obtained in exchange for the white salt they had sold; and other boats were seen in the backwaters of Puhar, "tied to rows of pegs and looking so many destriers."[13] The nature of the wood employed in these boats was resilient to the ferociousness of the sea and at any risk, they did not sink.[14] A seafarer who could stick to the boat in storms and high tides would safely reach the shore. The frequent loss of lives was prevented by these boats what checked the shortage that would arise in manpower and reduced the unwarranted fear about sea ventures.

With advancement in boat making technology, several varieties of the fishing net were also introduced. These enabled exploration into sea further easier. The man who hesitated to cross a limit in the sea was now able to not only move quicker on the surface of the water but also explored the depth with less effort. He went to areas close to Sri Lanka and identified the sand bars within the sea where reproduction of fish took place and their availability had been in large numbers. Tools required for catching bigger fish was also available and their use beyond the kitchen was also learnt. Huge fish of the cod family and their variables were caught for their medicinal value and oil was extracted from them. However, his way of life was not in violation of the laws of nature and was very much within the limit of sustainable development, for the nets that they employed prevented small fish and eggs from being caught.[15] The thread used in the nets did not make scratches on the fish causing them to spoil soon.[16] The fish after entering the net was also allowed with life for a longer duration so that it could reach the shore fresh and from there reached the interior faster. The total enterprise was planned in such a way to suit the requirements of time irrespective of the way they worked.[17] These developments suggest the not only greater interaction between the mainland and the coast but also the occupational specialisation that emerged along with that.

In the coastal context, the discovery of salt as food was a clear symbol of the surplus economy. Salt was manufactured in the coastal area, not with the same level of pain that otherwise was required for agricultural production. With time certain tools and techniques of easy and mass production were also evolved. Since rain and humidity in wind were the major challenges, it had seasonal strings attached to it. In a simple proportion, the use of salt to grain can be fixed even in a liberal calculation at 1:100. But the only source of salt was the coast and everywhere food was cooked with salt. The production in the coast had to cater to the need of all the people living in plains, hills, forests and deserts. Subsequently, other religious and political uses of salt were invented what increased the demand and value of it.[18]

With the learning of preservative qualities of salt, dry fish came into use. It was clearly made out of the extra produce, while at the same time the otherwise easily perishable product was preserved. Naturally, its importance to good health was widely publicised. By and large, the *Pearl Fishery Coast* addressed the demands of a wider world through the multitude varieties of dry fish. It became an important article of trade and was both exported to foreign lands as well as supplied to places in the plain, hills and forests. It possibly caused the early wave of *Parathavar* migration from coast to plain and as sine-qua-non settlements of stockiest evolved along the trade route. The traders were from a diversified background and did not always trace their origin from the fishing community although a predominant number of them were from within.[19]

If salt was a produce that came from the coast cutting across all boundaries including geographic and social, pearls were another produce that also came from the coast chiefly derived its value from the demands from abroad and catered to the need of people of the higher stratum of society. The importance of pearls in a society had to be understood in an economic context that was far ahead of the subsistence level. Together with chank, pearl processing also evolved into a regular industry since it involved a substantial strength of workforce in correspondence to the demand it generated from within and elsewhere.[20]

Impact of Economic Growth

The diversified articles of utility that were available at the coast impacted the overall living condition. That can be viewed starting from the production of salt although catching of fish remained the major occupation of the coast. The producers or the controllers of the salt-making mechanism were the *Parathavars*.[21] But they did not directly seem to have established effective linkages for the distribution of the produce. This surplus produce of the coast always awaited the service of the *Umanars*,[22] who constituted a significant part of the socio-economic life of the coastal region. They travelled in bands loading salt in carts and donkeys' back. Its value on sales was fixed on the basis of measure equivalent to grain.[23] Probably this included the profit margin they fixed for the article what was suggestive of lesser purchase value at the place of production. The need for grains and other vital needs of life not wholly available in the coast but found in abundance elsewhere would have possibly come through these *Umanars.* But they regulated their method of the transaction by establishing a guild namely *Umanchathu.* As far as the business motive of the *Parathavars* was concerned their general value could be stated as one of that did not always spin around profit making. They easily derived satisfaction with what they got at a time.[24]

Apart from the supply of salt, pearls and chanks were available in the *Pearl Fishery Coast.* Pearl and chank diving required skilled personnel ranging from those who located areas in the sea where pearls and chanks were found to those who controlled the sharks from attacking the divers respectively called *adapans* and *kadal kattis.*[25] Apart from these, there were also the divers themselves who were believed to be despised criminals forced into punishment for the sake of the state which probably monopolised the pearl and chank diving activities. Unlike pearls that were valued for its rarity, chanks were cheaply available and its use was more for decorative and ritual purposes. Their availability in large numbers caused the development of chank cutting into an industry that required persons to handle them from beyond the coast.

Once in a place, industries based on exports were developed, they continued to possess the industrial character despite fall of the demand for a product. Because industrial centres were developed by skilled people who created the chance for many to participate in the activities of production and when a group of people were relegated to the background other people fill the gap and contribute for the vibrancy of the locality.[26] The spirit of industrial development was in itself founded on such principles. Similarly, the nature of trade and articles that determined the character of the market varied from time to time but trade continued.

Overseas trade tended to develop with the availability of diversified articles of trade and development of the industry. The improvement in the quantum of articles of trade impacted the technology of shipbuilding in the one hand whereas in the other it attracted the attention of foreign countries. Simple fishing boats were evolved into larger ships usable for diverse purposes. There were references about powerful navy belonging to the *Cholas* which occupied a part of *Sri Lanka* in the II century B.C. As a matter of logic, ships had not been used for military purposes far earlier than they were utilised for trade. Also, the fact that constructing a naval ship needed improved skill and technology compared to a merchant's vessel should be accounted. Therefore, there must have been an active maritime trade much before II century B.C., on the basis of coastal shipping at the least with other parts of *India* and *Sri Lanka.* Subsequently, there had been some trade of mentionable nature with *Malaya* and other *South East Asian countries, China, Assyria, Palestine, Egypt* etc. Especially, Arabs as middlemen were said to have dominated the domain of trade before the discovery of monsoon winds by *Hippalus.* After the discovery of monsoon winds *Romans* were believed to have established direct trade with the sub-continent for which plentitude of numismatic evidence is available.[27]

The strengthening of economic activities in the coast together with the enhancement of agricultural production and supportive artisanship provided for the development of the cities and kingdoms from time to time – in the very early times it might have been *Adichchanallur* and sometimes later it could have been *Korkai*[28] and in the medieval periods it could have been *Tuticorin*. In the coastal front, the only possible threat via sea could be from *Sri Lanka*. But in the case of the *Pearl Fishery Coast* the parallel region in the *Sri Lankan Coast* was also seemed to have remained under the influence – direct or indirect – of the Tamil people.[29]

In contrast to sea, the land was a stable unit with definite boundaries. It provided scope for unrestricted movement of people. Under the kings, the land became a source of economic value. The surplus that was generated by land was basic for maintaining a kingdom. Therefore, within the Tamil country, fertile regions became the bone of contention among rulers, both major and minor. As a result in the one hand cities like *Madurai* and *Uraiyur* became strongholds from where the agrarian economy was secured and in the other coastal towns like *Korkai* and *Puhar* were maintained as significant ports.

It in no way means that the economic importance of the coast was replaced by the agrarian economy. Rather it was all about bringing a balance between the two regions. In order to strike a compromise among the divergent citizenry and accommodate dissent, certain symbols were evolved. In the case of the *Pandyan kings,* despite their shifting the capital to *Madurai* owing to the importance of the *Pearl Fishery Coast,* they adopted *fish* as their symbol of the flag. Similarly, the *Cholas* shifted their capital from *Kaveripattinam* to *Uraiyur.*

The shifting of capital was reflective of the expanding demand and supply and consequently the widening of commodity markets with the increase in the number of items for trade. The capitals emerged as the lifeline of the economic activities of the time. References in *Madurai-kkanci* vividly depicted the picture of the market activities at *Madurai*. Eminent historian *N. Subrahmanian* inferred *Madurai-kkanci* and stated: "in the evening bazaar in Madurai, the following person were busy selling and buying; the grocers, the sellers of conch-bangles, goldsmiths, appraisers of and gold articles dealers in foreign cloth like Kalingam,[30] other textile dealers in perfumes, flowers and sandal paste."[31] Similar references were also available in *Pattinapalai,* and therefore, *N. Subrahmanian's* description would fit for all the markets in the capital. Not only products like conch-bangles originated from the coast, but also other articles of trade that were not available locally could also have come via sea routes.

Apart from the markets located in the capital, there were also *peripheral markets* wherein *Parathavars* would have played a key role.[32] When activities of exports and imports were to be undertaken, capitals physically situated away from the coast could have played only a marginal role. *Parathavars* were known to have purchased merchandise from these markets mainly to play the role of intermediaries. They carried these items bought in the *peripheral markets* for sale to *Ilam, Sri Lanka, South East Asia* and other distant lands.[33] These markets seemed to have diversified their interests and increased their participation in coastal trade. Apart from the comparatively larger peripheral markets, there had been a multitude of weekly markets in the trade route mentioned above wherein *Parathavars* played a significant role as retail and traders.[34]

Migration of traders from the hinterland – chiefly from infertile regions – towards the coast took place as also the movement from the coast towards hinterland as it was with the case of the *Umanars*.[35] In the western direction of the *Pearl Fishery Coast,* trade routes[36] towards *Kerala* developed and settlements of the Parathavars along the route evolved with it.[37] The emergence of traders with adequate manpower and support base also provided the impetus for agriculture. Traders most often converted their savings into agrarian wealth and became absentee landlords. In some cases, successful fisherman also directly carried out agricultural activities.

Foreign trade altered their life – if not for all for a major section – and provided with the improved living condition.[38] Both villages and towns emerged in the coastal area. But it had been always difficult to distinguish between the ordinary fishermen in both the places in their life pattern. At the most, it can be stated that there had been a better quantum of demand in the towns in reciprocity to the population. But with a higher density of fishermen in the coastal towns, this advantageous position was also doubtful. The class difference was reflected in the settlement pattern. In a situation wherein traders with secure economic base coexisted with fishermen who lived their everyday life, these differences tended to exist. Suggestive of this, *Kaveripattinam* was said to have had two parts, namely *Pattinapakkam* and *Maruvurpakkam*.[39] *Pattinapakkam* was the residential area whereas Maruvurpakkam was the coastal area where merchants and fishermen had their separate settlements.[40]

Rise of Hierarchical Structure

The class difference that emerged in the coastal life owing to the inroads made by surplus and markets at various levels sought to undermine the tribal nature of economic life. Skill specialization contributed towards the rise of individuals in the sphere of trade and warfare. Such individuals moved out of the common fishing folk, formed a separate class and segmented their class interest. A socio-economic life characterized by definite hierarchy emerged. In such a context, with the support of available sources, a five-dimensional projection could be observed in the coast. At the first category can be located the leadership of the *Parathavar* people that was appointed by the ruling monarchs. The leadership of this kind was important insofar their being associated with the residential life of the *Parathavars*. As a class, they stood at the top of the hierarchy and were represented in the *Sangam* literature by individuals portrayed as '*Serpan*' and '*Palamban*' moving in large chariots.[41] In the later periods, officials like *Arayans* and *Kanakapulais* who remained part and parcel of the coastal life seemed to have been viewed by the people as representing the government for the purpose of tax collection and related works for the state. Possibly the governmental support strengthened the hands of this segment of people in consolidating their economic position.

Similarly, there were also references from the *Sangam* sources about persons like *Konkan, Thuraivan* and *Parappan*.[42] These officials seemed to have had a role in the administration of the ports.[43] The *Parathavars* never claimed the monopoly over the wealth of the sea. They did not hinder access for other people to explore the resources of the sea to carve out a living.[44] Therefore, the officials who were depicted in the context of the port may not be necessarily belonging to the *Parathavar* community and constituted by diverse caste category. As far as the residential settlements pertaining to these officials were concerned, they lived with their respective caste people. Parallel to the officials mentioned in the *Sangam* texts belonging to this category were the later officials such as *sammatties*,[45] *mandradies, Tandals* and etc.[46] Nevertheless, all these officials also contributed for the crystallization of the hierarchy – both in the internal and external facets of caste – and directly shook the foundation of the tribal mode of life.[47]

Thirdly, the need for marketing the surplus produce created a class of intermediaries and traders in the fishing and related enterprise that formed a vital part of the coastal economy. These intermediaries were also from diverse caste groups – though a dominant section was from the Parathavar caste – and was responsible for linking the coast with the mainland in a greater way.[48] They in a way ensured assurance of livelihood by way of purchasing the total produce. However, the value was fixed by them not always in favor of the producer. The transactions between the fishermen and the middlemen were not directly regulated by the state unlike that happened in the agrarian economy of the Northern India characterized by infuedation and sub-infuedation. However, as the system was reflective of absentee-landlordism, it was not difficult to ascertain that the intermediaries hardly had any interest in the overall socio-economic development of the coast than their personal profit.

It can also be assumed that these intermediaries with their ability to control the demand and supply mechanism would have gradually occupied other related fields of surplus production including salt manufacture, trade in pearls[49] and processing of dry-fish in large scale in order to meet the requirements of export. They had the ability to employ human labor required for such purposes. As far as dry-fish was concerned, the Tamil country had the special advantage owed to constant sun-shine throughout the year that was not the same with countries in the West. Dry-fish processing was an every home enterprise which gave the opportunity for the female-folks of the community to participate in the production process and strengthened their position within families.[50] How far the intermediaries networked with the women was not clearly known. But what can be assumed was the fact that, by virtue of their all-pervasive economic character they emerged as the cornerstone of hierarchy.

The dominant class thus constituted by the officials appointed by the government and the intermediaries were mostly the owners of the cattle needed for transportation and supply of milk.[51] Their settlement often was not close to the sea, if at all near the sea it was located in elevated planes. Near their settlement, adequate grazing land required for the maintenance of cattle was always available. For both of these requirements, persons who thoroughly relied on sea resources must have depended upon them. During periods of crises – both at the individual and group levels – the humble fishermen was expectant of support from this dominant class of people. With their command in the overseas trade, particularly with Ceylon, they were believed to wield the capacity to determine the fortune of ordinary families.

Fourthly, the possibility of the overarching growth of the dominant class within the caste was checked by the caste leader who later came to be known as *Pandyapathy*. His very position as caste leader was suggestive of the fact that the *Parathavars* over a period of time constituted a separate category separated from other administrative divisions based on lands such as *Mandalam, Nadu* and *Valanadu*. He was privileged with the right to hereditary succession. The possibility of his family having had entered a matrimonial alliance with the *Pandyan kings* cannot be ruled out. Because during their heydays, the leaders were identified at par with the king and became subject matter for eulogy in the religious literature such as *Periyapuranam*.[52] His position was secured by his knowledge on oceanography pertaining to the abode of pearls which he maintained in secret and transmitted to his successors. He evolved his own emblems and symbols of authority[53] to which he allowed access to every male individual during specific occasions. This was not to mean that there was a total absence of disaffection.[54] In fact, the *Parathavar* people were thought to be freedom lovers who hated the weight of individual authority and governance.[55]

Loyalty remained the hallmark of administration in the political history of the Tamil country before colonization through which leadership at various levels made subtle networking. The kings during the *Sangam* period derived unflinching loyalty and in turn, he recognized the sovereignty of the elements of local governance. In the subsequent periods also there was no evidence or hint for the possible change in the political ethos and values.[56] However, during the rule of the later *Pandyan kings* with *Varman* title, differences emerged between them and the *Parathavars*.[57] Whether that was directed against the leader of the *Parathavars* and his followers or *Parathavars* outside the command of the particular leader under focus was not clear. Nevertheless, what can be said for certain was the limitation of the caste leader to exercise military powers.

Finally, it was the importance of the *Ur* organization.[58] The Caste leader had judicial powers over his people who lived spread over several villages known as *Urs*. He supervised the administration of the village through the *Ur* organization and recognized the elected members known as *seethathimar* of a village. The occupational diversity of the *Parathavars* found expression in the constitution of the body of *seethathimars*.[59] The qualifications required for the members of the *Ur* were the same throughout the Tamil country.[60] It laid more stress upon the individual character of the members over their economic attainment. However, notable was the presence of multiple layers of power that ranged from authoritarian to republic denuding the possibility of concentration of power at a few hands what characterized feudalism.

Life in the Peripheral Regions

If the authority of *Pandyapathy* contained the domination of a class of people above him at the local level it was the *Ur* which checked the phenomenon. In general, the everyday life of the coastal people was one of a community life. To manage the affairs of the community, the *Ur* took the responsibility. In its outlook, the *Ur* reflected one of a tribal oligarchy wherein the chosen elders managed the everyday activity of the village. In the case of the Parathavars, the membership of the *Ur* and of the *jati* was one and the same. All the married men were members of the *Ur* and in exceptional cases, bachelors senior in age were given membership. Those who did not belong to the *jati* but resident of the village cannot become a member of the *Ur* although the term reflected a strong geographical connotation. At the same time, those natives belonging to the *jati* who migrated and left the village can continue to be members until a signal contribution was made by way of yearly presence during festival occasions or by undertaking certain expenditure of the *Ur*.[61]

The *Ur* elected a signal head although it worked only collectively. The position of the *headman* was not one of hereditary. He derived his strength from his personal skills and the image he developed among his fellowmen both within and outside the village. The head was constantly watched and the growth of his authority was checked through criticism.[62] A successful head was one who ensured the solidarity of the people in matters of common cause. He shall not expect any special treatment or status than what was permitted by conventions and traditions.[63]

Those who opposed the authority of the *Ur* – particularly the activities of the persons in responsibility – splintered and found a new settlement in the vicinity.[64] They sought to establish an administration in the shade of the erstwhile *Ur* in which they were members. With time, they were either subsumed as a satellite village or the division became permanent. In the case of the former, dependence on certain matters continued to exist whereas in the latter enmity became permanent. Therefore, the community attempted to neutralize differences that emerged over the overarching growth of the authority of the *Ur*.

The *Ur* had the power to inflict punishments upon the violating members. It maintained a link with the *Urs* of other villages and updated itself with the events that occurred around. The important elders and individuals were known and made acquaintance with. Common issues of the wider *jati* often became subject matter for discussion when elders of different *Urs* happened to meet. This was significant in shaping the dispute resolving mechanism beyond the village. The *Ur* took the responsibility of the safety and security of the lives and properties of the members. At times, when differences emerged between villages either through direct confrontation or on account of embarkment upon one's area of work in the sea, it was expressed by way of the abduction of the property or attack and capture of persons. At a situation like this, the *Urs* gave unto themselves the duty of negotiation. The general rule followed during such occasions was that the members were allowed to assault a person in the sea. But once they planted their legs in the land, the Ur came to protect the person and treat the abducted with grace.[65] If this was violated then the problem went beyond control.[66] Hence, the *Urs* have to ensure a greater sense of justice to avoid ethical criticism that often turned satirical.[67] On account of that was stated above, among the villages, one could see traditional friends and enemies for generations, and therefore, matrimonial alliances were entered into only after seeking the permission of the *Ur*.

The external agents of power operated through the *Ur* and never trespassed without their cooperation.[68] The autonomy of economic life as well as the confrontation that invited external agents were identified and avoided. One important article that required them to go out of the village was intoxicants often where problems crept out. The coastal landscape was known for grooves of palm and coconut trees both of which yielded toddy. The *Nadars* controlled the toddy-tapping enterprise. The *Nadar* community and the *Parathavars* were traditionally opposed to each other although they formed dichotomous organs of the coastal life.[69] The *Parathavar* people preferred to buy even *jaggery* one of the food products of the *Nadar* community only in an indirect mode than entering into the direct transaction. Nevertheless, since consuming of intoxicants was not uncommon,[70] it was procured directly from the sellers and sold out for a higher rate to the needed members by the seniors of the 'Ur.'[71] It prevented excess use and the profit was used for public purposes.

The *Ur* also performed, to a certain extent, the functions of a professional Guild. It evolved certain rules and regulations in accordance with tradition and law of the land and maintained order and peace. It attempted to control the middlemen and tried to have a say in the price fixation and marketing of the produce as also maintained contact with castes of people who depended upon the retailing of seafood for livelihood. It took into view the factors of demand and supply while deciding on price fixation. In transactions, the *Ur* never compromised on the possible profit chances of the retailer. It also supported the destitute women by way of allowing them some role in the sales of seafood. During off-seasons, it took the responsibility of feeding the people.[72]

The *Ur* also organized and headed the temple festivals.[73] The properties of the temple were constituted by the contributions of the people maintained by the *Ur*. Hence it was limited in nature when compared to the properties of the Brahminical temple. Therefore the people that benefitted from the proceeds of the temple were only a rare phenomenon. *Ur* also declared the role of every family in the peaceful conduct of the festival. Personal enmities were glossed until smooth conduct of the festival was attained. It was a creative occasion for expressing the group solidarity.[74] Unlike in the cases of non-tribal societies, the conducting of the festival was not used to express the position of leadership.[75] This was not to say that there remained only a single group in the village. Most often there were factions. But every faction registered its presence collectively.

The *Ur* also had the power to declare *menakadan* and *therippu*. Unlike agriculture where every day the farmer had to at the least shed water to the crops, in the coastal life it was not compulsory on the individual to enter the sea every day. Halting of the economic activity at sea on occasions did not hinder the economic life. Rather it became symbolic of the group solidarity. The concept of *menakadan* was established on that count.[76] Most often occasions of misery like death were causes for the declaration of *menakadan*. Similarly, *therippu* was also a collective gesture by which the coastal community offered either a part or the total output of their labor for a collective cause. Possibly it was a popular method of collecting the taxes. The *Ur* may call for *therippu* any day in a week or month and auction the total produce of the village and utilized the generated value for a public cause – predominantly a religious cause.

The *Ur* in its unconscious function as guild also undertook the duty of training of young people who intended to opt for sea bound life. It also maintained service personnel including the barber, the carpenter, the lime-makers, medicine-man and etc. Certain differences based on the physical spread and economic strength of the village determined the employing of service personnel. In case of the barber – also known as *kudimagan* – in big villages with strong economic base, there were more persons who hailed from the particular caste of *maruthuvar*.[77] In such villages, a *kudimagan* served only a few families for which his ancestors performed service. He had the right to claim a share on the produce. Through him the honorific symbols of the caste such as the umbrella and the carpet were used in public during wedding ceremonies.[78] During such occasions they were duly honored with valuable gifts.[79] In small villages, the duty was performed by a person of the Parathavar caste itself.[80] In both kinds of villages, if the *Ur* approved, they got direct access to sea resources. The *maruthuvars*, as a community were also physicians at local level. Popular family of physicians emerged only in certain villages. They often moved out of the village for the sake of treating the people.

The *Ur* also recognized the services of the carpenter who designed and repaired the catamarans. There were some carpenters who were also known, fishermen. Those who emerged from within were locally called as *Odavy*. But the carpenters belonging to the caste of *Viswakarma* were more skilled in the selection and handling of wood. By virtue of either being located in the plains or through kinship and professional contact, they also possessed knowledge about the availability of suitable wood. The *Ur* sought to project a favorable image to derive the services of the carpenter. It was most important because the aspiration of every individual within society was to have a strong fleet of boats in the village.

Conclusion

The tools and methods of fishing that included pearl diving required greater cooperation and interdependence among the coastal people. It maintained the tribal nature of life characterized by sharing of both income and loss. The breakthrough in the technological front – such as that in the art of boat-making – caused surplus production. The periods of scarcity together with surplus production caused the movement of people from the coast to mainland and vice-versa as well as from across the sea. The cheap availability of articles such as salt, dry fish, pearls and chanks maintained the vibrancy of movement and generated income to a considerable number of people. This together with the other causes of surplus production such as emergence of cities and introduction of a system of governance gave signals of eroding the basic premise of tribal life because it created hierarchical structure within the coastal life in which the trading class formed a vital component.

The hierarchical structure was not formed exclusively from the *Parathavar* community but by all the beneficiaries of the trade. One of the reasons for scholars like *Noburu Karasimha* for having included other communities over *Parathavars* in their discussions on trading classes possibly owed to this reason. The caste structure in the coast was also fluid in nature which was in itself marked more by alliances and enmity among the people of various castes than purity and pollution. In the case of the *Parathavars* of the *Pearl Fishery Coast,* the hierarchical structure was reflected in their domains of settlement conditioned by internal class division and external caste division.

Despite production of surplus and rise of hierarchical structure, the tribal elements of life were maintained. The *Ur* organization was chiefly responsible for that. Though the *Ur* gave its allegiance to a central head known as *Pandyapathy,* at the local level it had concrete powers upon the members. It prevented the clash of interests with other castes and stemmed the assertion of individuals or group of individuals over the community. For that purpose it established control over not only the production mechanism but also over the service personnel of the locality.

Endnotes

1   K.A. Nilakanta Sastri, *A History of South India: From Prehistoric Times to the Fall of Vijayanagar* (New Delhi: Oxford University, 1958), p. 119.

2   In a national seminar on the topic Folk Traditions of Sankam Age organized by the Department of Folklore, St. Xavier's College, Palayamkottai, between 23rd and 24th February 2007a scholar with anthropological moorings named Bhakthavatchala Bharathi expressed these views.

3   Rajan Gurukkal et. Al, *History of India: Earliest Times to 800 A.D.,* Booklet – 7 (New Delhi: Indira Gandhi National Open University, 1990), p 14.

4   Ibid.

5   The nature of the soil should be classified. In the field visits conducted at places like Oovari and Idinthakarai plant species observable at severe cold regions such as *Pinus sylvestris* popularly known as Christmas-tree are grown. At Manapad and Vembar near the sea stand pipal trees found in large numbers in the forests and in few numbers in plains.

6   The construction of the Kallanai by the Chola King Karikala could be cited as an example for development in the ideas of water management.

7   D.P. Chattopadyaya, *Madhamum, Samugamum* (Tamil), (Chennai: New Century Book House, 2009) p. 40.

8   Ibid. p. 30.

9   K. Rajan, *Situating the Beginning of Early Historic Times in Tamil Nadu: Some Issues and Reflections,* Social Scientist, (_______) pp. 40–78; He fixes the period of similar developments in the 1st millennium B.C.

10   It was generally believed that the Parathavars were associated only with the sea, and therefore, they could only form a coastal fishing community. But field visits conducted at a place called Maramangalam located near Korkai provided evidence for Parathavar fresh-water fishermen.

11   Pattinapalai: 90.

12   N. Subrahmanian, *Sangam Polity: The Administration and Social Life of the Sangam Tamils* (Madras: Asia publishing House, 1966), p. 241.

13   Ibid.

14   Interview with Mr. Parabaran (22), Fisherman of Manapad on 8-01-10.

15   Ibid.

16   Interview with Mr. Chandrasekharan Fernando (55), Founder member of Parathavar Welfare Association, Tuticorin on 11/03/10.

17   In most families, food was cooked for the whole day in the morning. Therefore the surplus fish that remained after self-use was supplied to the nearby region in the early morning itself and the fishing enterprise was planned accordingly. Similarly, fishing ventures targeting a rare variety of fish had middlemen for procurement. In such case, the middlemen awaited the arrival of the fishermen regardless of time. However, such activities were only performed by a few fishermen.

18   Salt attained a sacred status and constituted part of offerings to gods. Similarly, it was also part of taxes levied by the government.

19   Field visit conducted at Idinthakarai on 24-09-2011; as far the retail business of fish was concerned Nadars, Maravars, Padaiyatchis and others have formed an important part of it. Apart from these groups, Vania Chettiars seemed to have taken an active part in the overseas trade.

20   N. Athiyaman, *Pearl and Chank Diving of South Indian Coast (A Historical and Ethnographical Perspective)* (Thanjavur: Tamil University Press, 2000) p.35.

21   A. Sivasubramanian, *Uppittavarai* (Chennai: Kalachuvadu Pathipagam, 2009) p. 33.

22   Field visits conducted at various places identify people like the Nadars (earlier known as Shanars), the Arayars, the Parayars etc. constituting a significant part of the coastal life. There must have been similar communities forming part of coastal life beyond the Pearl Fishery Coast. One or more than one of these communities must have been identified as Umanars. In the opinion of the present researcher, with their access to the sea and entrepreneurial values, Nadars most probably would have been known as Umanars. This indigenous group of people was not known through any other nomenclature in the Sangam literature.

23   Akananuru 140: 7–8.

24   Interview with Mr. Chandrasekharan Fernando of Tuticorin on 11/03/10.; he spoke out of experience gathered in his service at Tuticorin harbour. In actuality, the share of the Parathavars as investors in salt manufacturing enterprise has come to a marginal level. Particularly in Pazhyakayal almost they do not have any say in the business. Persons from Nadar community dominate in the field.

25   N. Athiyaman, Op. Cit., p. 65.

26   H.R. Pate, *Tinnevelly District Gazetteer (1916),* (Tirunelveli: Manonmaniam Sundaranar University, 1993) p. 227; there existed aconch-bangle industry in Korkai. After its decline wax-bangle industry emerged in Maramangalam near Korkai. But it was developed by Kavarai Nayakkans who also took the chetti title.

27   Rajan Gurukkal et. Al, Op. Cit., p.30.

28   H.R. Pate, Op. Cit., p. 40; the author records a tradition according to which the origin of the three monarchs namely Chera, Chola and Pandya was traced from Korkai.

29   Kandhiah Arundhavaraja in K.A. Manikumar and Vinod Vincent Rajesh (eds.), *Southern Tamil Nadu through the Ages,* (Tirunelveli: Dept. of History, M.S. University, 2011) pp. 164–176.

30   Kalinga was the early name of the state of Odisha. There were contacts with the region through the indigenously built Toni with Bengal and Kalinga.

31 N. Subrahmanian, *Sangam Polity,* pp. 233–234.

32 R. Champakalakshmi, Trade, Ideology and Urbanisation: South India 300 B.C. to A.D. 1300 (New Delhi: Oxford University Press, 1996) p.104.

33 Ibid.

34 Interview with Mr. Joseph Irudhaya Xavier, Resident of Palayamkottai (Assc. Prof of Tamil, St. Xavier's College, Palayamkottai) on 22-11-2011; the interviewees ancestral native was informed to be Idinthakarai. But his great grand-father and grandfather migrated from there targeting the weekly markets that were organized in places like Karungulam, Chingikulam, etc.

35 A. Sivasubramanian, *Uppittavarai,* pp. 39–43.

36 L.F. Benedetto (ed.), *The Travels of Marco Polo,* (New Delhi: Asian Educational Services, 1994) p. 304; Marco Polo discusses the security provided to the travelers in the trade routes and that security can be inferred as part of security arrangement provided for the settlements nearby.

37 Places like Alwarthirunagari, Karungulam, Palayamkottai, Pettai, Thirupudaimarudhur on the Tamiraparani Coast carry traces of Parathavar settlement and influence.

38 R. Champakalakshmi, Op. Cit., p. 104.

39 *Akananuru* 73:10.

40 Ibid.

41 *Akananuru*: 140.

42 *Narrinai*: 4:4, 38:5, 72:5, 138:5, 145:4, 149:8, 163:12, 175:5, 187:9, 194:4.

43 The term *Thurai* in Tamil denotes port. Similarly, parappu means expanse. Therefore, there is more possibility for the term *Parappan* to give out a meaning related to the administration of port.

44 Sailing in small boats was more challenging that required apart from support and training, childhood socialization from the family whereas sailing in ships was more technical that required collaboration of many people like the carpenter, trader etc.

45 D. Henson Jebamani, *Ohlzindhu Kondirukkum Manidhargal,* Unpublished M. Phil thesis in History submitted to Manonmaniam Sundaranar University, Tirunelveli, 2011, p._; the scholar identifies sammatties as a sub-caste of vanniars what is suggestive of the possibility of convergence of several castes within the broader Parathavar category.

46 R.N. Joe d'cruz, Korkai, (Chennai: Kalachuvadu Pathipagam, 2009) pp. 717–719.

47 Uniquely in the coastal context, caste alliances and caste equality based on each caste claiming superiority over other marked by the rejection of the claim by the subjected caste that in turn claimed superiority over the former was very common. The Maravars, Vanniars and Parathavars seemed to have formed an alliance whereas the nadars were subjected to domination which they rejected and claimed superiority.

48 Interview with Mr. Parabaran of Manapad on 08-01-10.

49 *The Travels of Marco Polo,* pp. 303–304; he explains how young boys were trained in the selling of pearls.

50   In general fishing communities were believed to have elements of matrilineal society owing to the scope available for them to express in the economic front.

51   Interview with Mr. Joseph Gregory Babylaus Fernando (72), Retired School Teacher of Veerapandianpattanam on 02/01/10; in some of the families in the lower stratum, goats sheep and hen were grown. Particularly women seemed to have taken the responsibility of herding them. These women who went to the nearby regions for selling fish possibly took the goats and sheep along with them for grazing.

52   Edgar Thurston, *Castes and Tribes of South India Vol. VI* (Madras: Government Press, 1909), pp. 142–148.

53   Unpublished manuscripts of Capt. Berchmans Motha, Grandson and Successor of Parathar Jati Thalaivanmor, referred at his home in Tuticorin on 21/04/2010.

54   Though Parathavars were depicted as inhabiting the entire coastal stretch of Tamil Nadu and Kerala in the Sangam literature, their leader was identified to have settled near Rameswaram in later literature. However, by the time of their conversion, only a section of the community that inhabited seven coastal villages seemed to have recognized the authority of the caste leader. It cannot be surely ascertained as to when the internal divisions started.

55   *The Travels of Marco Polo*, p. 299; Marco Polo, as well as British ethnographers in the subsequent periods, considered the Tamil people including the Parathavars as poor soldiers. The parameter for the latter to declare martial character of a people took into purview discipline as a major criterion than physical exploits. In the perception of the Westerners in general, discipline stood on the premise of self-surrender to the established hierarchy. Since the Tamil people were thought to be lacking in it and they were not considered as good soldiers.

56   Ibid., p. 296; he refers to persons who died with the King on the latter's death. The same kind of ethic existed during the Sangam period also.

57   Velvikudi Copper plate of Pandyan King Nedunchadaiyanparanthakan; he seemed to have ruled between 765 and 790 A.D. In this copper plate, he has mentioned his suppression of the Parathavars.

58   T.V. Sadasiva Pandarathar, *Pandyar Varalaru*, (Chennai: Nam Thamilar Pathipagam, 2007) pp. 120–128; he discusses the Ur administration based on the converging information collected from Uttiramerur and Sankarankoil inscriptions.

59   Unpublished Manuscripts of Capt. Berchmans Motha.

60   Ibid.

61   Interview with Mr. Alangara Michael Nallathambi Fernando (67), President, Parathavar Vadakku Ur, Kottar on 27-11-08.

62   It's a kind of 'everyday forms of resistance' discussed by James Scott. Pessimistic criticism within the community was very common and there was hardly any marriage or funeral without it.

63   He surrendered his personal ambitions and emotions for the sake of the welfare of the community. In that way, he lost his personal freedom comparatively than gaining anything else.

64   Interview with Mr. Amaladas, (65), Fisherman of Alandalai on 02/01/10. In a confrontation among the fishermen of Alandalai a splintering group founded the Amalipuram settlement and separated itself.

65   R.N. Joe d'Cruz, *Aazhi Sul Ulagu* (Tamil), (Chennai: Tamizhini, 2004) pp. 325–326; the person taken into custody was given food and new clothes and freedom of restricted movement within the village.

66   Ibid.

67   Interview with Mr. Alangara Michael Nallathambi Fernando (67) of Kottar on 27-11-08; every village or town was known with certain values. While matrimonial alliances were made these values became the deciding factor.

68   The experience during field visit inform that when visitors cross residential area and try to go beyond it, somebody immediately ventures and makes inquiry about the person trespassing. Usually, a youth while observing visitors voluntarily takes the responsibility of vigilance.

69   In places like Kallamozhi, Tharuvaikulam etc. the Nadars take to sea as fishermen. They also control the salt industry and the marketing of fish.

70   Letter of Francis Xavier from Manapad dated 14-03-1544.

71   Interview with Mr. Joseph Gregory Babylaus Fernando of Veerapandianpattanam on 02/01/10

72   Interview with Mr. Parabaran of Manapad on 08-01-10.

73   Unpublished Manuscripts of Capt. Berchmans Motha; what can be inferred from his manuscripts was the division of great tradition and small tradition in worship pattern. In small tradition, there were temples for lesser divinities such as Kizhavan and Kizhavi, male and female respectively. Festivals were organized for these divinities annually.

74   According to some traditions the Parathavars were believed to be Palanquin bearers. In the coastal area, owing to sand wheeled vehicles for gods were not preferred. Particularly, in the temple of Tiruchendur, they had the right to lift the palanquin. Similar practice on a smaller scale they seemed to have had in every village temple.

75   It was the research finding of Arjun Appadurai and Breckenridge. Earlier when the seat of the leadership was located at Uttarakosamagay the temple festival was reflective of the status of the caste headmen. After conversion into Christianity, the headman was relocated at Tuticorin where the same kind of practice continued. In ordinary villages, collective expression was in view.

76   R.N. Joe d'cruz, *Aazhi Sul Ulagu,* pp. 147–148.

77   Interview with Mr. Chandrasekharan Fernando of Tuticorin on 11/03/10.

78   Interview with Mr. Parabaran of Manapad on 08-01-10.

79   R.N. Joe d'cruz, *Korkai* , p. 620.

80   Interview with Mr. William Villavarayar (34), Tea Stall Proprietor of Pazhyakayal on 10/09/10; a person of Pieris family belonging to the Parathavar caste performs this duty not only in Pazhyakayal but also in a few other coastal villages.

V

From Totemic Worship to Sanskritic Gods:
A Study of Religious Practices of Early Parathavar

Introduction

The shape and character of tools that were required for the effective negotiation of the man with nature were determined by the level in which he understood its features. In the oceanic context, since mysterious elements that made the possible understanding complex continued to dominate the tools evolved were not sufficient enough to eliminate the feeling of uncertainty[1] from the minds of the people. In the world of ideas, the history of uncertainty was traceable from the myth on *Lemuria*. Since at the popular level uncertainty of life was ultimately linked with death it had wider meaning beyond sensory perceptions. Though sensory perception was stressed by materialists philosophers like Democritis, in the context of Lemuria –rejected as a mere myth by recent scholars[2] – the Platonic perception of the preexistence of ideas hold greater validity. It meant apart from individual memory there always existed in any social formation a collective memory which was external to man and internal to society.[3] It was because a perfect idea of oceanic disaster found expression among the coastal people though it did not always happen in their contemporary life.

In a tribal way of life – among others – people's capability of externalizing their shared subjective experience on the level of ideas that resulted in collective representation was important.[4] Though this was absent in a band – that preexisted the tribal formation – it was doubtful in the coastal life whether the appeal of the sea in its magnificence contributed for diverse internal opinions. However, with the rise of caste structure the uncertainty of life in the coast that provided minimum scope for the people to relate themselves in terms of a well-defined social action[5] coalesced with the religious system[6] that did not strictly distinguish between good and bad or *God* and *Satan*.[7] For uncertainty that led towards materialist life often tended to remain incompatible with the spirituality taught by institutional religions. Therefore, the present study seeks to explore the religious expression of the uncertainty of life in the *Pearl Fishery Coast* both independently as well as when it evolved a correspondence with other regions.

Nevertheless, in the present context, an attempt has been made to view the belief system that pertains to the external element through the prism of the economy for changes that occur in the sphere of the economy have bearing in the socio-religious processes. It is not to state that such perceptions are not without limitations for it helps only to give a general outline against stressing particular developments. It also denudes the possibility of understanding the regional variations in the socio-religious dialogue of the *Pearl Fishery Coast*.

As far as the present researcher was concerned, the economic approach to religion was an impact of the readings made on *D. P. Chattopadyaya* who borrowed from *L. H. Morgan, Gordon Childe* etc to establish his ideas. According to these scholars with predominantly *Marxist* orientation, the history of world religions was classifiable into two stages – the stage of mystical performances and the stage of god's spirit coming in contact with the man.[8] The second stage was distinguishable from the first on the grounds of surplus formation that was enabled by the discoveries[9] of the third millennium B.C. In the present study on the belief system of the *Pearl Fishery Coast*, a period of transition has been located between both the periods mentioned above. It enabled the sketch of details that pertained to *totemic worship*. The viewpoints of scholars *R.N. Joe d'Cruz, T.K.V. Subramanian, R. Pavananthi Vembulu, James Hornell, H.R. Pate, Edgar Thurston, A. Dhananjayan, and T. Paramasivan* have immensely contributed to the shaping of the ideas.

The primary sources used for the study included significantly the Sangam literature. It was viewed in the sense as it was located in a midpoint that enabled the observation of the trends in the past and helped the identification of the seeds of the future. Sangam literature – particularly *Pattinapalai* – were highly informative on both pre-surplus and post-surplus reflections of the belief system. However, in the present study extensive quotations were avoided. Particularly, information about *Karma* and *transmigration of the soul* were commonly found in *Sangam literature* that made the need for separate footnotes unimportant. In the treatment of the Sangam literature, the present researcher concurred with eminent scholar *Kailasapathy's* opinion that the so-called Sangam literature were products of ordinary performers predominantly independent of the royal court. Other primary sources included for the study were the *Travelogue* of *Marco Polo, Archaeological Report, Epigraphic* and *Puranic Information*. The primary sources were cross-referred through information gathered in field visits.

Methodologically, the article has been structured into categories based on the understanding of the features of nature and man's response to it in the tool-making domain. Thus there were three stages in chronological order in which the belief system was sought to be discussed. First was a stage in which nature was understood to a bare-minimum level as a consequence of which tools of stones, bones, wood etc. were designed. In the second stage, nature was well understood to the extent making boats. Finally was the stage of surplus production wherein man asserted his control over nature and constructed ships. In other words, the three stages of band, tribe and caste tended to guide the logical basis of the writing. However, in the style of writing, basic ideas have been borrowed from the disciplines of philosophy[10] and anthropology.[11] Particularly, an attempt has been made to synthesize cosmological view with evolutionary theory.[12]

Evolution of External Beliefs

Irrespective of the regions such as the coast, plain, hill etc. in a historical situation before the discovery of agriculture, potter's wheel, bullock cart, boat etc. life was highly miserable.[13] Any adverse change in weather or climate undermined the productive capacity of nature and caused famines in which innumerable human lives were either lost or subjected to migration. The simple tools that were developed out of stones, wood, bones and etc were not sufficient enough to encounter the challenges unleashed by nature. Every man and woman were directly involved in the search for food. The scarcity of resources made people form into bands. Since there was hardly any scope for the individuals to manifest their talents in matters of food-collection the cause of the collectivity remained pivotal to all within every band. The perception that pertained to other bands was rooted in the ideology of 'might was right.'

For any individual, most of the observed elements were believed to be mightier than the band itself. The primitive mind constantly attempted to understand them in their entirety but without success. Similar attempt through diverse methods was also made with the sea chiefly because of its vastness in the spread and its very nature that was characterized by mysteries never holistically comprehended through human senses. The rationalization based on land had its impact. Yet sea marked the height of nature.[14] Unlike land which was comparatively a stable phenomenon, the sea was always restless suggestive of the presence of life in it. It's production of sound and expression of mood by incorporation of change in colour added to the awe in the minds of the observer. More frequently than the land it violated the pattern of regularity and did not allow easy access to its resource.[15] All these aspects delivered to it – in the sensory world – the status of 'a being than which no greater can be conceived.'[16]

Familiarity made in the sensory world was followed by the realization of the comprehensiveness in the world of ideas. The link between the sensory world and the world of ideas was provided by the experience underwent while in the dream. As a result of the interpretation of dreams, the primitive mind arrived at the belief in duality. Accordingly, a physical element and its other together made life possible. Within every physical element – at the least, those showed symptoms of change such as growth, decay, etc. by virtue of the presence of life in them – was ingrained with other [17]which was not thoroughly subjected to the control of its place of residence. The other manifested itself in shadows which moved along with elements that had skills of mobility and remained stationery with immobile elements. In an imaginary situation, an individual believed that the other moved out of the body while in sleep as the others of other elements also similarly wandered. At times of sleep, the other of one of the strange elements entered into the body of the ego and offered experiences hitherto not underwent.

While the ideas on the other were evolved, it was grounded on the logic of correspondence based on the symmetry of size among objects. Therefore, the question of the other pertained to the sea did not arise. The other of the tree or snake or the like were believed to have frequently but irregularly and unsystematically swapped their location and returned to their original domain. At the same time, the dream experience made it clear if the sea observable through sensory perceptions was great, then the sea of the world of ideas was definitely greater. Moreover, innumerable creatures by virtue of symmetry of size had the possibility to correspond with human beings took asylum in the sea.

It caused not only an early impression of origin of life traceable from water[18] but also gave the idea of the singular complex.

The other was attributed to certain characteristics that were conditioned by objects that had best features. As said already, in the coastal context it was the sea that had the status of 'a being than which no greater can be conceived' and thereby assumed the nature of permanence. The other while viewed in the shade of sea was also assigned the status of permanence. Thus the other was not subject to death. Rather death of the physical element caused the disintegration of the other from it. It seemed that the other eagerly waited for the end of the physical element and started its free journey[19] and explored the hitherto unknown regions in the sea and thoroughly reintegrated itself with the sea.[20] In a time when uncertainty and chaos patterned the everyday life, it was doubtful whether the human person regardless of the presence other was frightened of death.

The singular complex nature of sea not only appealed the minds of the people mainly through its creative potential but also made them view it in the feminine gender. In a time when simple tools usable by men and women alike were in vogue, there was no space for gender difference. Since her contribution at the level of production was tangible, she was recognized as the source of fertility. Comparable to the women, the sea was also a source of wealth. Thus sea was associated with motherhood. [21]It was known as Anangu[22] that etymologically gave out several meanings that included human emotions such as sorrow and dread apart from spectra, beauty, divinity, madness and morbidity suggestive of the complexity that had gone into the comprehension of the sea.[23]

When motherly sentiments were developed with the sea, it became central to the group. Hence, migration from coast became an untenable option. Morbidity and beauty symbolized motherhood and virginity respectively. Sorrow and dread were associated with death. And the sea was the culmination of all of these. Therefore, whatever it offered was whole-heartedly accepted. Anything that occurred in the lap of the mother was nothing but honour.[24] Favourable disposition was expected through parallel communication that was evoked not only with the sea but also with those who were believed to have integrated themselves with it through death.

In sharp contrast to land where every element had scope to manifest its potential fully, the sea embalmed every element and appeared as a singular complex establishment of control upon which meant attainment of command upon its entire domain. Thus a parallel communication with the sea was made by the coastal people with the belief that it positively responded.[25] The stronger or in the other sense the better-skilled in the band evolved the communication as he wished. Predominantly, the motion of the waves and sounds of the wind became part and parcel of the communication system known as magic through which two major purposes were sought to be served.[26] One was to control the environment[27] – in the present case, the sea – in its social entirety and the other was to check misfortunes.[28] Variations evolved with every band.

It was possible that the Parathavar devil-dancers[29] not known in the Sangam literature were continuity from the band stage life. The Panars depicted in the Sangam literature associated with simple tools like fishing hooks were most probably a further development of Parathavar devil-dancers.[30] Panars were distinguished from other coastal people not only through the tools they used but also in their capacity as performers.[31] Similarly, the Nadukals and Virakals (Hero-stones) that were planted to commemorate dead heroes in fertile regions added special meaning in the coastal context to deaths that occurred at sea.

Totemic Worship

The constant attempts of human beings towards the comprehension of the secrets of nature brought to limelight the fact that there was an effective regularity present in its features. It's interdependent character was also evidenced through the realization of the impact of sun and moon upon the surface of the earth that included the sea as well. This, on the one hand, brought the lives of human beings under the purview of the functions of sun and moon[32] and on the other hand led to various discoveries followed by improvement in the technology of tools that resulted in the production of surplus. In a transition period that fell between the periods before and during surplus production, rudimentary clans based on *totemic worship*[33] seemed to have emerged. Importantly tribal clans named after the sun and the moon emerged at a broader level i.e. beyond the coast.

Usually, *totemic worship* was linked with the earliest stage of life. But in the context of the coast, it could be viewed as the next transient stage. It owed chiefly to the reason that unlike in land better skills were required for the exploration of the sea to come in contact with *totems*. One found the *Dolphin* and *Shark* in the spots located in the depths of the sea. Similarly in the case of the *Tortoise* – albeit the species was also found on the shore – they attained glorification in their action at sea that was thought to have provided the clue for the design of oars.[34] In order to view the *Dolphin, Shark* and *Tortoise* in action at the least a few logs of wood were required so that regions of depth could be reached. At the same time, these logs of wood were not sufficient enough to produce the surplus and to ensure economic security.

The rudimentary form of boat-building technology demanded considerable physical strength apart from courage.[35] Though the feminine character attributed to the sea was not questioned, it was the skill based on physical strength which gained recognition in society. Consequently, patriarchal elements emerged which undermined the participation of women in the economic activity. Since physical strength determined the course of life the social ideology that was consequently evolved justified the continuity of might as right. The relationship between groups was predominantly conditioned by numerical strength of members based on which a hierarchical structure arose. Those who were in the advantageous position sought to trace their origin from totems that were distinguishable from others by certain specific features[36]. Skilled men[37] took the role of priests and stood between the world of men and the world of *totems* and evolved a worship pattern which had variations at the local level. It meant the presence comparative differences among the range of *totemic worship*.

The holistic attribution of feminine aspects as in the case of the sea earlier was withdrawn. Rather it was related to particular elements on the basis of performance of unique functions. To be accurate, it was the resources of the sea that attained importance over the sea in its fullest form. The resources were unstable and undependable since they responded to climatic change. Uncertainty continued. Therefore, representative elements of the sea were identified and direct negotiations were made with them. The most common elements that were available from the sea were the fish and salt. Since the challenges unleashed by changes in the climate were sought to be solved by the mix of fish and salt,[38] both attained universal special status. The dry-fish thus produced not only enabled the tackle of famines to a great extent but also added meaning to *totemic worship*.

Though in general the nature of the sea was thought to be permanent, it was the resources that determined life, particularly when population dependent on it expanded. Among fish, the best in kind was identified. As a matter of fact, the universalism was corrupted as the selection of the best and rejection of other was a matter of appreciation determined by quality as well as quantity.[39] Therefore, in cases where the people's population tended to be higher, bigger fish such as the shark were given importance.

Among fish, the shark was distinguishable by its strength. The ferociousness of sea was thought to be manageable with the familiarization of the regularity present in the surface and bottom of the sea water and through advanced skills in the art of swimming. But a definite regularity on the behaviour of sharks could not be arrived at and the possible danger from them could not be predicted. At sea, it had the strength to capsize even well-built boats. It's capacity as mammal added to its image[40] which guided the development of the belief that the flesh of shark had medicinal value particularly relevant for pregnant women though in general it was also associated with longevity.[41] Therefore, as in any *totemic worship form* permission was sought from the *totem* before it was killed. The hunter of sharks was usually an experienced senior man who was recognized by others to hold the perquisites required from a priest. He planted bone remains of a pregnant shark[42] in a central place of their settlement and invoked the *other* to reside upon it. His communication with the totem went close to the mystic performance of the earlier stage.

As far as the worship of *tortoise* was concerned, it seemed to have dominated over other *totems*. It chiefly attained a unique status by virtue of its amphibious nature. As said already, it was believed to be a *progenitor*, as its movement in the sea by its limb was comparable with the oars of a boat. Its sacrifice was believed to cause the proliferation of tortoise population and therefore feasted with great joy.[43] Such occasions provided space for the priests to articulate their role. However, for the people in the non-coastal areas, its appearance was an ill-omen.[44] In sharp contrast to the worship of *tortoise*,[45] *dolphins* were never harmed and the sounds produced by them were believed to have the potential of prediction.

Totemic clans emerged when the worship of a particular *totem* became the exclusive perquisite of a particular people. The relationship between one clan and another was determined by convention established through mutual cooperation in oceanic operations.[46] The inimical relationship between one tribe and another was thought to have diffused at the level of *totems* which unleashed vengeance upon the enemies at various levels. At sea, they not only posed threat – either directly or indirectly – to the person and property but also had the capacity to cause scarcity of resources. At land, the *other* of the enemy *totems* had potential to disturb normal life since they caused endemic diseases and unforeseen events. Under such circumstances, the *clan totem* was depended upon for protection.[47] It was made to attend to its duties by constant provocation. Therefore, the totem that was sacred to one tribe was profane for another tribe.

Nevertheless, there were points of convergence that made these differences appear meaningless. Particularly the convergence was attained in the sacred front. *Chanks* were one of the important sacred *totems* invariably recognized as such by almost every people.[48] Like *dolphins,* it was also associated with sound that was thought to ward off profane elements.[49] Freely found in the sea as well as inshore, its relevance penetrated into all walks of life that started with birth. It's sacred status at the peak was depicted in the marriages in the coast wherein the groom tied a thread in which *chanks* were attached to the neck of the groom and concluded the process.[50]

In view of the presence of common sacred things and absence of a strong hierarchy among clans to the extent of the practice of mutual untouchability, it was doubtful whether the fluidity among clans was effectively contained. Thereby it can be ascertained that the status of sacred and profane was not strongly and permanently fixed. In such a situation, the status of the partial priests did not emerge beyond the identity of a tribe or clan. Therefore these trends in oscillation found different expression with the changes that occurred at the level of tools in particular and economy in general.

Trade

Further advancement of tools coincided with the discovery of the demand for pearls worldwide. The developments in the front of tools resulted in surplus production to the tune of promotion of trade – both inland and overseas. On the one hand, there was an increase in the traffic of ships with greater tonnage and on the other hand trade routes via land became vibrant. The isolation of coastal villages was disturbed and cities with diversified population emerged. With the appearance of trade and private property of higher magnitude, the difference between urban and village areas became highly visible.[51] Cross-cultural exchanges found expression at various levels and chiefly in the sphere of society and religion. By all means, states with a definite system of governance were established what was reflective of these exchanges. However, it could not effectively check the severe shock on the basement of tribal mode of life what started to move in the direction of caste. Nevertheless, the issues like the reduced role of women in the public domain went unnoticed in the eyes of the state.

The production of the surplus was followed by the problem pertained to distribution.[52] A group of people who were relieved from direct participation in the production process has to be fed.[53] These people by virtue of their skills made others believe that their role was most important but indirect. These skilled people were the *priests* and they were located in the urban towns along with the rulers.[54] The very emergence of the classes of *priests*, rulers and traders were suggestive of the assertion of the human race over the forces of nature and *totems*. In the world of new urban revolution, since the changes that occurred were sudden and drastic it became very difficult for people to encounter it.[55] The priests asserted that they have established control over the forces of nature and evolved ideas to prepare others to smoothly adapt to the new life.[56]

Interpretations as such were needed to maintain the society without serious frictions. Subsequently, it gave rise to pervasive and quasi-natured institutions with the central notion of *God's spirit in contact with the man*.[57] Human attributes were ascribed to the *God* that was conceptually conceived. Even in cases where the human attributes were rejected, certain ideals tended to remain the same. There were points of divergence and convergence on certain important matters among the institutions. Social values and morals were differentially defined by every major institution namely *Brahmanism, Jainism* and *Buddhism*. Thus was evolved the idea of *Karma* accepted by all religions that held sway in the minds of an average person and surpassed materialist thoughts.[58] Closely linked with *karma* was the idea of *transmigration of the soul* which pointed to the eternal nature of one part of human-beings.[59]

The *priests* claimed monopoly to interpret beliefs that pertained to the external life of man. They took material from the past and modified it to the need of their time. It gave an impression of accommodation at the first instance as the sacred and profane of every tribe found their way into the belief system in different forms but with positive power. They authored the *Puranas* to address such a purpose among others. The priests assumed the role of shark-charmers and made others believe that their spells were important to prevent attacks of the sharks during *Pearl Exploration*.[60] As a result, the fear on *Totems* was reduced as also enmity among different *totemic worshippers,* although at the local level the independent worship continued.

The belief pattern at the urban level was viewed as established standard and a gradual shift in focus took place.[61] One of the major reasons for the rise of the religion centered in urban areas laid in the capacity of the priestly class to explain the unexplainable. Particularly, the unfamiliarity with the *other* was explained in terms of the soul which was conceived as permanent. Endless questions about death were thus given an end and subsequently, life was taught as meaningful only when the contours of *Varna-samskara* were not violated and happiness sought within that. These concepts had a powerful reach that it percolated into the local faith and evolved linkages among faiths at various levels. However, the attraction of the local faiths that stemmed from their ability to offer cure during physical problems like chicken-pox and cholera could not be prevented. Similarly, they provided ventilation for the superstitious beliefs of the urban people.

Urbanism operated at various levels and it was the political capital that marked the peak of it as the income generated elsewhere was pooled there. Such transactions were made from *Korkai* to *Madurai*. Sine-qua-non with that was the transfer of the motherly sentiments attached with the sea. As said already, the priestly class was attracted towards the city of *Madurai,* who gave new meaning to the age-old practices. At the first head, they gave physical expression to the motherly sentiments and formed the icon of *Minakshi,* also called *Angayarkannamai;* both of the terms gave out the same meaning i.e. *fish-eyed* female. She was paired with *Lord Siva*[62] and their royal chaplain was *Sage Agastya.*[63] Their separation in folk tradition was understandable through the myths that inform about the birth of their children. The elder son *Lord Ganesha* was born out of the mother-goddesses body without any role of *Siva* whereas it was upside-down in the case of *Lord Murugan.*[64]

The priestly activities became an exclusive prerequisite of the males who planted a stronger frame of patriarchal view that transformed the gender of the sea from feminine to masculine as also the totems. They sought to explain the mysterious character associated with the sea through human attributes. Thus conceived was *Varuna,*[65] the *God* who carried with him the imprint of *Indus Valley Civilization*[66] as also impacts of contacts with the *Indo-Europeans.*[67] He was believed to be the primeval matter[68] and *Lord* of the *Waters* at the same time. He had the powers to remove the sins of people.[69] Though *Varuna* and *Indra*[70] were manifestations of the comprehension of the potentials of nature, the need of the new economy provided more space for divinities which came close to everyday life. Especially these icons were not able to shake the mother-goddess worship at the local level. Therefore, the functions of *Varuna* were soon taken over by *Lord Murugan* whose divine personality was sketched as an ideal son emotionally closer to the mother-goddess.

In the subsequent periods, much of the functions of *Varuna* that included removal of sin were shared also by *Vishnu,* a war-god with who *Vaishnavism* was associated. He smoothly accommodated into his personality the rudiments of *totemic worship.* A typical example of the metaphysical state of life,[71] the icon of *Vishnu* took several incarnations to protect the world through protection of *dharma.* Among these incarnations, the *fish* and the *tortoise* were the earliest. An eternal sleeper in the depths of an ideal sea, he as war-lord permanently carried a *chank* in one of his hands. Though his worship did not find royal patronage in the initial stages, his reach upon the subaltern classes was wide that could be located between the religious processes in the urban center and villages at the local level.[72] His iconography in collaboration with *Siva* was more influential at *Rameshwaram.* At the next level, in places like *Maranmangalam, Alwarthirunagari* and *Kulasekharapattinam* his worship attained significance.[73]

Both *Murugan* and *Vishnu* were conceived as *gods* with accommodative spirit. They extended the sacred rule of *Saivism* and *Vaishnavism* respectively by the extermination of demons that ruled lands beyond the sea. These demons were viewed as responsible for the spread of evil. In the case of *Murugan,* he defeated *Suran,* the demon, and converted him into cock and peacock what became his flag symbol and vehicle respectively. Apart from his association with totems like *fish, tortoise* and *chank,* Vishnu in his *Rama* incarnation was believed to have killed *Ravana.* He was also believed to have made friendship with *Vibhishana* – a brother of *demon-king Ravana* – at *Rameshwaram.*[74] These gods along with *Lord Siva* were easily paired with local mother-goddesses as said already. Thus icons of female divinities emerged at *Uttarakosamangay,*[75] *Thirumandhiranagar,*[76] *Kulasekharapattinam*[77] and *Kanyakumari.*[78]

It was doubtful whether the differences based on *Saivism* and *Vaishnavism* did really matter at the level of the fishing communities. By and large, the mutual recognition of *Saivism* and *Vaishnavism* contributed for the consolidation of the believers and it was only undermined when particular communities tended to shadow the role of other people through the introduction of elaborate rituals. Since the *Parathavars* had a definite say in the *Pearl Fisheries*[79]– the proceeds of which was shared by the *Brahmins[80]* – they could not be completely denied of the ritual status. Possibly for that matter, they were treated at par with the *Vellalas* as no mechanism stopped the *Parathavars* from assuming *Pillai* status like the former caste. Therefore the *Parathavars* were allowed to carry *Palanquin* in which *Gods* visited the devotees during festival occasions.

With the development of trade, there was an assertion of individuals with aspiration for individual recognition. Particularly in the urban regions where the tribal values already underwent erosion, the possibility of rising of disaffection was sought to be contained by extension of a chance in the sphere of religion to the most influential individual.[81] But when several individuals with diverse backgrounds tended to compete with each other, the disaffection thus caused not only had a repercussive effect at the local levels but also as a logical consequence cleared the ground for the spread of heterodox sects.

Particularly important among the heterodox sects was *Jainism* which sought to redefine the doctrine of the life to the new demand generated by the economy what was well manifested in the icon of *Kannagi*.[82] Strong morals were stressed upon normally materialistic minded people. Until 12th century A.D., the influence of *Jainism* was strong in the region.[83] Similarly, *Buddhism* also had its own followers from among the coastal people.[84] But thereafter, the reassertion of the *Bhakti Movement* caused the fall of the heterodox sects. By the time of the arrival of *Marco Polo* all those which were rediscovered by the *Bhakti Movement* underwent marked degeneration and left the way for *Christianity* to establish itself.

Conclusion

Every man – irrespective of the tools in his possession – somehow or other had related himself with the basic components of life that included most importantly water. It had the ever pervasive quality found in every particle as one of the greatest philosophers like *Berkley* had remarked. At any point of time life had remained inconceivable without water. *Sea* not only symbolized life but it also conditioned perceptions as such what resulted in the construction of imagery as to *a being greater than which nothing can be conceived.* It was also as an abstraction of both vision and sound apart from experiences in the physical and dream worlds. In other words, it meant that it had basic features that derived parallels from *Indo-European* religions that stood on the premise of vision as also from the *Semitic* religions that were grounded on sound.[85]

However, the development of tools in subsequent stages and the resultant tribal formation guided the religious pattern more towards the *Indo-European* form of religion. It started with the understanding of transaction between various natural elements and culminated in the worship of totems. It was not to state that the importance of sound was thoroughly supplanted for the sounds of *chanks* and *dolphins* were given adequate space in the belief system. Rather it meant the dominance of sacred objects over the sacred sound. The *totemic* world not only caused division of *sacred* and *profane* but also undermined the position of women since skill based on muscle-power became the monopoly of men. However, the fertility viewed in association with women continued and they became symbols of purity and prestige.

In the further stage marked by the advancement of tools, man's assertion over natural elements was thought to be attained. However, his authority was contained through the introduction of the concept of sin. *Gods* stood above the man with the potential to alleviate sin. The *Gods* thus evolved were attributed with human form physically though they were known for the larger than life characteristics. The *Indo-European Gods* and the local deities were intermingled. As *David Hume* outlined the popular mind adhered to cut and paste what in the diverse background produced *Gods* and *demons* with several heads and limbs.[86] Ideas on *virtue* and *sin* emerged. A class of priests came to the fore-front who interpreted the meanings of human deeds and socialized the people to easily encounter the changes that occurred in the sphere of economy. Social interaction tended to improve at various levels while it undermined the tribal nature of the coastal people.

It eventually resulted in the division of society at the least into the broad categories of 'great tradition' and 'little tradition' culmination of which found expression in the sphere of religion also. The 'little tradition' provided scope for the continuity of the faith system evolved during the tribal stages of life prior to surplus formation. Though it was not to say that there was no change at all in the 'little tradition,' the 'great tradition' grew at the cost of the 'little tradition' and shadowed the elements of the latter. However, all these culminated in the development of a hierarchy within religion what reflected the caste system. In the presence of such hierarchy, the fundamental sanity of *Hinduism* traced from the absence of *Satan* relegated to the latter status the multitude of *Gods* not venerated by the higher-caste.

Endnotes

1   Karu. Arumugatamilan in A.K. Perumal and N. Ramachandran (eds.), *Kanalam Perunthurai* (Tamil), (Chennai: Thamizhini, 2005), p. 227; their everyday life was surrounded by uncertainty and was half–way towards death. The author was of the opinion that, it was at the first head imperative to learn the dimensions of uncertainty for the effective understanding of coastal life.

2   S. Christopher Jayakaran, The Lemuria Myth, *Frontline,* Vol. 28 – Issue 08, Apr. 09–22, 2011, pp. 90–94.

3   For the sake of present research the preexistence of ideas is equated with the sociological concept of *Collective Memory* developed by *Maurice Halbwachs* in his book *On Collective Memory* published in 1950. *Halbwachs* was a sincere disciple of *Emile Durkheim.*

4   Tim Ingold, *The Appropriation of Nature: Essays on Human Ecology and Social Relations*, (Manchester: Manchester University Press, 1986), p. 236.

5   Eminent sociologist Talcott Parsons has classified *Social Action* as instrumental, expressive and moral actions. In the present researcher's opinion, the moral action takes its recognition from religion. A society which did not define moral action stood in a significant time-period in history only to allow reformers to define them in subsequent periods.

6   Noted Prof. Kunal Chakrabarty, who was the author of the book 'Religious Processes: The Puranas and Making of a Regional Tradition,' delivered a lecture on the character of Hinduism in a Refresher Course conducted by the UGC – ASC, Jawaharlal Nehru University, New Delhi

between 24/08/2009 and 18/09/2009 in which he put forth this view. According to him, a religion should qualify certain conditions. Among others, it should have a founder, a prescribed holy book, and an established institutional structure with a headship. Since Hinduism does not qualify these conditions it is only a belief system where mutually contradictory ideas pertaining to the external element find expression.

7   Romila Thapar, *The Penguin History of Early India: From the Origins to A.D. 1300* (New Delhi: Penguin Books India (P) Ltd, 2002), p. xviii.

8   D.P. Chattopadyaya, *Madhamum, Samugamum* (Tamil), (Chennai: New Century Book House, 2009) p.2.

9   Ibid.

10   Importantly a novel authored by Jostein Gaarder translated in Tamil by R. Sivakumar entitled *Sophiein Ulagam* published by Kalachuvadu publishers was of great use in enlightening the present researcher on the broad philosophical issues of the Western World.

11   Readings in anthropology were not made through prescribed textbooks. Rather they were information gathered from classroom notes dictated by teachers like Professor Subhas Mahapatra of Delhi University in the period between December 1999 and May 2000.

12   D.P. Chattopadyaya, Op. Cit., p. 8; the rudiments of Evolutionary Theory was developed by Auguste Comte and subsequently by Herbert Spencer. The latter was of the opinion that societies moved from simplicity to complexity in correspondence to the tools they developed from time to time. Marxism believes that the starting point to understand religion is the comprehensive knowledge about the evolutionary growth of society.

13   Ibid.

14   Naturism in the modern context has been predominantly taken for the practice of nudity. In the Western countries, even a hesitant person removes at least one of his clothes in the sea-shore. It goes to show both the importance as well as the uniqueness of sea in the broad world of nature.

15   R. Pavananthi Vembulu and R. John Suresh Kumar, *Circling the Triangle: Vulnerability, Social Exclusion and the Making of Disaster*, Research Paper Series, (Tirunelveli: Centre for the Study of Social Exclusion and Inclusive Policy, Manonmaniam Sundaranar University, 2010) p._.

16   T.K.V. Subramanian, *Religious Thoughts and Beliefs in India (Block 1)*, (New Delhi: Indira Gandhi National Open University, 2007) p. 9; this is patterned on the ontological view of religion to which philosophers like St. Anselm, Rene Descartes, Leibniz subscribed. But ontological view does not accept observation as a source of making an argument. With Rene Descartes and Leibniz, it laid much emphasis on mathematical perfection and coherence respectively which are not applicable either to sea or ideas on the sea.

17   The idea of the soul was a latter day development.

18   Jostein Gaarder, *Sophiein Ulagam,* (Nagerkoil: Kalachuvadu Publications, 2011) p. 49; noted natural philosopher *Thales* who lived a few centuries before the birth of Christ in the West was of the opinion that life emerged from the water and with death dissolved in water.

19 Ibid., pp. 98–106; *Plato* was of the opinion that the soul was permanent and it was endowed with the ability to visit the world of ideas against human senses which could relate only to the physical world.

20 R.N. Joe d'cruz, Korkai, (Chennai: Kalachuvadu Pathipagam, 2009) p. 192; the author narrates the risks in pearl and chank diving. At times the diver risks his life in the desire of seeing more oysters and chanks in the pristine beauty of the ocean. The second order meaning of that can be inferred as the struggle of life to liberate itself from the bodily prison as said by *Plato*.

21 Interview with Mr. Parabaran (22), Fisherman, Manapad on 8-01-10; he said even today if affected by Chickenpox the residents secretly attribute some rituals for the mother goddess located at Kulasekharapattinam.

22 A. Dhananjayan, *Kulakuriyeealum, Meenavar Valakarugalum* (Tamil), (Palayamkottai: Abidha Publications, 1996), pp. 170–175.

23 Ibid.

24 R.N. Joe d'Cruz, *Aazhi Sul Ulagu*, (Tamil), (Chennai: Tamizhini, 2004) p.267; the message of death that occurred at sea spread widely in short duration and caused the visit of elders from other coastal settlements.

25 D.P. Chattopadyaya, Op. Cit., pp. 13–15.

26 G. Duncan Mitchell (ed.), *A New Dictionary of Sociology*, (London: Routledge, 1999), pp. 115–116; in a book on the history of Christianity (exact name of the author and book not remembered) a reference pertaining to the Biblical Babel event occurs. It maintains that the quaking of strange sounds by Christians of certain new-born denominations in the recent past was begun as an intentional attempt to trace the universal language before the fall of Babel tower. However, the intention was lost and a new meaning of divine spirit entering the body of the worshipper was added. Similarly, a system of communication – irrespective of the question of rationality in it – was developed. In subsequent periods the sounds were converted into words with secret meaning and believed to have had an effect.

27 R.N. Joe d'Cruz, *Aazhi Sul Ulagu* 100; in this ethnographic novel that depicted Parathavar life in the twentieth century the author refers about a magician who controlled rainfall through his command over the oceanic currents.

28 G. Duncan Mitchell (ed.), Op. Cit., pp. 115–116. *See also* E.E. Evans-Pritchard, *Witchcraft, Oracles and Magic among the Azande,* 1937.

29 Edgar Thurston, *Castes and Tribes of South India Vol. VI* (Madras: Government Press, 1909), pp. 140–141.

30 Perumpanattrupadai: 280–286; *Panans* were depicted as skilled fishermen. Yet they catch fish with bait attached to a bamboo pole.

31 Sirupanattrupadai: 137–138; *Panans* were depicted as drummers. The people of the Parvatha Rajakulam trace their origin from the Panans.

32 Possibly the roots of native astronomy were traceable from this period.

33 G. Duncan Mitchell (ed.), Op. Cit., p. 230; according to the dictionary "a totem is a species of plant of animal or plant; or part of an animal or plant; or a natural object or phenomenon or the symbol of any of these…" The term totem has been used in the present study with this broad meaning which subsumes the need to distinguish among animism, fetishism and etc.

34 A. Dhananjayan, Op. Cit., p. 204.

35 Difference between men and women could not be made on the grounds of courage. Earlier women were able to partake in fishing activities at par with men because the simple nature of tools did not demand much of their physical strength.

36 Interview with Mr. Alangara Michael Nallathambi Fernando (67), President, Parathavar Vadakku Ur, Kottar on 27-11-08.

37 The demand that pertained to labour from agricultural lands was the physical strength of young people. To its contrast, the mysterious character of sea required the role of experienced men. Probably that was the reason why the protagonist of the novels like *The Old Man and the Sea* and *Aazhi Sul Ulagu* by Ernest Hemingway and R.N. Joe d'Cruz respectively were elderly people.

38 Salt was believed to contain intangible potential that could ward off evil power.

39 Interview with Mr. Parabaran (22), Fisherman, Manapad on 8-01-10; the interviewee identified a painting in a boat that depicted *Tuna*. It was preferred over other variety because *Tuna* was known for its taste. Hence it was not only most demanded but also economically valued more.

40 There are certain varieties of Sharks which belong to egg-laying variety also.

41 Among one of the shark families that belonged to mammal category, the she-fish mostly carried its small ones in its womb. This was believed to give strength to the pregnant women. Usually, fisherwomen were stronger and healthier than women in other parts. At times, the fisherwomen fed excess breast milk to weak children in the neighborhood.

42 Pattinapalai: 86–90.

43 Interview with Mr. Amaladas, (65), Fisherman of Alandalai on 02/01/10; the flesh and blood of Tortoise were among the most desired delicacies in the coast. However, its flesh is not easily digestible.

44 In the plains they maintain a phrase that 'aama pukundha veedu velangadhu'. Generally, they believed and still believe that a house visited by a tortoise would never flourish.

45 Pattinapalai: 63–65; they were depicted as feasting field-tortoise during a festival occasion.

46 R.N. Joe d'Cruz, *Aazhi Sul Ulagu*, p. 243.

47 Ibid., p. 145; there was the practice of instigation of the totems – chiefly big fish – against enemies.

48 H.R. Pate, *Tinnevelly District Gazetteer (1916)*, (Tirunelveli: Manonmaniam Sundaranar University, 1993), p. 146–147; he has discussed extensively a caste known both as Katasans and Sozhiya Vellalas who were associated with Chank-diving. Though a separate caste, the formation of one of their clans was traced from a marriage between a Katasan male and a Parathavar caste female.

49 James Hornell, The Indian Chank in Folklore and Religion, *Taylor and Francis,* Vol. 53, No. 2 (Jun, 1942), p. 114.

50 Ibid.

51 In the context of the *Pearl Fishery Coast, Korkai* emerged as an important urban town with port, mint etc. The proceeds of the *Pearl Fisheries* was chiefly responsible for the rise of *Korkai.* When better water management was learnt, it corresponded with threats of invasion. Therefore, *Madurai* assumed the status of capital.

52 D.P. Chattopadyaya, Op. Cit., p. 5.

53 Ibid. p. 31.

54 Ibid.

55 Ibid. p. 38.

56 Ibid.

57 Ibid. p.2.

58 Vinod Vincent Rajesh, *From Totemic Worship to Sanskritization: A Study of Early Parathavar History and Culture*, Unpublished M. Phil Dissertation submitted to Bharathidasan University, Trichy, 2007, p. 47; importantly Ajivika sect to which popular literary character such as *Kovalan* belonged had its survival in the Tamil Country before it disappeared.

59 Romila Thapar, *The Penguin History of Early India,* P. 169; but Buddhism was against the idea of the permanence of soul.

60 L.F. Benedetto (ed.), *The Travels of Marco Polo*, (New Delhi: Asian Educational Services, 1994) p. 293.

61 It comes close to Sanskritization explained by the eminent sociologist, *M.N. Srinivas* in terms of lower castes imitating the cultural practices of the upper caste and asserting rise in their caste ranking. These can also be viewed as part and parcel of the 'great tradition' and 'little tradition' dialogue.

62 William P. Harman, *The Sacred Marriage of a Hindu Goddess*, (Delhi: Motilal Banarsidas Publishers Pvt Ltd, 1992). p. 50.

63 K.A. Nilakanta Sastri, *A History of South India: From Prehistoric Times to the Fall of Vijayanagar,* (New Delhi: Oxford University, 1958), p. 67.

64 D.D. Kosambi, *Myth and Reality* (Bombay: Popular Prakashan Pvt Ltd, 1992), p. 3.

65 Clarence Thomas Maloney, *The Effect of Early Coastal Sea Traffic on the Development of Civilization in South India,* Unpublished Ph. D. thesis submitted to the Dept. of Anthropology, University of Pennsylvania in 1968, p. 74; Varuna was mentioned as a patron deity of several clans.

66 T.S. Subramanian, From Indus Valley to Coastal Tamil Nadu, *The Hindu* (Madurai edition), dated 3rd May 2008; the article seeks to identify parallels between *Tamil Culture* and *Indus Valley Civilization.* In view of that, the importance attributed to water through *Great Bath* in the *Indus Valley Civilization* instigated to associate *Varuna* in that angle also.

67 P. Balakrishnan, *"Neydal Nila Makkalin Valzviyal – Oru Aiyvu"* (Tamil), Unpublished M. Phil dissertation submitted to Manonmaniam Sundaranar University, Tirunelveli, 2005, p. 24.

68 Pushparani, C. *"Sangakala Panpaadu"* (Tamil), Unpublished M. Phil. dissertation submitted to Manonmaniam Sundaranar University, Tirunelveli, 2005, p. 61.

69 Pattinapalai: 99–100.

70 Clarence Thomas Maloney, Op. Cit., p. 74; he was mentioned as lord of the sea. However, both *Varuna* and *Indra* were linked with rain also. In the context of the coast, it marked the realization of the importance of rain. Rivers were dependent upon rain which in turn was depended by sea for minerals. Therefore, good rain meant an improvement of the resources of the sea.

71 Vishnu in his Krishna incarnation was associated with the delivery of Bhagavat Gita which expounded the philosophical basis of Hinduism at large.

72 T. Paramasivan in A.K. Perumal and N. Ramachandran (eds.) Op. Cit., p. 47.

73 Still in these places, settlements of the *Parathavar* people are found.

74 R.N. Joe d'Cruz, *Aazhi Sul Ulagu*, p. 212; in folklore, it was also maintained that the nose of Surpanaga – the sister of Ravana – was disfigured at a place called Mookaiyur located in the *Pearl Fishery Coast*.

75 Clarence Thomas Maloney, Op. Cit., p. 115; the name of the goddess ending with Mangay is notable. Mangai might have been an independent deity later identified as Lord Siva's spouse probably during Bhakti Movement. The place *Uttarakosamangay* was linked with the divine sports of *Lord Siva*. It is located in Ramnad district. *See* Edgar Thurston, *Castes and Tribes of Southern India*, Vol. I, (Madras: Government Press, 1909)

76 _____; Thirumandhiranagar was the early name of Tuticorin. Here Santhana Mariamman was the guardian deity of the *Parathavars*. It was a fortified temple.

77 Mutharamman is the guardian deity of *Kulasekharapattinam*. A chank has been placed before her image in the temple. Therefore, unlike other goddesses she was linked with *Vaishnavism*. Yet she also was endowed with capacity to cure chicken-pox.

78 At Kanyakumari the goddess was believed to be an eternal virgin and mother. The temple bears testimony to the historical links with the *Parathavar* people. Both Brahmin and non-Brahmin priests perform rituals to the goddess.

79 The impact of the coastal economy spread as far as *Thirupudaimarudhur* located approximately 80 kilometers away from the coast wherein murals testify the vibrancy of trade.

80 *The Travels of Marco Polo*, p. 293.

81 According to the research finding of Arjun Appadurai and Breckenridge the God seated in the *Chariot* during festivals represented the leader who organized the program.

82 S. Ramachandran, *Korkai Varalatril Sila Pudhiya Seidhigal* (Tamil), Archaeological Report of Curator, Korkai in a manuscript dated 13-06-2000 sent to headquarters, pp. 5–7.

83 In the Tirunelveli government museum, two Jain statues that belonged to 8th Century A.D. unearthed from *Uttarakosamangay* have been maintained. *Uttarakosamangay* was a well-

known place associated with the *Parathavar* history. During the days of Bhakti Movement, it was seemed to have been the capital of the *Parathavar* people.

84 Clarence Thomas Maloney, Op. Cit., pp. 112–115; the close and amicable relationship of the *Parthavars* with the *Sinhalese* was suggestive of their favourable attitude towards *Buddhism*.

85 Jostein Gaarder, Op. Cit., pp. 166–179.

86 Ibid., p. 298.

VI

Class Structure, Social Values, Gift Giving:
An Ethnographic Study of the Social Life of the Parathavars

Introduction

Life on the coast, in general, was believed to be tribal in nature. The social organization that started as band-like formations attained tribal characteristics with expansion in population and accommodation of diverse groups through the introduction of exogamy. With further expansion of population and diversification of economic activity, production of surplus as in agrarian economy ensued and it tended to introduce hierarchical segmentations based on the division of labour as observable in the caste system. In the context of ancient Coastal Tamil Nadu it not only contributed to the evolution of independent castes such as the *Panars,*[1] *Nulaiyars, Umanars Parathavars* etc. but also introduced complexity within these castes.

The dynamics of the social history of coastal Tamil Nadu could not be effectively comprehended in the light of *Varna* based hierarchical division.[2] Nevertheless, the influence of the conventional understanding of caste made with the agrarian village as the background was so very powerful to be totally avoided in any study that pertained to social history. Whether or not the three layers of caste; the tenants, the intermediaries and the overlords had parallels in the coast was a pertinent question. There were definitely huge traders in the coastal life at par with the agrarian overlords followed by the intermediaries and ordinary fishermen. The presence of these diverse social segments comparable with agrarian life was traceable since the *Sangam* period in the *Coast* of the *Tamil Country* – that included parts of present day *Kerala* as well. However, in the larger spectrum, the present study intends to research the complex dimensions in the social history of the *Parathavars* before their conversion to *Christianity.*

The literature of the *Sangam* period has depicted both public and personal lives in the coast inhabited by the *Parathavars* as marked by 'open siege'[3] and 'long separation of lovers'[4] respectively. It is suggestive of the division of the social domains of men and women. The present study seeks to investigate this hypothesis linking it with the nature of work in which the *Parathavar* people were involved. Thus the study has been structured into three compartments with a base structure on which two superstructures are perpendicularly placed. The base structure of the study is formed by

101

analyses of the *Parathavar* social identity that takes the cue from the deductive approach[5] and the superstructures to it are created through observations of the role of men and women in the society based on ethnographic approach.[6] The approach of the study is interdisciplinary insofar it takes into purview issues like *Sanskritization* that is more popular in sociology. An attempt has been made in the present study to incorporate dimensions of social exclusion and mechanisms of integration.

Ideas from scholars like R.N. Joe d'Cruz, Roche A. Patrick, J.H. Nelson, H.R. Pate, A. Sivasubramanian, A. Dhananjayan, S.N. Sadasivan, T.N. Sadasiva Pandarathar, R. Pavananthi Vembulu, R. Champakalakshmi, C.T. Maloney, S.C. Chitty, James Hornell, M.A. Durai Rangasamy, Poneelan, D.M. Persis Rajammal, George Hart and S.C. Kaufmann has been borrowed to enrich the article. Importantly, the classification of the *Parathavar* community into thirteen classes by S.C. Chitty and the memory of eminent novelist *R.N. Joe d'Cruz* recorded as an insider in two of his Tamil *Aazhi Sul Ulagu* and *Korkai* requires special mention.

Generally, the social history writing style stresses upon particular issues confining itself to a narrow geographical area. To its contrast, the present study attempts to capture the general social actions from a broader geographical area, namely, the *Pearl Fishery Coast*. A range of primary sources like the *Sangam Literatures, Tholhappiyam, Travelogue of Marco Polo* and *Letters of Francis Xavier* that cannot be classified into a single time period have been employed for the study. These have been also substantiated with information collected through field visits. Such an approach not only seeks to create a harmony between the inductive and deductive methods but also makes the standpoint of the researcher clear that the *Parathavars* live in the same epistemic period at the least from the *Sangam* period till their adoption of *Christianity* in the 16th century A.D.[7]

Class Structure

The entire coastal stretch inhabited by the Tamil speaking populace was known as *Neydal*. During the *Sangam* period, the people who were exclusively dependent upon the resources of the sea were the *Parathavars*. Therefore their identity was linked to geography that caused the appellation *Neydal Nila Makkal*. Since other communities mentioned in the *Sangam Literature* such as *Umanar*,[8] *Nulaiyar*,[9] *Thimilar*[10] and *Panar*[11] were partially dependent on the sea for livelihood they did not attain a status at par with the *Parathavar* people. However, in the post-*Sangam* periods, the *Parathavar* title lost its significance in places outside *Pearl Fishery Coast*. One finds *the* reference about various independent castes linked with the sea such as the *Sempadavar*,[12] *Meenavar, Valaignar*,[13] *Katasans*,[14] *Karaiyar*,[15] *Pattinavar*,[16] *Mukkuvar*,[17] *Kurup*[18], etc. [19] The variety owed its rise to geopolitical factors[20] and the trans-border market[21] dynamics that culminated in the emergence of diversification of economic activities and occupational specialization.

At a time when other categories emerged, the *Parathavars* within the *Pearl Fishery Coast* attained the character and features of a separate caste. The caste was grossly affected by the markets that emerged at the sub-regional level which was tied to the trans-border market at the higher level. The surplus formation and diversification of commodities in the market that ranged from *Pearls* to *betel leaves* together caused complex divisions within the *Parathavar* community. Though the vibrancy of these markets was maintained by the surplus produced in the coast i.e. fish and salt,[22] the people responsible for the production of surplus were socially relegated to the background against traders and others. This was not only suggestive of the presence of an elaborate class division within the *Parathavar* community but also of a mechanism that maintained internal cohesion.

Since historic period, the *Parathavars* were never a professionally homogeneous group. The occupational diversity of the *Parathavars* of the *Pearl Fishery Coast* largely segmented the community internally. These segments can be broadly classified into three major classes on the basis of their role in trade. They were the *economically assertive class, the intermediary class*, and *the excluded class*. Possibly the *headmen*[23], *dealers of clothes, owners of Thonies, Priests*[24] and *sailors* (in the rank of tandal) constituted the *economically assertive class.*[25] The scope for migration[26] from the coast for these people was wide. With migration, they further diversified their occupation and particularly entered into agricultural activities. The *intermediary class* was formed by *retailers in fish and other commodities, tailors and other professionals* and *personnel at the service of the government*. They were located either on the coast or mainland. But importantly they created the link with the mainland. The *excluded class* was constituted by *sailors* (below the rank of tandal), *the divers for corals, the divers for pearl-oysters, divers of chank, packers of clothes, tortoise-catchers, porpoise-catchers, catchers of sharks and other fish, palanquin bearers, peons of the headmen, crab-catchers,*[27] *wage earners in chank and salt industry* and those who *fish in freshwater.*[28] They were excluded from the benefits of trade and had minimum scope for migration. The agriculture that was evolved by them in the coastal environment was of negligible nature. At times of off-season, they performed simple agricultural works in the farms of other people.[29]

The class division within the caste did not assume the dimensions of internal purity and pollution what was evident from their collaboration in the ritual sphere. Mobility from below to the top was quite possible through diversification of economic activity and hard-work. The economic loss encountered at the top pulled people down to the level of fishermen. The class differences within the caste did not appeal the minds of an outsider who viewed all of them as mere fishermen. The *assertive class* did not feel embarrassed to be conceptually bracketed and identified with the ordinary fishermen since the latter were feared as desperadoes in the larger society.[30] Moreover, the *assertive class* did not take any special effort to evolve symbols to distinguish it from others. If at all there were certain symbols like turban, ribbon etc. the *excluded class* was not prevented to imitate it. The common image helped the *economically assertive class* and the *intermediary class* at various levels of business relationship.

The high frequency of death that marred the lives of the fishermen was a major factor that bridged the gap between classes. Apart from the life challenge imposed by nature i.e. sea, there were dangers of external invasion attracted by the wealth created by the *assertive class*. During such critical periods, it was the *excluded class* that offered protection. Therefore, it can be ascertained that the cultural core focused on death was formed from below i.e. by the *excluded class*. Death time and again reiterated the limitation of life. Since even the *assertive class* and the *intermediary class* were born from out of the wombs of the *excluded class,* the pervasive nature of the cultural core was logically understandable. Therefore, death maintained the nature of society in *tribal* form and the public-spirited outlook of the *assertive class* was due to it.[31] However, when a settlement was formed by different classes its social image was shaped by the bravery of the *excluded class,* the approach towards women of the *Intermediary class* and the numerical density of the *assertive-class.*[32]

The *economically assertive class* not only had better access to trans-border politico-economic powers beyond the coast but their dynamism created wealth that attracted people – both from abroad and within – and caused the birth of cities. With the population constituted by diverse classes and castes, many settlements in the *Pearl Fishery Coast* attained the status that went close to a city. The settlements in the coastal area, in general, were divided into *Pattinams, Pakkams* and *Cheris* during the Sangam period.[33] The residential division, in general, was reflective of both caste and class. In the *Pakkams* resided the wealthy people of diverse backgrounds whereas a *Cheri* was populated by the humble folks of a predominantly homogeneous caste. The *Intermediary class* lived either in the *Pakkams* or in the *Cheris* and their professional success was determined by the ability to hide their class identity although the social values of the community at large emerged from among them.

Economic necessities of a settlement determined the number of *Cheris.* Therefore, in wealthy settlements, there were *cheris* of the *Parayars* also apart from the *Fishermen Cheri.* Since the *Parathavars* were not professionals in house construction, the caste of *Parayars* seemed to have assisted them. As the *Parayars* were associated with the manufacture of lime, their services were inevitable particularly when bigger homes were constructed. But the settlements of the *Parayars* were located separately and sometimes gave the impression as buffer zones.[34] Even the pathways for both the settlements were separate. Though it was reflective of the hegemonic assertion of the *Parathavars,* the ill-treatment meted out was not all the same comparable with that of the plain. The *Parayars* were allowed limited access to the sea and were able to fish for personal consumption. It can also be stated as the *Parayars* who were placed in the lower rung in the social stratification of the Tamil society lived depending on the *Parathavars,* the latter's status also improved.

The *economically assertive class* facilitated the process of *Sanskritization* at all levels. By virtue of their command in the economic sphere, they directly imitated the *Brahmins* and *Vellalas.* For the *excluded class* it was the lifestyle and social practices of the *assertive class* that was largely available for imitation. By and large, the *sanguthali*[35] worn by the females of the community and the role of their men in temple festivals symbolized their social status as not low within the *Brahminical* social hierarchy.[36] Moreover, they were able to derive the service of the goldsmith – known as *Pon-aasary* – at their homes. At the professional side, they were able to procure the services of the carpenters – known as *Mara-aasary.* The barbers and the washer-men also provided their services directly in the residential hamlets of the people. Since these services were within the attainable limit, it can be effectively stated that the services of the *Brahmins* were not inaccessible to them.[37] Significantly, they were able to achieve such status despite the fact that a vast majority of the community was involved in a work that created stench.

The market demanded an accommodative spirit from among the *Parathavar community* in the social sphere. The *Parathavar* fishermen, in general, required the cooperation of castes such as the *Savalakarars* and the *Padaiatchis*[38] in fish-retail. With time, a substantial population from among these communities became dependent upon the *Parathavar* fishermen in the capacity of retailers. As a result, the caste-based differences were undermined and matrimonial alliances were made. Predominantly, alliances were made with the *intermediary class* and with the passage of time the caste based difference was underplayed. Such alliances were instrumental in causing migration from the coast towards the plain.

The *Ur* played a vital role in the debasement of incongruous projections in the society, and thereby, it disallowed the creation of a strict hierarchy against fluidity. It made best attempts to protect the tribal egalitarian character of the society. It recognized the significant members of the community by an honorific title known as *Kadalodi* – a generic term that referred all *Parathavars* professionally linked to the sea either directly or indirectly. Such persons were also addressed with *Pillai* title.[39] The first half of the term *Parathavar* i.e. *Parathu* possibly outlined the inclusive character of the *Ur* at large while it gave the meaning expanse.[40]

The *assertive class* entered into an economic transaction with the *Maravar* caste people who were employed as village watch-guards. But the relationship did not disturb the boundary between the castes. It was given a kinship form that was explained through a myth wherein the mutual relationship was said as that between father and children.[41] Since the people of the *assertive class* were highly class-conscious, they evolved a knowledge system that identified the background of people with their residential settlement. By and large, they predominantly preferred matrimonial alliance within the residential area.[42] However, within the residential area, the domains of men and women counterpoised each other.

Values: The World of Men

There were repercussions at various levels caused by the social division that was characterized by the absence of absolute solidarity within classes. In the capacity of traders and fishermen, the male members of the society were thought to be responsible for the maintenance of social balance and upward mobility what gave the society a patriarchal outlook. The patriarchy though pervasive not only did not become pivotal to the society but also derived substance from the lifestyle of the men of the *excluded class*. Therefore, it denuded the scope for the emergence of strong leadership from among the individuals rooted in the allegiance of substantial sections of the community. Rather, it gave way for the establishment of patron-client relationships within the community and caused the rise of multiple factions. In other words, the class division maintained the tribal characteristics of the society on the one hand while prevented the polarization of people on the other hand.

The patron-client transaction added complexity to the social system as each faction was constituted by a few families of the *economically assertive class* and a number of hierarchically positioned client families from among the *intermediary* and *excluded classes*. Undoubtedly, the factions were led by the families of the *economically assertive class* whose influence was not only appreciated by the latter but also was thought as shared by all members of the faction. It was also widely believed that such influence secured them in places beyond the coast.[43] Since such a benefit was enjoyed by the clients they in return gave their unflinching loyalty symbolized by free access to the fish in their nets. There were situations wherein the patron might not at all recognize the client. Yet, the general principle of the coast that allowed the discount[44] for those who procured fish from within the settlement for outside business was wholeheartedly followed by the fishermen for it largely benefitted their patrons.

As said already, the *economically assertive class* was not embarrassed to be identified with the humble fishermen for reasons that owed to the latter's image. Moreover, the life of the people who belonged to the *excluded class* was marked by regularity against the life of others. If a person of the *economically assertive class* met with misfortune, the available option of livelihood for him and his descendants was to take up the fishing occupation and join other fishermen. Same was in the case of migrants of the *intermediary class* who met with misfortune.[45] In such case, the fishermen assumed the role of a teacher and largely remained sympathetic. Since the fishermen imitated the lifestyle of the *economically assertive class* they viewed the arrival of the members of the latter class to their profession as prestigious. Thus the unsecured nature of life in the coast evoked certain unique patterns.

It was generally said that the complex nature of sea that paralleled the *Pearl Fishery Coast* demanded hard work and those who were able to cope with that can manage anywhere.[46] In such an environmental condition, constant engagement in physically rough work and easy access to healthy seafood made the appearance of the *Parathavar* fishermen muscular. Unlike other non-vegetarian foods such as mutton, chicken, beef and pork, fish was known for its variety. Among food, it was exchanged from the lowest to the highest value. Usually, *Chalai* (Sardines) and *Nethili* (Anchovy) were commonly available and were valued lower than vegetables. On the other hand, there were varieties like *Naimeen* (Indo-pacific king mackerel) and *Guthippu* (False Trevally) which were of higher economic value. Irrespective of the value, the fishermen had easy access to anyone of the kinds. Except in times of famine – usually during summers – they hardly took food without fish. Even during periods of scarcity they never hesitated to share the catch with the patrons, and thus, every day the families of the patron also took food with fish.

The mind-frame of the *Parathavar* fishermen was in nature a mix-of-extremes. They were normally considered magnanimous at heart and loyal to those who reposed trust. They were rarely calculative and settled for what they were offered.[47] They liberally offered their hard earned materials to the benefit of others. They allowed their women even to breastfeed children of other communities.[48] They were not only short-tempered people but also largely ignorant.[49] As viewed by members of other castes, the *Parathavars* generally maintained physical and emotional distance from other communities and were not always easily approachable. They were intolerant to criticisms and sarcastic remarks made by others what can also be stated as their love for freedom and social autonomy. A minor issue provoked conflict between two individuals. Anger was expressed in the range from verbal abuse with employment of foul words to physical assault. But they sank the difference in a shorter period of time and easily reconciled. However, they resorted to extreme steps when their women, children and elderly were disgraced.[50] In a conflict, they never disgraced these categories of people. Most often, there were intra-caste conflicts either between two fishermen hamlets or between two factions in the same hamlet.[51] Unity was a rare phenomenon though the *Ur* made best attempts to maintain it. They spontaneously united on issues that commonly affected them and dispersed when immediate goals were attained.

In popular perception, they were associated with weapons made of the remains of marine creatures that were camouflaged easily. These weapons were believed to cause incurable wounds in the body of the enemies.[52] Above all, the *Parathavars* were thought to have immersed their enemies in the sea what resulted in the inability to trace the evidence of the victim's body. The migrants from the coast to the plains were also viewed in the light of such perceptions since their link with the coast ensured regular supply of healthy food through the visits of muscular coastal men.

Over and above the fear the *Parathavars* generated in the minds of other people, they were also reduced to a level of mockery for gluttony and craze for expensive clothes.[53] Food, clothing and other mundane luxuries of life seemed to have constituted the matter of the prima facie importance of life against nurture of definitive plan for future. It was also true that the prestige of the individual members and families of the *Parathavar* community rested in the pomp and show that they demonstrated at times of public gatherings and ceremonies like the wedding. However, the differences that emerged in the perception of men and women at this juncture had to be accounted.[54]

The emotional insecurity that pertained to the life characterized the collective psyche of the *Parathavars* which did not provide adequate scope for long term plans. This was so at the bottom of the society at the least till social mobility was attained. Accumulation of wealth was not tolerated in the system. An individual who made a successful enterprise through fishing was viewed as a lucky man. The sea was venerated for its immense resources. But two fishermen that ventured into the sea on the same day returned with different volumes of catch. Mere experience and skill alone did not contribute to the success. At the same time, only those who meet with constant success could alone hope to improve his material status. Such persons were viewed as potential competitors and their well being was hindered. Attitudes of these kinds also denuded the community from the attainment of unity and evolution of a strong and uncontested leadership among them. Therefore, the hard work for which they were known for did not transpire into pathway towards progress.

The profession demanded physical commitment from the individuals. Normally men left their home in crews either in early morning or afternoon. On return, usually, one of the members picked the best fish from the catch and started cooking while the rest of the crew was involved in the distribution of the catch followed by drying and mending of the nets. The team was not dissolved until the works were completed. While the work was performed they discussed issues that ranged from personal to public without distinguishing the participants on the basis of age. The process of food preparation and miscellaneous works were completed almost simultaneously and the leisure was spent in liquor consumption. A similar lifestyle was imaginable in the case of *Pearl* and *Chank-divers* also.

The members of the crew that returned after catch were received by a member of their respective families – usually a male child – with porridge or some other food. A valuable fish was given as a reward to the child. Nobody worried about what he did with the reward. He converted the reward into his desires[55] what denuded life ambitions beyond the coast.[56] Most often, the male-children played near the place where the maintenance and miscellaneous works took place. The young minds were exposed to the conversations in which everyday experience at sea was a common theme. They were inspired by the recognition derived by fishermen who were distinguished on the basis of skill. In the coastal context, violation of routine was thought to be the first step in the direction of skill[57] and it went hand-in-hand with experience. Since age difference was not an important determinant in a relationship they freely conversed with the skilled and preferred to join their crew for training. They even imitated their habits such as chewing on betel leaves, consumption of liquor etc. They remained intractable for the females in the family to control.

Women: The Chief Gift Receivers

The females of the fisherman family collected fish for the family consumption from the nets of the male members every day. They were accountable to the fish only in cases where the males took food at home. Otherwise, the bulk of fish was dry-processed and converted into materials of value.[58] Predominantly, the dry-fish reached the market through the women. Most of the times, one of the senior women of the family took the responsibility of the procurement of essential items – that included chiefly food – with the proceeds earned from the dry-fish sold. With responsibility and command upon the domestic affairs, the mind of the females attained patriarchal character than feminine. They were equally short-tempered and sensitive. They chewed betel leaves, in several cases consumed intoxicants[59] and commonly employed foul words in everyday activities. Nevertheless, marriage was the factor that instigated change among women.

Polygamy was common.[60] As in any case, the number of wives taken by a man was determined by his economic status.[61] Since the *Pearl Fishery Coast* was viewed as the source of wealth, it attracted women of immoral nature.[62] The patriarchal element was so strongly ingrained in the minds of an ordinary coastal woman that they were socialized to tolerate the excesses of the masculine such as polygamy and prostitution at the personal level and appreciate it in general. The ability of a man was estimated on his economic potential to support as many people as he could. The personal ornamentations like growing of large mustache, wearing of earrings, finger-rings and other jewels, choice of dress, mode of personal transportation were thought to be depictive of the economic status of a man and attracted fellow human beings, particularly, women.

The females were expected to maintain control over their senses since chastity for which they were valued was linked to the moods of the sea. It was constantly taught to her that if she failed to control herself, the sea would punish the male members of the family while they explore it.[63] To its contrast, it was also said that the women with high morals were rewarded with invaluable gifts by the members of the family on several occasions in her lifetime. Dissemination of ideas like these controlled the frequency of love affairs.

This was not to understate the occurrence of love-marriages, the incidence of which was attributable to the socio-geographical condition of the coast. As said already, the home was only a place of food production and it provided only limited privacy for virgin girls. At the least for the purpose of procurement of water and fire-wood as also for everyday ablutions, the females left their homes.[64] Mingling at places where men were present was unavoidable. In fact, one of the two general values of the coast – placing of undue importance on clothing – was ingrained on the collective consciousness of *Parathavar* women which hardly confined them within the home. Those places where they roamed attracted men. Therefore, over and above the division of the domains of men and women, there existed certain places where young males and females happened to meet each other that led for mutual attraction.

As a matter of logic, there should not have been any problem when good-natured people were mutually attracted. But the tribal nature of the society was such that it did not allow the special character of individuals to glitter independently. As mentioned already, the *Parathavars* were short-tempered people who magnified minute issues and quarreled on that. In such a context, it remained difficult for any good natured person to project his personal values and be recognized. It undermined the possibility of love marriages. Apart from that the factional politics that gave way for the emergence of families associated with certain characteristics caused superficial division within the tribe and undermined the harmonious negotiation between the bride-takers and bride-givers. These families traditionally maintained alliance and animosity with other families which determined matrimonial negotiations. At indefinite intervals, changes took place in the family alliances. Dynamics of these kinds complicated the prospect of love marriage.

Apart from that, the *Ur* also exercised control over the moral life of the young people. It attempted to mitigate between the parents of the boy and girl in cases was both belonged to the *Parathavar* caste. Otherwise, social ostracism was imposed upon the defective member what made him ineligible for life-rituals that reiterated social status. The bridegroom who married within the same caste was honoured with a gift of garland[65] and recognized as eligible to hold various offices of the *Ur*. Similarly, the girl who married as wished by her parents was blessed with the dowry which constituted a substantial part of the family savings and other gifts from time to time. Her children found special recognition within the family.

It was thought prestigious to enter into matrimonial alliance with the higher classes, namely the *economically assertive class* and the *intermediary class*. Since there were differences in the lifestyle of these classes and the humble fishermen, the former preferred to take only the brides than grooms if at all there were any alliances. It necessitated long-period plan from the side of the bride's family for it was chiefly the quantum of dowry that determined such matrimonial alliances. Most often, the bride migrated to a strange place and family as wished by her parental family. She willfully did that when convinced that the alliance would improve the status of her parental family. In the case of migration,[66] the female carried with her the fame of her place and family. Therefore, it was the responsibility of the elderly females in the fisherman's family to train the young girls in house-keeping.

The adaptive nature of a girl was associated with her personal character against smartness. As brides, their chief duty was to venerate not only her in-laws but also the values they evolved for their family over a period of time. The bride-takers preferred a girl of high morals to a girl of charms. Equally important was the culinary skills of the girl. Not only a girl was expected to know the least preparation method of a few varieties of different regions but also the difference between the cooking pattern of the coast and the plain.[67]

Kinship tie was another important criterion that culminated in marriage. The *Parathavars* had the practice of both concluding marriage between cross-cousins as well as between maternal uncle and niece.[68] However, it did not stem the system of dowry. Even after marriage, the daughters were visited by the members of the parental family with gifts – usually dry-processed fish. There were several food items which were specific to the coastal area. Such food items were gifted to the married daughter from time to time. As in typical patriarchal set-up, it was considered dishonour not only to accept gifts in reciprocation from the daughter but also to spend more time in her home. The joint family characterized by the presence of multiple members under one roof prescribed elaborate rules to the disadvantage of the bride-givers. The *Ur* and the public, in general, expected these rules to be observed with sincerity for without them the status of the caste was thought to be reduced.

The joint family did not leave adequate scope for married couple to spend time privately in the home. There were other places away from home meant for married couples where at nights the movement of young people was kept in control. The elderly people were smart enough to recognize the presence of couples and maintained a safe distance. Predominantly, the couples met in public farmyards.[69] Similarly, there was hardly any mechanism to maintain cleanliness in the surroundings. The stench created by the human and fish waste caused contagious diseases like cholera.[70] Though there were native-physicians to cure ailments, the civic sense towards prevention of diseases was absent.

Improvement of family status was a responsibility chiefly of the females. Since they had the ability to control the affairs of the family, they were the repositories of the confidence of the males. They took care of the health of all the members especially of the aged. Therefore, a home was not only a place to cook and conserve valuables – that included food-grains – but was symbolic embodiment of the power of the females. Though in certain cases men remained blind-eyed to the economic condition of the home, few women were disaffected by the misfortunes of the men at sea. The general criticism that associated the arrival of a wife with misfortune was one of the major reasons for the enthusiasm women showed in the quantum of fish-catch. They resorted to sorcery through which they either sought to improve the fortune of the men in their families or in a few cases even attempted to play spoil on the good fortune of others.

By and large, it can be stated that women were not viewed as burdensome in the *Parathavar* society. Their birth was rarely viewed with pessimism. As potential receivers of gifts of voluntary nature, they were normally looked after with care and affection in the family what reflected in the rituals. Their attainment of puberty was celebrated in the company of kinsmen and neighbours. On the occasion of wedding, the groomer of the bride was given the status of an emperor.[71] Their pregnancy after such a celebrated wedding attracted invaluable gifts from their parental families. Her presence was not expected in the funeral grounds. An ideal woman – virgin or married – was made into an icon in the family after her death and was believed to have entrusted with divine powers to protect the members of the family.

In view of the security provided to the widows within the system,[72] it can be said that remarriage of widows was not generally encouraged though it was not totally ruled out. Women formed their own groups within their free domain. The ideas that came out of these groups were of orthodox nature which celebrated the observance of widowhood in the name of living off-springs or dead husband. Though widowhood derived the sympathy of other women, it provided scope for gossip. A remarried girl was subjected to indifferent look and oral comments in her everyday life. Like in any orthodox society marriage was associated with the virginity of a female. A man who married a female who was not a virgin was subjected to satire in his domain. Therefore, widows and women deserted by husbands who were socialized in a background as such from childhood hardly had any desire for remarriage.[73] It was only with the interference of elderly people of the joint-family, remarriages within kinship group were arranged. Yet it was doubtful whether females who remarried under such circumstances escaped gossips. It can be stated that they preferred a respectable status through the adoption of orthodox values.

Conclusion

The necessities generated by the economy made the social life in the *Pearl Fishery Coast* vibrant. The participation of a large number of people in the trade was an inevitable precondition to maintaining the balance of trade in a favorable position. In such a context, the *Parathavars* –the major participants and beneficiaries of the trade – evolved a life in response to the situation. For them, life was at any moment sandwiched between the dangers caused by invaders and the calamities caused by nature. Therefore, though the seeds of trade sought to divide the society into classes, the elements of tribal life that stood on the premise of inclusion and integration was maintained by the *Ur* which derived its legitimacy and overarching power from the situation itself. Apart from strengthening the tribal egalitarianism, on the one hand, the *Ur* administrations on the other hand indirectly cultivated martial arrogance among the *Parathavar* men.

It was the waiting for the arrival of death that vastly influenced the value system of the *Parathavars*. Their life pattern dominated by consumerism and short-tempered emotions were attributable to the emotional preparedness to encounter death. The contextual meaning of death was different for men and women. Though men were subjected to encounter death in many situations, it affected the women more. It was one of the major reasons why it was difficult to classify the *Parathavar* society into either patriarchal or matriarchal forms despite the dominance of patriarchal elements. In actuality, how an individual related himself or herself with the uncertainty of life and the values evoked by that conditioned his or her *Parathavar* identity. An indefinite life as such has been rightly mentioned in the *Tholhappiyam* as marked by an *open siege* that meant not just the invasion of enemies but by death itself.

The domain of woman was segregated and they were thoroughly involved in the management of domestic works as it was considered taboo for women to venture into the sea for the purpose of fishing.[74] On an average, a man who spent much time with women was subjected to satire. The nature of work allowed only minimum time to devote to family. Nevertheless, a woman was expected to live a morally committed life since their chastity was linked to the safety of her husband in the sea. They migrated to far-off places for the interest of men and remained in isolation in the custody of their in-laws. Their lives were also consonant to the viewpoint of *Tholhappiyam* that associated *long separation of lovers* with coastal life.

Endnotes

1   K.A. Nilakanta Sastri, *A History of South India: From Prehistoric Times to the Fall of Vijayanagar* (New Delhi: Oxford University, 1958), p. 118; in *Purananuru* he finds mention of only four castes namely Tudiyan, Panan, Paraiyan and Kadamban. The Panans were representative of coastal life and possibly ancestors of all castes associated with the coast.

2   S.K. Pillai (ed.), *The Ancient Tamils as depicted in Tholhappiyam Poruladhiharam Part I*, (Madras,_____, 1934), p. 67.

3   Ibid, p. 86.

4   Ibid, p. 48.

5   Ravinder Kumar, *Essays in the Social History of Modern India*, (New Delhi: Oxford University Press, 1983); in this book he extensively speaks about the efficacy of Marxist deductive method in informing Indian caste system.

6   G. Duncan Mitchell (ed.), *A New Dictionary of Sociology*, (London: Routledge, 1999), p.70; according to this dictionary, ethnographic approach means 'depth study of a society through personal contact over a period of a year or more'. It is in the same meaning the present researcher also adopts the ethnographic approach.

7   A. Patrick Roche, *Fishermen of the Coromandel-A Social Study of the Paravas of the Coromandel*, (New Delhi,: Manohar, 1984) , p. 3; the scholar classifies their social history as falling into 3 categories – 1) pre-colonial, 2) Portuguese and Dutch and 3) Post-1860. The present researcher does not concur with this view.

8   A. Sivasubramanian, *Uppittavarai,* (Chennai: Kalachuvadu Pathipagam, 2009), p. 31; *Umanars* were distinguished by the scholar from the *Parathavars* and they were said to have bought salt from the latter for the purpose of trade.

9   Sirupanattrupadai: 157–159; the poem speaks about the food prepared by the women of the *Nulaiyar* caste. In parts of *Kanyakumari,* people who belonged to the barber community were remarked as *Nulaiyar.*

10   S.K. Pillai (ed.), Op. Cit., p.50; they were mentioned merely as owners of boats.

11   Some scholars tended to trace the origin of *Parvatha Rajakulam* community from the *Panars.* However, the *Panars* identified in the coastal context by the *Sangam literature* were not directly associated with the same geographical region in the subsequent periods.

12   J.H. Nelson, *The Madura Country A Manual,* Part II (New Delhi: Asian Educational Services, 1989),, p. 73; they were said as engaged in fishing in freshwater.

13   R.N. Joe d'Cruz, *Korkai,* (Tamil), (Chennai: Kalachuvadu Pathipagam, 2009), p. 540; there are three sub-divisions among the *Valaignars,* namely, *Mutharayars, Ambalakarars* and *Valaignars.* Unlike the *Parathavars,* they were chiefly engaged in coastal fishing. The term *Arayan* is very important. In the Malabar, Kadalarayans linked with the sea were a significant tribe. In the field visit conducted at *Vembar,* a settlement of *Mutharayans* was located along with that of the *Parathavars* and *Nadars.* There were also people within *Parathavar* community with titles like *Poobalarayan, Villavarayan* etc. It was possible that the government officials employed in the coastal area over a period of time merged with the *Parathavar* community.

14   H.R. Pate, *Tinnevelly District Gazetteer (1916),* (Tirunelveli: Manonmaniam Sundaranar University, 1993), pp. 145–147; they were associated with making of fish traps. They took the title *Choliya Vellalan* probably because they collected *Choli* from the sea. As in the *Parathavar* community, their headmen were also called as *Pattangatti.* They had seven internal sub-divisions among which one known as *Nettali* was believed to have formed in association with the *Parathavars.*

15   Britto Vincent (ed.), *Thooya Saveriar Kadithangal* (Palayamkottai: FRRC, 2002), p. 2; a place by name *Kombuthurai* was mentioned to have been inhabited by people of the *Karayar* community.

16   A. Dhananjayan, *Kulakuriyeealum, Meenavar Valakarugalum* (Tamil), (Palayamkottai: Abidha Publications, 1996); this book deals with the fishing communities known as *Periyapattinavar* and *Chinnapattinavar.*

17   S.N. Sadasivan, *A Social History of India* (New Delhi: A.P. H. Publishing Corporation, 2007), p. 357; they were the fishermen who predominantly inhabited the *Malabar Coast.* It was believed that they were settled in the Coastal area West of *Kanyakumari* by the *Travancore kings* after evacuating the natives. They formed a '*sept-endogamy*' within the four *illams,* namely, *Kattotillam, Karottillam, Chempottillam* and *Ponnettillam.*

18   Ibid; it was predominantly a title taken by a section of fishermen in *Malabar* who took to the profession of *shell collection* and *Lime-burning.*

19   The geographical limit of the *Pearl Fishery Coast* was maintained as the coastal strip between *Rameshwaram* and *Kanyakumari.* Therefore *other places* during Sangam period included parts of Kerala also. With the emergence of language based differences though geographical division became concrete via land, such divisions did not extend into the sea.

20 T.V. Sadasiva Pandarathar, *Pandyar Varalaru*, (Chennai: Nam Thamilar Pathipagam, 2007), pp. 72–80; he narrates the unrest from the ninth century A.D. to the thirteenth century A.D. caused by the wars between the Cholas and the Pandyas what altered the socio-political life of the people across the states.

21 R. Champakalakshmi, Trade, Ideology and Urbanisation: South India 300 B.C. to A.D. 1300 (New Delhi: Oxford University Press, 1996), p.104; they carried trade constantly with *Ilam, Sri Lanka, South East Asia* and other distant countries.

22 A. Sivasubramanian, *Uppittavarai,* p. 32; he attributes the production of salt to the *Parathavars* and distribution to the *umanars*.

23 Known as Adepans and Pattangattis, they chiefly exercised control over resources of the sea and land respectively.

24 A. Patrick Roche, Op. Cit., p. 17; there were *Dharmakartarkal* who gave themselves to the service of the temple. A group of *Parathavar* people took 'Pandarathar' title suggestive of their role as temple priests.

25 Simon Casie Chitty, Remarks on the Origin and History of the Parawas, *Journal of the Royal Asiatic Society of Great Britain and Ireland*, Vol. 4, No. 1 (1837), p. 133; the scholar in all enumerates 13 sub-classes within the community.

26 Clarence Thomas Maloney, *The Effect of Early Coastal Sea Traffic on the Development of Civilization in South India,* Unpublished Ph. D. thesis submitted in the Dept. of Anthropology, University of Pennsylvania in 1968, p. 115; the author discusses the traditions of *Parathavar* immigration to *Sri Lanka*. He records the *Sinhalese* proverb that states 'Parathavar people are like our people'. But in the present context, the term migration underlines both inland and overseas migration.

27 Simon Casie Chitty, Op. Cit.; p. 133.

28 In a field visit conducted at Maranmangalam (4 Kms from Korkai) a settlement of *Parathavar* engaged in fresh-water fishing was identified. Neither Simon Casie Chitty nor any other scholars have included these people in their research.

29 Information collected through conducting of field visit at *Punnaikayal* on 10-09-2010.

30 L.F. Benedetto (ed.), *The Travels of Marco Polo*, (New Delhi: Asian Educational Services, 1994) p. 293.

31 H.R. Pate, Op. Cit., p. 122; in their capacity as *headmen,* the members of the *assertive class* were expected to visit the homes of persons that died in the sea, and thereby, they were more exposed to death and related experiences. However, Pate intended a thoroughly economic meaning through the expression 'public spirited'.

32 Every settlement was associated with a specific character based on bravery and treatment of the bride. But a uniform opinion about any settlement by all members of the spread-community never arrived.

33 D.M. Persis Rajammal *"Ceris of Tamil Nadu: Paratavar Ceri,"* Dissertation submitted to Manonmaniam Sundaranar University, Tirunelveli, 1997, pp. 22–23; the term *cheri* should not

be equated with its modern meaning of it for during the Sangam age even the 'Andanars' are said to have resided in *Cheris*. However, there were also *cheris* that reflected class division such as *Minvilainarcheri, Valaivalnarcheri, Muthukulippavarcheri, Chankukulippavarcheri* and etc.

34	At *Veerapandianpattanam* their settlement was located near the sea. Any attack via sea or by waves of the sea would first affect the *Parayars*. In *Manapad* since a ridge-like formation protects the settlements naturally, the *Parayars* were located at the entrance. They will be the first casualties in any enemy attacks. In both the places, the pathways to the *Parayar* settlement were separate.

35	James Hornell, The Indian Chank in Folklore and Religion, *Taylor and Francis,* Vol. 53, No. 2 (Jun, 1942), p. 120.

36	A. Patrick Roche, op. Cit., p. 26; he states that the 'depictions of Siva, Varuna and Parvati as progenitors of the Jati was a forceful argument in claims for a prominent place in the social hierarchy'.

37	*The Travels of Marco Polo*, p. 293; since the *Brahmins* profited from the *Pearl* harvest, it was logical that they accorded favourable status upon the *Parathavars.*

38	J.H. Nelson, Op. Cit., p. 57 and 73; both these castes were treated as separate from one another. The *Savalakarars* were mentioned as salt-water fishermen. But by field experience in the Tirunelveli and Kanyakumari districts, these communities form part of the larger Vanniyar community.

39	R.N. Joe d'Cruz, *Aazhi Sul Ulagu,* (Tamil), (Chennai: Tamizhini, 2004); in this ethnographic novel on the *Parathavar* community, elderly male characters were predominantly addressed with the suffix *Pillai* attached to the name.

40	M. A. Durai Rangasamy, *The Surnames of the Cankam Age: Literary and Tribal* (Madras: Manorama Press, 1968), p. 130.

41	R.N. Joe d'Cruz, *Korkai,* pp. 325–326.

42	Interview with Mr. Joseph Gregory Babylaus Fernando (72), Resident of Veerapandianpattanam on 02/01/2010; the informant said that they can identify the background of a person by their names.

43	A. Patrick Roche, Op. Cit., pp. 22–23; the people of the wealthy section known as *dharmakartarkal* meaning 'philanthropists at the cause of religion' extended patronage into areas beyond the coast – sometimes as far as Thirupudaimarudhur. In such case, the respect given to the wealthy *dharmakartarkal* was also given to their clients.

44	R.N. Joe d'Cruz, *Aazhi Sul Ulagu,* p. 153; the discount is one-tenth of the value and known as *Pidivaadu.*

45	Even in the recent times, the priority of the *assertive class* was large scale export-import business whereas the *intermediary class* preferred sailing in fishing vessels and cargo ships.

46	Interview with Mr. R. Pavananthi Vembulu, Field Worker in Tsunami Project on 14/09/2008; the reason was chiefly attributable to the geographical diversity of the region.

47	Interview with Mr. Chandrasekhar, Ex-President of Parathavar Welfare Association, Tuticorin on 11-03-2010.

48 Interview with Mr. Joseph Gregory Babylaus Fernando (72), Resident of Veerapandianpattanam on 02/01/2010; there were varieties of fish – particularly sharks – with a medicinal quality that strengthened the body of women during pregnancy and enhanced the lactating capacity in them. The tribal mode of sharing ensured the constant supply of such fish.

49 Poneelan in A.K. Perumal and N. Ramachandran (eds.), Op. Cit., p. 227; Poneelan was of the opinion that there was effectively present a relationship between the *Parathavars* and the *Nadars*. Therefore they mutually addressed each other as '*uyirakara*' that meant 'intimate dear. He also has narrated a story in which he explained the ignorance of a *Parathavar* community man and smartness of *Nadar* community man. However, the *Nadars* and the *Parathavars* as distinct groups hardly developed an amicable relationship. The people of the *Parathavar* community asserted social superiority over the *Nadars* and the latter did the vice-versa. But from the information gathered from the field visits, there was no case of *Nadars* having dependent caste like the *Parayars* as in the case of *Parathavars*.

50 R.N. Joe d'Cruz, *Aazhi Sul Ulagu*, p. 326.

51 Ibid; throughout the novel, the author discusses the factional politics within a settlement.

52 It was the popular belief of non-coastal people about the *Parathavars*.

53 Interview with Mr. Amaladas, (65), Fisherman of Alandalai on 02/01/10.

54 R.N. Joe d'Cruz, *Aazhi Sul Ulagu*, p. 290; it was spending on food and liquor which made a celebration grand for men. But for women, the quantum of expensive durable-goods used during celebrations determined the grandeur. It became customary to distribute cigar for men on occasions of death.

55 Interview with Mr. Parabaran (22), Fisherman, Manapad on 8-01-10; according to the informant, such rewards were responsible for disinterest in formal learning.

56 *The Travels of Marco Polo*, pp. 303–304; he records similar practice in pearl fishing where the children directly take pearls to the traders and made a profit.

57 If the majority confined itself to a secured life by opting to catch small harmless fish, the most skilled preferred catching of sharks which required a few days of hard work in the sea. Dedication and endurance were other requirements from such people.

58 A. Sivasubramanian, *Uppittavarai*, p. 36; the author speaks about the exchange of grain for salt in the context of *Umanars*. It can be inferred that a similar exchange of dry-fish for grain existed in the case of the *Parathavars*.

59 Letter of Francis Xavier from Manapad dated 14 March 1544.

60 R.N. Joe d'Cruz, *Aazhi Sul Ulagu*, pp. 91–92; an *amba* song (songs sung while performing physically rough work such as pushing the boat into the sea and pulling back) recorded by the novelist speaks about a younger wife.

61 *The Travels of Marco Polo*, pp. 295–296; the chieftain took more than five hundred wives and many concubines most of who committed Sati with the death of the former. The chieftain even

took the wife of his brother. From this picture, it can be ascertained that polygamy was common and the general position of women was not appreciable.

62   Letter of Francis Xavier from Manapad dated 12 September 1544; Xavier mentions about dancing girls on whom the men spent a substantial sum of money.

63   George Hart, *The Poems of Ancient Tamil: Their Milieu and Their Sanskrit Counterpart,* (New Delhi: Oxford University Press, 1999) pp. 101–102; he infers from Thakazhi Sivasankara Pillai's novel Chemmeen where a mother character is being depicted as advising her daughter. Though the novel unfolds in the background of Malabar, it has applicability in the context of *Pearl Fishery Coast* also.

64   Unlike in agricultural belts, the number of wells was less in the coast. It was not always located near the house. Therefore, the frequency of the movement of females in public domain was higher.

65   Interview with Mr. Alangara Michael Nallathambi Fernando (67), President, Parathavar Vadakku Ur, Kottar on 27-11-08.

66   S.B. Kaufmann, A Christian Caste in a Hindu Society: Religious Leadership and Social Conflict among the Paravas of Southern Tamil Nadu, *Modern Asian Studies*, Vol. 15, No. 2 (1981), p. 228; since there were settlements as far as *Chinnakadai* in *Kollam* district the distance involved in migration cannot be clearly mentioned.

67   Interview with Mr. Amaladas, (65), Fisherman of Alandalai on 02/01/10; in the coast, the excessive cleaning of fish before cooking was thought to be wasting of food whereas in the plain inhabited by the bulk of the *assertive class* and the *intermediary class* it was difficult to eat without thorough cleaning. Similarly, the latter classes use vegetables such as drumstick and mango along with fish curry. But the ordinary fisherman preferred the pure taste of fish.

68   Interview with Mr. Parabaran (22), Fisherman, Manapad on 8-01-10; on the day of field visit one such marriage was reported by the informant. But these kinds of marriages are becoming uncommon.

69   Interview with Mr. R. Pavananthi Vembulu, Field Worker in Tsunami Project on 14/09/2008; the informant shared his experience of how without exposure to coastal life some volunteers deemed the pairing of a couple in public farmyards as immoral. There were landlords to who the farmyards belonged. But until there was any robbery, they never treated entry into their land as trespass.

70   R.N. Joe d'Cruz, *Aazhi Sul Ulagu,* p. 334.

71   ________, *Korkai,* P. 447–450.

72   Interview with Mr. Parabaran (22), Fisherman, Manapad on 8-01-10; they were helped by the *Ur* in procuring fish for sales.

73   R.N. Joe d'Cruz, *Aazhi Sul Ulagu,* p. 66.

74   R. Pavananthi Vembulu and R. John Suresh Kumar, *Circling the Triangle.*

VII

Embracing Christianity:

Tracing Parathavar Conversion in the Light of Sixteenth Century Socio-political Ruptures

Introduction

Until 13th century A.D., the *Parathavars* were able to maintain a command over the economy of the *Pearl Fishery Coast*. They were engaged in diverse occupations such as business in pearls, salt manufacture, fishing and etc. Their contribution to the exchequer of the *Pandyan* state was immense and that was acknowledged through the incorporation of fish as the symbol of the kingdom. The effect of the economy was felt in the sphere of the *Parathavar* religion wherein a correspondent pluralism that ranged from deities at the family level to the *Brahmanical Gods* emerged. With access to not only *Brahmanical Gods* but also to rival religions such as *Jainism, Buddhism* etc. the *Parathavar* upper class constituted by traders and headmen gave an impression of having distanced themselves from other people. Despite the presence of hierarchy, the nature of coastal social life was such that the internal class difference determined by economy was never permanent. Therefore as rightly pointed out by the anonymous author of the *Chronicles of the Pearl Fishery Coast,* they constituted a nation unto themselves.

The turn of the 13th Century A.D. century witnessed the assertion of the *Muslims* that directly undermined the position of the *Parathavars* in the coastal economy. Since the members of the economically assertive class within the *Parathavar* society were losing hold, the internal social difference determined by wealth was reduced. It, on the one hand, enhanced the internal solidarity and on the other hand questioned their position vis-à-vis other communities in terms of *Sanskritization.* At this juncture, one has to remember the point that the rise of the *Muslims* corresponded with the decline of heterogeneous sects such as *Buddhism* and *Jainism* due to the spread of the *Bhakti Movement* and loss of political patronage.

The conventional understandings about the Indian sub-continent as made by the nationalist historians stressed upon the tolerant side of the natives and issues like unity in diversity etc. They have maintained that the division of people based on identity was a colonial product. To its contrast, the history of the *Parathavar Conversion* contained seeds of idea that could germinate and project the colonial powers to have effectively utilized the existing division among the people. In the caste based

119

society of India, the oppressed people hardly had any chance to unite and organize themselves against the perpetrators of oppression. In the case of the *Parathavars,* they were not a subdued people in the caste hierarchy, and therefore, had scope to decide upon the course of their social life. But with their conversion to *Christianity,* the pertinent question that why they were not able to sustain within the majority religion remains to be answered.

The present article intends to survey the major dimensions that led towards conversion in the light of the political economy characterized by the competition between the *Muslims* and *Portuguese.* It also seeks to explore the methods in which the *Parathavars* related themselves in the new economy. The primary sources used for the study is very limited and includes the travels of *Marco Polo* and *Letters of St. Francis Xavier.* Rather analytical narration based on information culled out from secondary sources guide the course of the article. As such ideas of historians like H.R. Pate, Roche A. Patrick, Maria Augusta Lima Cruz, Luis Filipe F.R. Thomaz, Jorge Manuel Flores, Teotonio R. de. Souza, T.K. Oommen, Hunter P. Mabry, Fatima da Silva Gracias, Clarence Thomas Maloney, S. Decla, R. Pavananthi Vembulu, R. John Suresh Kumar and C. Veeramuthu have contributed to the consolidation of the subject matter of the article. The rational that is reached by the survey of both primary and secondary sources necessitate a pattern of narrative that starts from the history of the *Muslims* in the *Pearl Fishery Coast,* followed by the *Portuguese* interruption and *Parathavar* conversion. Therefore, such an approach has been followed.

The Muslim Assertion and the Political Situation

The *Muslims* from *Arabia* entered *South India* chiefly as traders. They were smart traders that they not only made huge wealth but also dominated the business.[1] Particularly in the *Tamil* country, they made a good profit by selling horses. They gradually evolved political aspirations what was reflected in their literature wherein they recorded that *Ibrahim Sultan* of *Arabia* defeated a *Pandyan* ruler.[2] With the invasion of *Malik Kafur* and subsequent establishment of the *Sultanate of Madurai,* their power reached the peak. They unleashed repressive activities against the natives that caused irreparable resentment in the minds of the natives. Nevertheless, the *Sultanate of Madurai* was able to rule only for a brief period from 1324 to 1372 A.D. and was routed out by *Kampana Udayar.*[3] With that, the majority of the *Muslim* population moved either towards *Keelakarai* or *Kayalpatnam* where already existed a considerable number of *Arab Muslims* for want of trade opportunities and related economic benefits dwindled at *Madurai.*[4] Moreover the *Pandyans* located in the South required horses and contributed for the vibrancy of trade in *Keelakarai* or *Kayalpatnam* regions.

The society of the *Muslims* who settled at *Kayalpatnam* was constituted by people with diverse backgrounds. At the top were the *Arabs*[5] who took the honorific *Marakayar* title.[6] Over a period of time, they were identified with the location and came to be mentioned as *Kayalars* also. They gradually diversified their occupation yet maintained links with the *Arab* settlements in other parts of *Malabar.* Their assertion in the *Pearl Fishery Coast* was coterminous with the political decline of the native *Pandyan* rulers. They learned the *Tamil* language and gave indications of assimilation with the natives though it did not actually happen. They proved to be good soldiers and a substantial section of *Muslim* soldiers along with other tradesmen migrated from *Kayalpatnam*[7] to *Ceylon*.[8] When the degeneration of political life[9] had its toll in the native armed forces, the military strength of the *Muslims* was consolidated.

The *Muslims* of *Kayalpatnam* lived an orderly life in a chaotic situation and maintained social purity what can be termed as *Arabization*. The concept of *Arabization* was a model of social mobility wherein the practices of those in the highest stratum of society were observed and followed by the inferiors. Since the *Arabs* were placed at the highest level of the society, *Arabization* denoted imitation of their lifestyle. The *Arab Muslims* formed an endogamous group and excluded the native *Muslims*.[10] Their women covered their physic with *Purdah*.[11] Although they learnt the vernacular language, they followed *Arab scripts* in transaction and their dressing style and appearance had resemblance of the *Arabs*.[12] They lived in separate streets and constructed homes in a style unfamiliar to the natives.[13] They established a mosque imitative of that in *Mecca* and followed rational principles compared to other *Muslims* and allowed little scope for superstition.[14]

For the *non-Arab Muslims,* it was their ability to relate themselves with the *Marakayars* that determined their status. This section of *Muslims* was constituted by the converts from the communities of *Parathavar* and *Katasans* who were chiefly residents of *Kayalpatnam*.[15] With the conversion, they seemed to have constituted an endogamous group based on religion and limited their previous caste ties.[16] It was unlikely that these people were largely discriminated within the local fold of *Islam* for without their support the exploration of marine resources was a mere impossibility. Even if the *new-Muslims* were not treated at par with the *Arabs,* by virtue of their residential settlement at *Kayalpatnam* they were identified by outsiders as *Kayalars* which enhanced their prestige. In order to improve their status further, the *new-Muslims* sought to *Arabize* their lifestyle. Possibly, the orthodoxy of the *Arabs* was corrupted – to the advantage of the *new-Muslims* – when migrations like that occurred during *Kampana Udayar* took place.

In spite of an effective social hierarchy comparable with the stereotyped Indian social system, the *Muslims* undermined their internal differences and demonstrated unity at times of a collective crisis. But the fourteenth and fifteenth centuries never witnessed the reassertion of the *Muslims* at *Madurai* – the political headquarters – as the rulers of *Vijayanagar* seemed to have backed at first the *Udayars* and then a line of *Pandyans* and then *Nayakkans* and not the *Muslims*.[17] At the time of the *Parathavar* conversion, it was the *Zamorin* of *Calicut* who came forward to collaborate with the *Muslims*. He realized the potential of the *Muslims* at the sea front and possibly thought of balancing the *Portuguese* influence in the region through them. Similarly, the *Maharaja* seated at *Kanyakumari* expected their alliance against the *Vijayanagar* kingdom, and therefore, allowed them to reap benefits of *Pearl Fishery*. The rulers of *Kollam* and *Cochin* predominantly supported the *Portuguese*[18] as also the rulers of *Ceylon* such as *Bhuvaneka Bahu* of *Kotte, Mayadunne* of *Sitawaka*[19] and *Sekkarasa Sekaran* of *Jaffna*.[20] The political trend was suggestive of the fact that irrespective of whether the *Muslims* united or not, other people viewed them as a holistically united society. The arrival of the *Portuguese* further complicated the socio-political trends.

The Portuguese

For long the kingdom of *Portugal* remained loyal to the *Popes* of the *Roman Catholic Church*. They recognized the spiritual suzerainty of the *Popes* and least bothered when that embarked upon the temporal authority. On their own right, the rulers of the Catholic world in general and of Portugal, in particular, were committed to the cause of the spread and protection of *Christianity*. As early as 1310, *Dom Dinis*, the *King of Portugal* founded the *Order of the Knights of Christ* to prevent his country and the *Christian* world from the onslaught of the *Muslims*[21]. The *Christian Kings*, who shared the frame of mind of *Dom Dinis*, believed that the interests of the *Christians* and that of the *Muslims* were mutually opposed and the latter believed vice versa.[22] Perceptions as such heightened since the fall of *Constantinople* in 1453 that culminated in the closure of the land route between the east and the west to the great disadvantage of the traders. It was widely realized that the counter balance rested in oceanic explorations, and therefore, in 1493 Pope Alexander III issued the *Inter Caetera* that sought to divide the globe between the *Portuguese* and the *Spaniards*.[23] Through the *Inter Caetera*, the *Portuguese* expansion towards the East was recognized. It gave an impression of spiritual motives being placed above trade motives.

The spiritual motive took twists and turns in a very short period with the assertion of *Dom Manuel* in the place of *John II*. Apart from the nationality based competition with the *Spaniards,* there was also a drastic shift in the frame of mind of the new *King of Portugal*. Particularly, he considered the discovery of a *route to India* as *Divine Providence* embalmed with a special message to him.[24] He was inspired by the writings of *Joachim of Fiore*[25] who expressed his disaffection over the institutional church and believed in the emergence of a *Saviour King*.[26] *King Dom Manuel* believed that he was the chosen *Saviour King* of the *Universal Empire*.[27] It was logical that he realized his ambitions required a huge support of men and material. When the *Portuguese* reached the *Western Coast* of *India* they witnessed the presence of *St. Thomas Christians*. However, these *Christians* were not important for *King Manuel's* ambitious program since the background of these *Native Christians* was not martial.[28] Irrespective of that and unlikely of the *Roman Catholic Church*, he was accommodative of the differences at the level of *Christian* practices for he thought he represented all *Christians*.[29] He also aspired to establish control over *Mylapore* where *St. Thomas* was believed to be buried since that could enhance his overall image and for the spiritual support of the saint in his mundane activities.[30]

In a brief period of time, the *Portuguese* established their factories in the *Coast of Malabar*. The viceroys of the *Portuguese King* sought to give expression to the ambitions of the latter. They proved their ability not only as a competent maritime force but also as soldiers and diplomats. Notable viceroy among the *Portuguese* was *Afonso de Albuquerque* (1510-1515) who on the one hand challenged the weak *Bahmani Kingdom* while on the other hand established an amicable relationship with *Vijayanagar Empire*.[31] He also signed treaties with the *Zamorin* of *Calicut* according to which all ships that entered *Calicut* from *Coromandal, Kayalpatnam, Jaffna* and *Ceylon* were required to procure *Cartaz* from the *Portuguese* prior to their arrival.[32] He realized that the *Portuguese* required more collaborators in India to support and sustain the imperialist ideas of the crown. Therefore, he attempted to reform the practices of *Native Christians*. He also encouraged his sailors to marry *Indian women* so that the children born out of such wedlock would adopt *Christianity* and remain loyal to the *Portuguese* crown.[33] Possibly his opinion on the *Latin practices* as best among all *Christian practices* did not clash with the views of his master *King Manuel*. Therefore, he thought of moulding *Indian Christian converts* in *Latin* spiritual lifestyle[34] so that the distance between the *Europeans* and the *natives* would be reduced.

Both the *Portuguese king* and *Albuquerque* substantiated their reforms with service.[35] *Albuquerque* also established hospitals initially for the benefit of the *Portuguese* upper class which was later extended to the *Indian Christians* also by the order of the king.[36] The declaration of *Padroado* by the *Pope* in 1514 gave an impetus to the activities initiated by *Albuquerque*. It was not clear whether or not the announcement of *Padroado* was a strategic move of *Pope Leo X* but it further strengthened the position of the *King* and his *Order of the Knights of Christ* vis-a-vis the monks since the *King* for a greater part relied upon the latter to execute welfare schemes.[37] Through the *Padroado,* the *King* of *Portugal* was empowered to appoint *Bishops* though it mandated the formalization by the *Pope*.[38] Any monk or *Orders* within *Roman Catholic Church* cannot operate within the provinces ruled by the *Portuguese* without prior permission.[39] The *King* was also made responsible for the establishment of seminaries, schools, hospitals, orphanages etc. as also to meet out the expenses incurred on maintenance and salary.[40]

The focus of the *Portuguese* shifted from the *West Coast* after the period of *Albuquerque*. Nevertheless, his policy of conquests and alliances was continued by his successors.[41] They realized the strategic importance of the *Strait of Ceylon* to dominate *Asian Trade*. Though it did not enable the control of long range trade-routes, it helped to control trade between the *Coramandal* and *Ceylon*.[42] Particularly, when import of rice by *Ceylon* was blocked it enabled in the bargain of *cinnamon* from it. Also, *Estado da India* cannot neglect the interest of the *private settlers* who traded in other articles from the *Coramandal* region.[43] Therefore, they established a fortress at *Ceylon* in 1518.[44]

Coincidental to their landing at *Ceylon* was the conflict that ensued in the *Gulf of Mannar* between *Khadhi Rayannah*[45] of *Kayalpatnam* and *Bhuvaneka Bahu* of *Kotte* in *Ceylon* for the reason that the former crossed the natural sea boundary and indulged in *pearl exploration* in *Ceylonese* waters.[46] When the head of *Kayalpatnam* faced setback it was the duty of *Raja Marthandavarma,* the ruler seated then at *Kanyakumari* to stand by him since the latter was the receiver of tribute from the former. But *Raja Marthandavarma* lacked in marine force, and therefore, *Mudalaiyar,*[47] the successor of *Khadhi Rayannah* to the headship of *Kayalpatnam* sought protection from *Antonio Miranda,* the *Portuguese officer* in-charge of the *Colombo Fort* and offered to pay a substantial amount.[48]

Antonio Miranda did not decide upon the issue immediately.[49] Hitherto, the *Portuguese* have treated *Muslims* with hatred and enmity and vice versa. It continued to be so in *Europe* and *West Asia*. Despite all that the *Muslims of Kayalpatnam* – constituted largely by local populace –sought assistance. In such a context *Antonio Miranda* must have thought that he was not competent authority to decide on such a sensitive issue. Therefore, he wrote a detailed letter to the *King of Portugal* and awaited his reply. However, by 1521 *King Manuel* was succeeded by *King John III* who replaced the policies of the former with thoroughly commercial policies.[50] He ordered the *Governor of Goa* to send a ship to *Kayalpatnam* and capture it.[51] He also further ordered to lend lease the *Pearl* and *chank diving* in the name of the *Portuguese Government*.[52] Therefore, *Kayalpatnam* was invaded by 1523 and the *Muslims* who lived there sought help from *Calicut*. Leaders of the *Muslims* like *Pate Marakkar, Kunjali Marakkar* and *Ali Ibrahim* came to the protection of the *Muslims* and their influence had its own impact on the *King of Calicut*. As a result, the *Treaty of 1513* that enabled the collection of revenue through *Cartaz* was brought to an end. Though it contributed to revenue loss, a substantial amount was earned from the proceeds of the *Pearl Fishery Coast*.[53] However, it led to continuous battles in the *Gulf of Mannar* from 1525–1539. The battles were characterized by ups and downs on both sides. On their side, the *Portuguese* realized that they need the support of at the least one community which had some martial character in the region.

Parathavar

At a time when the *Portuguese* were looking for potential allies, the *Parathavars* were also awaiting for potential collaborators. Since the fall of the *Pandyan kingdom*, their political and economic influence in the region underwent degeneration. The arrival of *Muslims* followed by the *Nayaks* of *Vijayanagar* further undermined their interest. The rise of *Kayalpatnam* adversely affected the interest of the *Parathavars*. With a better network of trade and technologically advanced sea vessels, they challenged the *economically assertive class* of the *Parathavar* society. It can be ascertained that with the control of the *Pearl Fisheries* and support of the *King Marthanda Varma* of *Kanyakumari,* that the dominance of the *Muslims* in the sea became absolute and it had its bearing in boat traffic to the disadvantage of ordinary fishermen.

The difference in the power axis did not contribute for eliciting the loyalty of the *Parathavars* in favour of the *Muslims*. In such a context, the scope for suspicion among *Muslims* about *Parathavar* supporting the *Sinhalese* during the conflict cannot be ruled out.[54] Moreover, there could have been a positive gesture from the side of the *Parathavars* to the dismay of the *Muslims,* when the *Portuguese* arrived at the *Pearl Fishery Coast*. All these happened despite the *Parathavars* and the majority of the *Muslims* shared *the Tamil* language in common. They also shared common life space in both sides of the *Gulf of Mannar* i.e. the *Pearl Fishery Coast* and *Ceylon*.

In the opinion of the present researcher, the mood for a shift towards the *Portuguese* camp could have occurred at the minds of the *Parathavar elite* ever since they observed the active presence in the *Pearl Fishery Coast*. Though the *Sinhalese* were friendly, they neither aspired to conquer any part of *India* nor founded permanent settlements in the *Tamil* speaking world. To its contrast, the *Portuguese* freely spread throughout the regions where there was some trade activity and owned superior ships. They had the capacity to diversify trade. They also mingled with the local people to the extent of marrying them and such marriages were further supported by patronization. The *Portuguese* and their dependents were governed by a better legal system than that was in force at that time among the rulers who partitioned the *Pearl Fishery Coast* and ruled it. Trends like these naturally took the *Parathavars* closer to the *Portuguese.*

The event that was said to have sparked a civil strife between the *Parathavars* and the *Muslims*[55] could be effectively viewed from this angle. The event was depictive of the unsympathetic attitude of other communities against the *Parathavars.* It was also self-explanatory of the unequal positioning of the *Parathavars* vis-à-vis the *Muslims* and other natives since the *Parathavars* as a group were not able to stop the onslaught by their religious fellows by offering a higher sum either for a *Muslim* head or for their protection. It landed the *Parathavar* people in an utterly chaotic condition and there was hardly any mechanism from outside the caste to restore normalcy. The rulers of the region such as the *Pandyan King* based on *Kayathar* named *Vettum Perumal, Thumibchi Nayakkar* who controlled *Vembar, Vaippar* and *Keelakarai* and *Marthanda Varma of Kanyakumari* did not take the effort to control the *Muslim* onslaught.[56] Therefore, the community at large resorted to three steps – initial protection, long term protection and retaliation.

The event thoroughly affected all the sections of the society. Those who had access to *catamarans, vallams* and *thonies* took asylum in the tiny islands located parallel to the *Pearl Fishery Coast.*[57] They were made to violate the professional norms that had considered women stepping into the fishing vessel to be taboo.[58] They were very well aware of the fact that the islands where they took refuge could not provide adequate water and sanitation facilities for long. The higher and middle segments of the society that were located at some distance from the coast were worst hit.[59] Apart from their lives property was also threatened.[60] Though, there was a requirement of urgent settlement it was also very well understood by these people that the situation warranted long term solution.

Since there was no other option, they sought protection from the *Portuguese.* The *Portuguese* were cautious at the initial stage and seemed to have vacillated. However, the *Parathavars* found a suitable mediator in *John de Cruz* who by virtue of his personal relationship with the *King of Portugal* had considerable influence among the *Portuguese Officers.* For the *Parathavars,* his was a personal example of the benefits attainable from association with the *Portuguese.* He was recognized by the *King of Portugal* to carry out tax-free trade in the horse as also recognized as tax-collector in the *Pearl Fishery Coast.*[61] As a *Chevalier* in the *Order of the Knights of Christ* and *God-son* of *King John III of Portugal,* he was bound by the duty to explain the tenets of *Christianity* and the spiritual intent of the *Portuguese* government. As a native, he successfully convinced the *Parathavars* guided the *Pattangattins* in the right track. He also made the *Portuguese* to understand the motive of the *Parathavars* and possibly about the latter's abilities.

The process of conversion into *Christianity* was with the *baptism* of 15 *Pattangattins.* Subsequently, other *Pattangattins* followed and mass conversion of the *Parathavar* people took place. They were not only admitted into the fold of the *Roman Catholic Church* but were also deemed as *Portuguese citizens* eligible for the protection and other benefits released by the *King of Portugal*.[62] The *Christian monks* visited the coastal villages and desecrated the temples hitherto venerated by the *Parathavars*.[63] The conflict between the *Portuguese* and the *Muslims* in the straits of *Ceylon* included the *Parathavars* within it. *John de Cruz* was made to associate with the family of the *Parathavar* leaders and was honoured.

The adoption of *Christianity* by the *Parathavars* contained seeds of reconciliation for they were placed closer to the *Muslims* than before as far as their new socio-religious practices were concerned. The *Muslims* in general and particularly of *India* hated idolaters than *Christians* who like them believed in the exposure of *God* through holy words. Moreover, the shrine of *St. Thomas* that attained the status of a pilgrimage center for *Christians* was equally venerated by the *Muslims*.[64] Like the *Muslims*, the *Parathavar* converts also desecrated the temples in their surroundings. The ethics of the new *Christians* did not alienate the *Muslims* for the reason that they were beef-eaters. Therefore, conversion in the long run tended.

Conclusion

Identity shaped by religion played a very limited role in the Tamil society when compared to identity shaped by caste. But yet there were harmonious negotiations effectively present among castes what even culminated in the conclusion of marriage bonds.[65] Events as such occurred during the *Sangam* period wherein political stability was well established. To its contrast, the assertion of one social group over another was possible only in a situation of a political void. Therefore, the differences based on the identity of people as to *Muslims, Parathavars* etc. were attributable to the failure of the political mechanism to maintain a balance among contestants. The invasion of the *Sultanate* of *Madurai* and areas further south by Kampana Udayar, in the long run, caused the birth of small chieftaincies that fought among themselves. In chaotic situations, the relevance of social values like tolerance, adjustments, etc was naturally under-stressed.[66]

As far as the *Muslims* were concerned they were a numerical minority – though dominant in the sphere of economy – and were bound to protect their identity. Their extra caution was the only natural which delayed their integration with the mainstream society. The integration was further undermined by the rivalry over the resources of the *Pearl Fishery Coast*. The rivalry found expression in the division of other beneficiaries of the *Pearl Fishery Coast* into *pro-Muslims* and *pro-Parathavars*. It was unfortunate that the *Parathavars* found only a minimum support from other people. An introspection of the situation by the *Parathavars* easily explained the dimension of religion within it. The arrival of *Portuguese* who gave a tough time to the *Muslims* in the field of trade occurred at that time.

The gradual expansion of the *Portuguese* – traceable from their superior status in the technology of ships, weapons etc. – was followed by implementation of several welfare policies. Those who volunteered to associate with the *Portuguese* happened to confirm their loyalty by the adoption of *Christianity*. But in the case of the *Parathavars*, the organization and military strength of the *Portuguese* had more meaning than these welfare policies. Moreover, those who volunteered to collaborate with the *Portuguese* at the very first instance was the *Parathavars* of the *economically assertive class* whose support was also required by the former to establish themselves on both sides of the *Gulf of Mannar.*

In such a backdrop, their adoption of *Christianity* en masse in reaction to a civil strife was but an excuse to protect their economic interest. The fabric of the Indian society of that time was tolerant as pointed out by the *Nationalist Historians* insofar there remained hardly any mechanism to either prevent or to reconvert the *Parathavar* into the majority religion.[67] Nevertheless, there was also effectively present scope for mass conversion to remain just an expression of disaffection over the erstwhile fellows of the majority religion. Therefore, it required a monk like *St. Xavier* either in person or as imagery to actually guide the people in the tenets of the newly adopted religion.

Endnotes

1   L.F. Benedetto (ed.), *The Travels of Marco Polo*, (New Delhi: Asian Educational Services, 1994), pp. 296–297; they never informed the need for farriers or the systematic method of horse maintenance. Therefore, out of 2000 horses bought every year by the *Pandyan King* only 100 horses sustained. The amount they fixed per horse was also comparatively higher.

2   A. Patrick Roche, *Fishermen of the Coromandel-A Social Study of the Paravas of the Coromandel*, (New Delhi,: Manohar, 1984), p. 39; he infers from *Theenerivilakam,* a thirteenth-century work on the political history of the *Muslims* of *Kayalpatnam.*

3   J.H. Nelson, *The Madura Country A Manual*, Part II (New Delhi: Asian Educational Services, 1989), pp. 80–81.

4   Robert Caldwell, *Thirunelveli Sarithiram* (Chennai: Kavya, 1977) p. 81; their migration was explained through a myth according to which the area between the Vijayanagar Kingdom and Kanyakumari was conquered by Mujahid Shah. This may be considered only as their influence continuing in the said region.

5   J.H. Nelson, Op. Cit., p. 86; these were the Saiyads, Sheks, and Pathans. The Saiyads claimed that they were the descendants of the Prophet, the Sheks asserted their lineage from the friends and followers of the Prophet.

6   H.R. Pate, *Tinnevelly District Gazetteer (1916),* (Tirunelveli: Manonmaniam Sundaranar University, 1993) Op. Cit., p. 98.

7   In a discussion with Mr. Vellaithamby Ameerdeen, Assoc. Prof of Political Science, Peradeniya University, Sri Lanka during our stay at the Jawaharlal Nehru University between July and August 2002, he stated that the Tamil Muslims of Sri Lanka have Moorish physical features and they trace their origin from Kayalpatnam.

8   *Marco Polo*, p. 291; he has stated that there were no native soldiers in Ceylon and at times of military needs they made use of the *Saracens.*

9   The social life as projected by Marco Polo was suggestive of this degeneration wherein features of chastity and martial character seemed to have disappeared.

10 Ibid. pp. 499–500.

11 Ibid.

12 Ibid.

13 Ibid.

14 Ibid.

15 Ibid. p. 500; he traces the converts chiefly from *Katasans*.

16 The *Parathavar* men were addressed as *Chacha* by the *new-Muslims*. The contextual kinship meaning was that the *Muslims* could not enter into matrimonial alliance with the *Parathavars* since the latter avoid parallel-cousin marriage.

17 J.H. Nelson, Op. Cit., pp. 82–83; the *Udayars* ruled from 1374 to 1451, the *Pandyans* ruled from 1451 to 1500 and thereafter the *Nayakkans*.

18 Jorge Manuel Flores in Sanjay Subrahmanyam (ed.), *Sinners and Saints The Successors of Vasco Da Gama,* (New Delhi: Oxford University Press, 2000), p. 60.

19 Ibid., p. 59.

20 Britto Vincent (ed.), *Thooya Saveriar Kadithangal* (Palayamkottai: FRRC, 2002), Letter of Francis Xavier from Punnaikayal dated 16 June 1544; the letter mentions that the commander stationed at *Nagapattinam* had considerable influence upon the *King* of *Jaffna*. But in a Letter of Francis Xavier from Cochin dated 18 December 1544, the *King* of *Jaffna* was said to have rendered some serious injustice to the *Christian* converts. This makes clear the point that there was intolerance upon people who opted out of a religion followed by the majority.

21 *Thuthukudi Maraimavatta Kaiyedu Ponvizha Vezhiyeedu, 1923–1973,* (Tuticorin: The Diocesan Pastoral Centre, 1973) p. 25.

22 Maria Augusta Lima Cruz in Sanjay Subrahmanyam (ed.), Op. cit., pp. 13–14;

23 *Thuthukudi Maraimavatta Kaiyedu,* p. 26; it was popularly known as *Papal Line of Demarcation.*

24 Luis Filipe F.R. Thomaz in K.S. Mathew, Tcotonio R. de. Souza and Pius Malekandathil (eds.), *The Portuguese and the Socio-Cultural Changes in India,* (Tellicherry: Fundacao Oriente, 2001), p. 32.

25 Ibid. p. 31; He was a *Calabrese* monk who lived between 1130 and 1202. He divided the history of Human life into three phases and related it with the *Holy Trinity*. The first phase was that of *God the Father* viewable in the *Old Testament* followed by *God the Son* viewable in the *New Testament*. The lapses of the institutional church in the second phase would lead towards the third phase inspired by the *Holy Spirit*. In this phase, purity will be ascertained and monks will lead the society.

26 Ibid.

27 Ibid, pp. 29–35.

28 Ibid.

29 Ibid; many of the practices of the native St. Thomas Christians were branded as heresy by priests of the Roman Catholic order.

30 Ibid.; the scholar states that King Manuel had such ambitions since 1501.

31 Maria Augusta Lima Cruz in Sanjay Subrahmanyam (ed.), Op. Cit.

32 Jorge Manuel Flores in Sanjay Subrahmanyam (ed.), Op. Cit., p.62;

33 Teotonio R. de. Souza in K.S. Mathew et. al. (eds.), Op. Cit., pp. 440–442; the *Portuguese* sailors married Muslim women who they took as captives and Hindu women they liked. But they were reportedly bored with their Indian consorts.

34 T.K. Oommen and Hunter P. Mabry, *The Christian Clergy in India Vol. I, Social Structure and Social Roles,* (New Delhi: Sage Publications, 2000), pp. 43–45.

35 Fatima da Silva Gracias in K.S. Mathew et. al. (eds.), Op. Cit., pp. 280–281; alms were regularly distributed by the king whereas Albuquerque ordered the release of financial assistance to poor Native Christians and Indo-Portuguese children.

36 Ibid. p. 279.

37 Ibid. p. 280.

38 *Thuthukudi Maraimavatta Kaiyedu,* p. 26.

39 Ibid.

40 Ibid.

41 Jorge Manuel Flores, in Sanjay Subrahmanyam (ed.), Op. Cit., p. 58.

42 Ibid. p. 60.

43 Ibid., p. 62.

44 Ibid., p. 58.

45 Name as transliterated from the Tamil source *Thuthukudi Maraimavatta Kaiyedu Ponvizha Vezhiyeedu, 1923–1973.*

46 *Thuthukudi Maraimavatta Kaiyedu,* p. 29

47 Name as transliterated from the Tamil source *Thuthukudi Maraimavatta Kaiyedu.*

48 *Thuthukudi Maraimavatta Kaiyedu,* p. 29.

49 Ibid.

50 Luis Filipe F.R. Thomaz in K.S. Mathew, et. al., Op. Cit., p. 36.

51 *Thuthukudi Maraimavatta Kaiyedu,* p. 30.

52 Ibid.

53 Ibid.

54 Clarence Thomas Maloney, *The Effect of Early Coastal Sea Traffic on the Development of Civilization in South India,* Unpublished Ph. D. thesis submitted in the Dept. of Anthropology, University of Pennsylvania in 1968, p. 115; the author records the *Sinhalese* proverb that states '*Parathavar* people are like our people'. He also discusses the traditions of *Parathavar* immigration to *Sri Lanka.*

55 S. Decla, *Muthukulithuraiyil Porchukeesiyar* (Tamil), (Chennai: New Century Book House, 2009), pp. 22–23; There seemed to have emerged a quarrel between a *Parathavar* man and a few *Muslim* men since the latter eve-teased the former's wife at Tuticorin harbor sometimes around

the early 1530s. The *Parathavar* man was insulted by cutting off of his ear with the ring. This triggered a scuffle between *Parathavars* and the *Muslims.* The *Parathavars* initially killed a few *Muslims.* The *Muslims* retaliated heavily by declaring that they will give five panams for every *Parathavar* head. The *non-Muslims* slaughtered *Parathavar* men in large numbers and ceased only when the amount was lowered.

56 *Thuthukudi Maraimavatta Kaiyedu,* p. 33.

57 Letter of Francis Xavier from Manapad dated 16 June 1544 and from Alandalai dated 5 September 1544; at times of crisis caused by politically powerful enemies they took refuge in any one of the three coral reefs located to the South East of Kanyakumari. There were also islands such as *Kosal Yeri, Vaan Theevu* and *Pandyan Theevu* (also called *Muyal Theevu*).

58 R. Pavananthi Vembulu and R. John Suresh Kumar, *Circling the Triangle: Vulnerability, Social Exclusion and the Making of Disaster,* Research Paper Series, (Tirunelveli: Centre for the Study of Social Exclusion and Inclusive Policy, Manonmaniam Sundaranar University, 2010), p._.

59 Letter of Francis Xavier from Manapad dated 19 August 1544; it could be inferred from the letter that these people took asylum in the forest areas that was not familiar to them as much as it was to their rivals.

60 Ibid. dated 3 August, 1544; the letter highlights the importance of ransom in conflicts of that period.

61 *Thuthukudi Maraimavatta Kaiyedu,* p. 33.

62 C. Veeramuthu in K.A. Manikumar and Vinod Vincent Rajesh (eds.), *Southern Tamil Nadu through the Ages,* (Tirunelveli: Dept. of History, M.S. University, 2011), p. 101.

63 *Thuthukudi Maraimavatta Kaiyedu,* p. 35.

64 *The Travels of Marco Polo,* p. 309.

65 A. Sivasubramanian, *Uppittavarai ,* (Chennai: Kalachuvadu Pathipagam, 2009)p._.

66 Interview of S.P. Udhayakumar in *Kalachuvadu* dated November 2006, p. 26; he states that tolerance is one of the internal features of *Parathavar* society.

67 During the mass conversion that occurred at Meenakshipuram political parties like BJP attempted to prevent conversion. Leaders at the National level paid a personal visit to the village. There were also sympathizers for the converts from among the communist parties.

VIII

St. Xavier:
A Lesser Known Reformer of the Parathavar Community

Introduction

Insofar the fundamental essence of all religions since the birth of civilizations was concerned the undercurrent tended to remain the same based on 'ideas on god's spirit in relation to human beings.'[1] The doctrines of every religion were only manifestations of the necessities generated in the sphere of economy.[2] The history of the religions that spread in the *Pearl-Fishery Coast* was not an exemption to this pattern. Though traceable from the pre-Christian era, the history of the *Pearl-Fishery Coast* landed in an interesting episode by the thirteenth century. The region known for its riches on the one hand correspondingly caused degeneration of social values on the other hand.[3] The continuous attacks by the *Muslims* and subsequently by the rulers of the *Vijayanagara* Empire culminated in the introspection of the *Parathavar* community from within by the first half of sixteenth century.[4] In such a context the chief inhabitants of the region i.e. the Parathavars opted to embrace *Christianity* en-masse reposing faith on the *Portuguese colonial* agents.

These developments had their reflections on the economic sphere in terms of shifting of the control of the *Pearl Fishery Coast* from the *Muslims* to the *Portuguese* who used conversion in the most appropriate time to elicit unflinching support and allegiance of the *Parathavars* to the ruler of *Portugal.* However, it was to be noticed that the *Parathavar* alliance with the *Portuguese* did not lead to any great change or alteration in the basic tools of production and thereby in the overall economic fabric.[5] Therefore the repercussive effect of the *Portuguese* intrusion failed to reach the cultural core as it was expected.

Notable here was the fact that in sharp contrast to the case of *Latin America,* religious conversion of the *Parathavars* was not a logical consequence of an invasion.[6] Therefore, ideological justification of master and protégé relationship characterized by exploitation of the latter's resources without total subjugation was necessitated. That could be effectively done by the priests whose function was to alter the ideological fabric of the society to the needs and demands of the economy.[7] Even an exalted figure like *St. Francis Xavier* himself gave impressions of falling within this frame of view. Since conversion to *Christianity* was only a by-product of colonialism scholarly perceptions like these

131

were common. Therefore, in order to arrive at objectivity, pertinent questions such as 'on which side the missionaries including Xavier stood during situations and periods of crises,' and 'what were the values developed by the converts since adopting *Christianity?*' assumed importance.[8] The encounter of both the questions could be effectively made through understanding the general background of the native people in terms of conversion while contextualizing the scope and limitation of missionary activities.

In the present research, the dimensions of the economy in determining the course of religious conversion have been attempted. It would give a broader framework to discuss the particular achievements of *Francis Xavier* on the social front. Through deliberately allowing confrontation of mutually opposite views an assessment of *St. Francis Xavier* as a social reformer has been made. Fundamental hypothetical questions that guide the discussion come from the article of *Ines Zupanov* wherein he thoroughly breaks the hagiographical perceptions on the Saint developed by *Sebastiao Goncalves*. In view of oral traditions and popular folklore that depict *Francis Xavier* in a brighter frame and attribute several myths and legends on his saintly personality, the present article intends to strike a balance between *Zupanov* and *Goncalves*. The principles of historicism have been taken into account in order to prevent a replica of both of the scholars.

The structure of the article has been laid out with ideas of comparative religion but not so much adopting of the grammar of the discipline. Thus locating the general background on the arrival of missionaries and the converts has been sketched. This is followed by discussions on the points of convergence and departure infused by missionaries in general and *Xavier* in particular. The estimate of the developments has been made in the conclusion. The terms priests and missionaries have been used to denote religious professionals from among the natives and foreigners respectively for the sake of maintaining the difference although even the latter can be mentioned as priests.

The primary sources of the study ranged from the travelogues of *Marco Polo* and *Caesar Frederic* and Letters of *Fr. Francis Xavier* all of which contain hints of a social situation in the *Pearl Fishery Coast*. Insights developed through field visits also contribute in shaping the arguments. Apart from *Ines Zupanov*, ideas of *D.P. Chattopadyaya, A. Sivasubramanian, Rowena Robinson* and *Kenneth Mcpherson* have evoked key questions that went into the making of the article. The viewpoints of the elites of the coastal community[9] such as *R.N. Joe D'Cruz,*[10] *Vareethiah Constantine*[11] and *Capt. Berchmans Motha*[12] have been incorporated to verify the past. Therefore, a dialogue based on the present perceptions of the community since the occurrence of *Tsunami* with the events that emerged in the beginning of the conversion has also been attempted.

Need for the Missionaries

The arrival of *Fr. Francis Xavier* and his subsequent works were conditioned by several historical factors in the background independent of the economic crisis in the host land. *Xavier* was part of the *Society of Jesus* agenda. The purpose of the missionaries of this *Order* in the first half of the sixteenth century was to check the degeneration of morals of the sailors and traders who came in contact with other people.[13] These sailors and traders were the colonial elements at the lowest level that had very limited say in the production mechanism though in actuality traveled extensively between *Europe* and other parts of the world and on requirement resided in different places. Since the time of *Marco Polo,* the *Pearl Fishery Coast* was said to have been undergoing a period of degeneracy, wherein there was the absence of morality in sexual contact, there was a need to oversee the activities of these people.[14] There was a fear that the *Europeans* who came in contact with these people would embrace paganism.[15] The Missionaries were expected chiefly to address this problem.

Every *missionary* including *Francis Xavier* had limitations in other counts also. The renaissance and reformation movements that occurred in *Europe* segmented the respective domains of operations of the missionaries and the mercantilists in whose hands rested the control of the economy. Despite points of convergence, the missionaries at large remained helpless. The demand of time from a missionary in a strange land was to maintain a balance between the foreigners and the natives. Linking of both remained difficult in the absence of control over the economy.[16] The problem was one nurtured by the imperialist mindset of the time that aimed to introduce *Christianity* as a matter of diplomacy followed by strategies for retention.[17] The interest of the merchants was kept in the forefront at the diplomatic side whereas the services of the priests were used for retention.

At the native side, an irking situation ensued ever since they adopted *Christianity.* Owing to the unfamiliarity of the people with the new religion and its tenets there was a need for spiritual mentors who could instruct them on the basic principles of the religion. By the time of *Xavier's* arrival, the natives knew nothing about the religion than calling themselves '*Christians.*'[18] Without liberating the minds from the moorings of the early faiths and beliefs, the process of religious conversion was not completed. In fact, a brief gap that fell between the date of conversion and the arrival of the spiritual mentor was marked by great vacillation and return to the pre-conversion life and faith. It meant a departure from the newly introduced *Christian* values such as monogamy, ceasing of sexual indulgence outside wedlock and consumption of intoxicants by women,[19] etc. on the social level.

In a situation wherein these values continued, even if there had been a priest, it was doubtful whether in the popular perception they could have distinguished between a foreign missionary and a native priest in their fundamental functioning was concerned. For them a priest stood in a higher position in the socio-economic apparatus, for in the case of the *Parathavars* prior to conversion, the priests had an important role in the economic life in their capacity as shark-charmers.[20] The easy access of foreign missionaries to the European powers stationed locally had the possibility of projecting them in the native mould. It was reflected in the rituals of both the religions where priests of the native system used *the Sanskrit* language as the medium of communication between them and god while the *Missionaries* used *European* languages – particularly Latin. Both did not reach the minds of the ordinary people. Therefore, both the religions equally had the seeds of alienating their followers by developing a gap through the role of the native priests and missionaries.

However, in contrast to the native religions, the missionaries introduced the rituals of *Christianity* with a more inclusive component attached to it. Apart from weekly *holy-mass,* every significant occasion of life such as birth, marriage and death required the sanction of the Church – a mechanism by which even the irregular members were made to depend on the Church. Important among all of the above was death. In the joint family system of the natives, every man wished to have his funeral performed by dear ones. In the native religion, mere existence without membership in any other religion was sufficient for a man to have a peaceful funeral. But, for a *Christian,* he underwent certain basic rituals – that started from *baptism* – to make himself eligible for his funeral. The inactive members of the Church and the defectors of faith were kept under constant pressure by the priests through the kin-group with the threat of denial of a place in the cemetery.

Before conversion, the relevance of a priest – for that matter even God – for a community marred by a high frequency of crisis was not aimed at addressing the philosophical need of the people though there was a requirement for that. In the absence of a philosophical basis that reflected the internalization of life crisis, there was more possibility for the mind of an average inhabitant of the coast for having unconsciously embalmed with *charvaka* philosophy that stood on the premise of 'eat, drink and make merry for tomorrow cannot be certain.'[21] Therefore the requirement for a *missionary* after their conversion was aimed at linking the converts with a philosophical world propounded by *Christ,* while at the same time checking the continuity of elements that were incompatible with Christianity.

In the case of the Parathavars – like any other community that had fishing as its central activity – life had been always half-way towards death. The receptiveness to Christianity was only natural and what was required was a creative delivery of the principles. Among all teachings of *Christ, His* life was the greatest message that chiefly sought to explain in details every man's questions and pestering confusions on *death.* The *Christian missionaries* effectively introduced the concept of sin and forgiveness.[22] Thereby they kept the followers in a state of preparedness to encounter death. With stagnation in the economic front and expansion of population that depended on fishing for livelihood, the ensued poverty intermingled with the ideas of *Christianity* on life, death and salvation that guaranteed happiness in the next world i.e. heaven, on an average appealed the minds of the people.

Though these kinds of doctrines were needed to facilitate the smooth exploitation of the resources *Pearl-Fishery Coast,* for the *Parathavars,* conversion meant – importantly among others – establishing access to the religion of the masters of the sea which improved their social status in the eyes of other castes as like the higher castes they evolved a separate philosophy of life anchored on virtue and sin.[23] Nevertheless, as for as *Francis Xavier* in his role of pioneer missionary was concerned, though he cannot be completely relieved of the colonial mindset,[24] at the same time, he did not adhere to direct manipulation that caused exploitation. He always placed trade interests subservient to the spread of *Christianity.*[25] Even when he was in need of money he did not generate it from the poor people of the community.[26] He negotiated with the native rulers and at times even struggled to withstand their challenges only for the benefit of the converts.[27] Therefore, he cannot be blamed of exploitation. In fact, his activities went close to reversing the life of the *Parathavars* towards the days of *Bhakti Movement* than *Latinizing* local life.

Parallels with Native Practices

Being a pioneer, *Xavier* sowed the seeds of social change among the *Christian* converts in the coastal belt that covered *Ramanathapuram, Tuticorin, Tirunelveli* and *Kanyakumari* districts of the present day. The social environment that was structured with the ideas of the priests was replaced with those of the missionaries. As there did not occur any change in the tools of production correspondingly the cultural life did not emerge out of the chaotic situation created by the *Muslims* and *Vijayanagara rulers.* Therefore, the *missionaries* happened to infuse *a* certain degree of adjustment and accommodation in the *Christianity* they preached in order to pull the followers in their line. The coincidence of the continuity of the rudiments of the *Bhakti Movement*[28] in the *Pearl-Fishery Coast* among the dominant castes with the period of *Parathavar* mass conversion and the period that followed provided scope for the articulation of the ideas of adjustment.[29] The *missionaries* were the sole authorities that expound the doctrines of the religion. Since the implementation was particularized with the *Parathavars,* with the support of their loyalists the *missionaries* were able to effectively check the adaptation and violation of the rules.

It gave an impression of the *missionaries* reversing the life course of the *Parathavars* only towards the past days of vigorous *Bhakti Movement* more because of their inability to place the converts closer with the fellow *European Christians* by imparting the doctrines of *Christianity.* Commonalities that existed between *Hinduism* of the *Bhakti movement* period and *Christianity* of the sixteenth century in matters pertaining to virtue and sin contributed for the synthesis of ideas and thereby facilitated the work of the missionaries.[30] The missionaries capitalized on the commonalities of religions while desperately underlined and highlighted the differences. *Francis Xavier* was not an exemption to it.

The *Karma theory* that earmarked *Bhakti Movement* was the social philosophy of the higher castes. As in the *theory of Karma, Christianity* preached by *Francis Xavier* also highlighted the idea of soul – more particularly at the individual level. As a religion, while admitting all human beings to the presence of God, *Christianity* introduced a terrain ruled by *Satan.* It also introduced the idea of the need to prevent the extension of his rule into the world of humans. These were only the major departing points from the native religion. However, the prevention of the extension of the rule of *Satan* was convinced to be possible only through thoroughly dedicating the soul to God by deriving strength through the teachings of Christ. Thus, the biblical passage often repeated by *Xavier* "for what profit is it to a man if he gains the whole world, and he loses his own soul?" became the central point of his teachings.[31]

In the discourse between God and his devotees what was manifested in the holy mass, the latter sang in unison to raise up the individual souls to reach the expectation of God. The process of the holy mass was schematized with the accompaniment of music that came close to the cultural elements of the natives.[32] These were the features of the *Bhakti Movement.* While the *missionaries* drew parallels with *Bhakti Movement,* they tended to give an impression of elevating the ordinary folk to a level of equality with the higher castes. At the same time, by way of introducing the devotion of *Mother Mary,* the *missionaries* also incorporated the elements of local cult worship.[33] In turn, it contributed to the development of iconography on *Mother Mary.*

As in the *Bhakti Movement,* the saints who carried the message became important. At the least, the legends of *St. Thomas,*[34] *St. Antony,*[35] *St. Mathew*[36] and *St. Paul*[37] were introduced among the followers. The sober lifestyle of the *missionaries*, especially their commitment to celibacy improved their image. Although *Christianity* did not undermine family life, the importance attributed to celibacy what became an essential qualification for priesthood had its own positive effects. The ethics based on celibacy was not new in the context of the *Pearl-Fishery Coast*. The *Jain Monks* who had strong roots in the region before and during the *Bhakti Movement* were associated with the idea of purity through celibacy. During the period of degeneracy, celibacy was viewed as the symbol of magical power. Moreover, narrations of the physical challenges underwent by *Missionaries* paralleled with the imagery of *Christ*[38] enhanced their overall image in the perception of the natives. Even *Xavier* underwent certain difficulties owing to the tropical climate.[39]

Moreover, what can be assumed in the context of the absence of historically rooted inquiry among the native people was the possibility for the development of beliefs like the *missionaries* being considered direct disciples of *Jesus Christ*.[40] In the life before conversion, the natives at large were familiar with the native *epics* and *Puranas* wherein larger than life characters were presented.[41] It was doubtful whether the *missionaries* attempted to liberate the minds of the natives from the thematic obsession caused by the *epics* and *Puranas*. In view of the popularity of myths and legends that pertained to the *Christian Saints* spread by the *missionaries*, it was easy to assume that there were no such attempts. In practice, such perceptions facilitated the process of effective dissemination of the doctrines of *Christianity*.

In this background, it subsequently became inevitable to project an appealing image of the *Christian priests* in order to make the masses believe what Christ performed can also be performed by the disciples.[42] Though it was one of the novel strategies for retention, in this wavelength of thinking even *Xavier* was attributed with mystical powers at par with *Christ* to the tune of resurrecting dead people.[43] In one of his letters, *Xavier* had only confessed of having relieved a woman from labour pain.[44] But ascribing several miracles to him without adequate evidence were later day interpolations authored after his death for which *Xavier* cannot be blamed. Canonization of *Xavier* with sainthood and the dissemination of the news of his corpse remaining unaffected without any need for preservation for a longer period in the Church of Goa supplied motive and material for the germination of myths of several kinds. Over a period of time, this helped his successors to develop the iconography of *Xavier* which facilitated the process of consolidation. The major problem that the missionaries had in the reversing process was the cleansing of the native minds from idol worship[45] based iconography and the idea of transmigration of the soul. It was ironic that the chief missionaries like *Xavier* were himself idolized.

Networking

The reversing process would have failed if it had ignored the strength of the temples and their impact on social life. With immense landed property and invaluable jewels under their disposal, the temples were symbols of the native people's faith at the highest level. But, in its capacity as an institution, whether temples contributed in the shaping of the solid consciousness of the religious identity among ordinary people was highly doubtful. There had been several neutral elements least bothered of the control mechanism of the temple that maintained social and other transactions with the *Parathavars* for generations which did not either necessitate or compel the forming of a religious identity.[46] Although ritually marginalized, during the heydays of their past life the *Parathavar* people contributed immensely to the development of the temple economy[47] consolidating which the temples generated employment and schematized other benefits. Since in the popular perception the *Parathavars* were known as desperadoes they were excluded from the benefits and the chief beneficiaries hailed from other castes among who the temple established its effective control.

The stagnation in the economic front and the volatile situation marked by frequent invasions combined with plunder and massacre required an institutional inclusive mechanism for the benefit of the *Parathavars*. The *missionaries* were in the realization of it in their process of developing the *Church* as an institution in the physical sense. Any insensible attempt was feared to culminate in riots and bloodshed. The *missionaries* of that time like *Francis Xavier* carried the memory of the crusade wars in them.[48] With a clear mandate to spread *Christianity*, they viewed all the problems of the converts as always having a religious connotation. In the beginning, the solution was believed to lie in isolating the particular set of people from others and thereby protect them from becoming a numerical minority through unification at the level of all castes eliminating all internal differences. Therefore, in order to ensure the physical safety of the *Parathavar* converts, the *missionaries* like *Xavier* conceived of a comprehensive and separate settlement plan.[49] Since the plan failed, the *missionaries* thought of introducing a pattern similar to the temple among the *Christians* with changes mainly to benefit the *Parathavars*. The plan of creating institutional parallels with native religion had the potential not only to contain the wrath of the upper castes,[50] but also thought to prevent the social confrontations at other levels from becoming permanent.

The Church also had scope to score on other fronts. The tendency towards vegetarianism that gradually attained importance in the belief system of the natives had the seeds of alienating all those involved in the supply of non-vegetarian food.[51] It possibly generated a feeling of guilt among the *Parathavars* pertaining to their profession, since fishing was also killing of life.[52] But, *Christianity* subordinated all living beings to the need of man and the priests themselves nourished all kinds of non-vegetarian foods.[53] For them, it was not the everyday food which determined personal purity, rather the participation in the divine feast – compulsorily on *Sabbath* and optional on other days – in which symbolically the blood and body of *Christ* were offered as food. To be a Christian meant observance of certain holy rules that included attributing the first day of a week to God i.e. Sunday, which departed from the native practice of observing Friday as a sacred day. On the holy day of the natives, the rule of purity of food was strictly observed while it was the opposite in *Christian* life. This mechanism removed the alienating string and further extended the ideas of inclusion.

These helped the *missionaries* like *Xavier* to successfully evolve a religious consciousness – at the least to a minimum level – among the *Parathavar* people on the grounds of which they internally linked several of the fishing villages. It meant underplaying of the religious identity of the dependents located outside the villages while over stressing upon the identity of the internal dependents such as the barbers,[54] who were allowed to continue service only after adopting Christianity.[55] This was well manifested in the regions south of *Punnaikayal*. During a time of crisis, *Francis Xavier* was able to utilize the men and material that belonged to some of the villages for the well-being of another village.[56] Since in the regions north of *Punnaikayal* the control of the *Kayathar* based *Pandyan* king *Vettum Perumal* was solid, the *missionaries* were not able to make much headway. Therefore, *Xavier* caused migration of people from that region to places like *Kottar*.[57]

In order to ensure the well-being of the *Parathavar* community, *Xavier* entered into a diplomatic relationship with the native rulers. In fact, it was his success on that front which gave way for finding settlements like *Kottar*. He was well aware of the fact that he along with the converts were bound by the laws decreed by the native rulers and did not aspire to violate it.[58] Paradoxically, in his efforts, he faced more challenges that stemmed from the selfish motives of some of the *Portuguese* officers who wanted to make a profit through trading in the horse with the *Pandya* king *Vettum Perumal*.[59] Therefore, most of *Xavier's* activities were confined to the areas south of river *Tamiraparani* and in the coastal line South of *Punnaikayal,* as it formed the physical boundary of the king *Unni Keralavarman* of *Travancore* with who he maintained constant touch.

In a period of crisis on which the control of the *Pearl-Fishery* was no more under the thorough control of the *Parathavar* people, they required a better method of administration. *Fr. Francis Xavier* in the realization of that introduced it through the Church. His principle of governance – although brief in time – was unto itself based on feudal order what can be termed as paternal despotism.[60] He was critical of the nature of the people and often apologetic of his difficulty in understanding them.[61] He was usually sympathetic but insisted upon punishments for repeated lapses.[62] In several instances, he decided upon the duties of the individuals and groups even in matters that were beyond the purview of the Church and had a hold on the economic life of the people. He identified some individuals as adopted children and maintained a father-son relationship in the event of the latter meeting with his expectations.[63] Similarly, he maintained the friendship with a few.[64] Usually, absolute loyalty towards the religion and dedicated service to the growth of the Church were the chief expectations from out of these relationships which were often rewarded with gifts when performance was satisfactory. This naturally created reference points among young people who desired to follow it. As a result, bands of young people dedicated to the cause of *Xavier's* dream emerged.[65]

Along with these supportive elements that included both people and ideas, *Xavier* aspired to strongly establish the Church in comparison with the temple. They identified public spirited individuals that could donate liberally for the cause of the establishment of the Church.[66] As an institution, the Church imposed a tax upon the believers. To a limited extent, the *king of Portugal* also provided financial assistance.[67] These funds were chiefly used to reach the minds of the *Parathavar* converts.

Particularly, they appointed language translators and spiritual instructors and offered them incentives in cash.[68]

Importantly, in contrast to the native religion, the Church did not want to ignore the perceived evil habits of the desperadoes such as consuming intoxicants, spending on dancing girls, etc.[69] Moral education was realized as the key to cleanse them. The content of such a moral education was planned to suit the requirements at the local level and uniformity was maintained wherever the Catholic priests or its instructors operated. Thereby, an attempt was made to institutionalize the faith at the local level and it was integrated with higher order located at *Kollam* or *Goa*. In the system innovatively initiated by *Francis Xavier* in the *Pearl-Fishery Coast,* the *missionaries* stood as cornerstone in-between the people and the external authority of the Church.

Family life was never discouraged in *Christianity* as propagated by *Xavier.* It championed moral discipline among its followers through the instruction of the 'Ten Commandments.'[70] The presence and role of women and children in the proceedings of the Church were important. 'The idea of the purity of human body' in the native religion was associated with women.[71] Women were secluded from all sacred places especially during the menstrual cycle. But in *Christianity,* they were free to visit the Church at any time and nothing could stop them. Since *Christianity* urged upon monogamy their status improved. Although free mingling with men was not encouraged,[72] women contributed significantly to the development of the Church as members of the choir and spiritual development societies where they outstood men. They not only dedicated much of their leisure time in attending the mass but also motivated and socialized the children to give their loyalty to the Church.

Fr. Francis Xavier appointed *Pattangattis* – headmen of the village – and his deputies and expected them to perform such other duties instructed by him and the Church from time to time.[73] It amounted to the extent of interfering with the autonomy of the *Ur* because appointments to the posts of *Pattangattis* were made on receipt of a payment against the convention of oligarchy.[74] However, the major function was to check defection from faith and practices that were incompatible with the ethics of Christianity. As in the temples, these *Pattangattis* were laymen who were expected to look after the external functioning of the Church in coordination with the priests.[75] In his physical absence, *Xavier* commanded the *Pattangattis* through letters and unleashed coercion on those who failed to fulfill his expectations and aspirations.[76] By and large, the power structure that existed prior to the arrival of the *Portuguese* in the region particularly among the *Parathavars* was now absorbed by the Church with certain modifications.

Conclusion

Every activity of the missionaries gave an impression of subordinating the natives and their economy to the colonial interests. Though *Xavier* was largely opposed to the officers at the local level, he gave his loyalty to the *king of Portugal* and to the society to which he belonged. Therefore, he also conformed to the conventional expectations from a priest. His teachings were also responsible for the emasculation of the people of their potential to protect the *Pearl-Fisheries* and made the exploitation easier. But, the priests of the native religion were also doing the same on behalf of the ruling class of their region and time. While doing that they also made a huge personal profit. The Nayaka rulers were beautifying their kingdom at the cost of the native people. But, in contrast, *Xavier* did not have material motives. He withstood physical pains and challenges only for the sake of the spread of *Christianity* and the welfare of the *Christian* converts.

Xavier – consciously or unconsciously – drew parallels with the *Bhakti Movement.* It had its own positive results in the long run for it gave a feeling of improvement of caste status and concretized loyalty. On the one hand, it helped to withstand the provocation of the *Dutch Colonialists* that came in the form of 'conversion to protestant faith rewarded by a share in cotton trade' and, on the other hand, it supported in the retaining of local identity. The *Parathavars* through the *Portuguese* contact attached honorific titles with their *European* names. But, their cultural life did not depart from that of other natives. There was more space for mutual accommodation than confrontation. Religious-riots were rare occurrences although only a caste-riot was responsible for their conversion.

Importantly *Xavier* was able to introduce a set of morals in the life of the *Parathavars.* The polygamous system of life gave way to monogamy to the great advantage of women. The consumption of intoxicants – particularly by women – was put to effective check. His negotiations with the local monarchs were reflective of his love and care for the *Christian* converts. Therefore, *Xavier* when viewed in the context of *Pearl-Fishery Coast* through the indicators such as time, the overall situation, contacts with local people and long-term effects of his activities was not a negative personality as projected by *Zupanov.* He had remained true to the people he converted and thus left a legacy behind him.

Endnotes

1   D.P. Chattopadyaya, *Madhamum, Samugamum* (Tamil), (Chennai: New Century Book House, 2009), pp. 2–4.

2   Ibid., pp. 30–31.

3   L.F. Benedetto (ed.), *The Travels of Marco Polo*, (New Delhi: Asian Educational Services, 1994)**,** pp. 292–305; Marco Polo elaborately discusses the pathetic situation of women that ranged from subjection to the males in a polygamous marriage system to erotic group dancing in front of divine idols.

4   Britto Vincent (ed.), *Thooya Saveriar Kadithangal* (Palayamkottai: FRRC, 2002), Letter of Francis Xavier from Manapad dated 30 June 1544. *See also* A. Sivasubramanian, *Kirittavamum Tamizccuuzalum* (Tamil), (Nagercoil: Kalachuvadu Pathipagam, 2010).

5   From the *catamaran* that was used at the local level to the *Toni* maintained for the purpose of overseas trade in the ports there was no change of mentionable importance was infused. In fact, the number of important ports also dwindled subsequently after the Portuguese arrival. The *Toni* traffic depicted in the background of Kulasekharapattinam, Veerapandyanpattinam, Manapad, Kanyakumari, etc. was limited to Tuticorin in the post-independence scenario.

6   Ines G. Zupanov in Sanjay Subrahmanyam (ed.), *Sinners and Saints The Successors of Vasco Da Gama,* (New Delhi: Oxford University Press, 2000), p. 135.

7   D.P. Chattopadyaya, Op. Cit., p.20.

8   A. Sivasubramanian, *Kirittavamum Tamizccuuzalum* (Tamil), (Nagercoil: Kalachuvadu Pathipagam, 2010), p. 126.

9   In contrast to popular folklore, the elites of the community have viewed conversion into Christianity as a curse. Since the starting point was traced to the contemporaneous period of Francis Xavier, these views attain importance. In the aftermath of Tsunami, these views were widely shared by other members of the community. It was only in the anti-Kudankulam movement of 2011–12 the Church directly took the cause of the community on a larger scale.

10   As the author of Tamil novels such as *Aazhi Sul Ulagu* and *Korkai* and insider belonging to the *Parathavar* community, he predominantly attacked the attitude of the priests of the Church in his novels.

11   A scholar from the *Mukkuva* community, he is known for his book *Neydal Suvadugal* (Tamil), (Nagerkoil: Tamil Nadu Meen Thozhilalar Union, 2005). He underlines the commonalities of his communities with Parathavar community. He is also critical of the Church in its contribution to the communities' development.

12   He was the grandson and successor of the last *Parathar Jati Thalaivanmor* who lived in Tuticorin and popularly known as Pandyapathy ('literally meant the head of the Pandyas'). He compiled the memories of his ancestors in manuscripts. Presently no more, he was also critical of the role of the Church in shaping the lives of the *Parathavars*.

13   Ines G. Zupanov in Sanjay Subrahmanyam (ed.), Op. Cit., p. 150.

14   *The Travels of Marco Polo*, p. 301, Letters of Francis Xavier from Manapad dated 14 March 1544, from Tuticorin dated 14 May 1544 and from Punnaikayal dated 12 September 1544. In the opinion of Marco Polo, no form of lechery was considered to be a sin in the region. In the case of Francis Xavier, he observed several evil habits associated with the *Parathavar* people that included spending on dancing-girls – probably devadasis. By nature, these people were also found to be difficult to understand.

15   Ines G. Zupanov in Sanjay Subrahmanyam (ed.), Op. Cit., pp. 150–151; they took one or more Indian wives probably without making them convert to Christianity.

16   Several letters of Francis Xavier depict the gap between the officials and the missionaries.

17   In a national workshop entitled *Towards a Theoretical Understanding on Tamil Society: Text/Praxis/Memories* conducted at St. Xavier's College, Palayamkottai, between 10-11-2008 and 16-11-2008 Mr. A. Sivasubramanian delivered a lecture in which he shared his views on retention. According to him, the missionaries viewed conversion as self-realization of the natives for they were greatest sinners only because of venerating other gods opposed to Christianity. There was no attempt in the missionary side to know the essence of the native religion during the 16th century.

18   Letter of Francis Xavier from Tuticorin dated 28 October 1542.

19   Ibid; from Manapad dated 14 March 1544.

20   *The Travels of Marco Polo*, p. 293.

21   Ibid.; According to Marco Polo, since the *Parathavars* were considered desperadoes their witness was not accepted in law courts. When an attempt was made during the British rule to attribute martial status upon groups of people, they rejected several groups on the grounds of lack of discipline. *Parathavars* were one of them. By that, it can be inferred that their life philosophy differed from that of others.

22   Letter of Francis Xavier from Cochin dated 15 January 1544; the people were trained in their own language on doctrines of *Apostle's Creed* and *Ten Commandments*.

23   Caesar Frederic in N. Athiyaman (ed.), Op. Cit., p. 115; Frederic who visited the *Pearl-Fishery Coast* between 1563 and 1581 observed that all those involved in Pearl-fishing were Christians and they paid duty to the king of Portugal and the Church of St. Paul for the pearls they harvested.

24   Letter of Francis Xavier from Manapad dated 10 November 1544; in this letter, his feeling of Portuguese and other Europeans as owners of the sea is being expressed.

25   Ibid; from Manapad dated 20 March 1544; in this letter, his intention of protecting the native converts from Portuguese officials was clearly depicted.

26   Ibid; from Manapad dated 30 June 1544.

27   T.S. Subramanian, Tamil Nadu temple murals portray Tamiraparani battle? *The Hindu* (Madurai edition) dated 10/09/2011; Since after the battle of *Tamiraparani* that took place a few years before his arrival extended the frontier of the Travancore State up to Punnaikayal located in the Pearl-Fishery Coast, he happened to face two kings. Among them, the king of Travancore was in friendly terms whereas the Pandyan king of Kayathar was opposed to him. However, he respected the laws and conventions of the host land.

28   In the heydays of the *Pandyan rule,* the economy in correlation with the social thoughts of the dominant castes shaped the *Bhakti Movement* and derived the subordination of the ordinary people and contributed for conformity to social status-quo based on economic inequality and caste-hierarchy.

29   For example, at Kulasekharapattinam one of the important ports of the Pearl-Fishery Coast, Vaishnava temples exhibited trends of *Bhakti Movement* till the seventeenth century.

30   Letter of Francis Xavier from Tuticorin dated 28 October 1542; The Ten Commandments mentioned in the Old Testament elaborates upon virtue and sin for Christians. An ideal Christian has to strictly follow it. Similarly, the idea of *karma* in the native system was clear in its standpoint that a right action will be rewarded with right ultimate effect and vice-versa. But according to the need of the time, certain of the ethics were given importance by the priests for they had the authority over the interpretation of the scriptures. For instance, *Xavier* lauded the killing of non-Christians by the Portuguese Governor though non-killing was a universal value postulated by Christianity.

31 New Testament Psalms, *Matthew 16:26, See also* Ines G. Zupanov in Sanjay Subrahmanyam (ed.), Op. Cit., p. 140.

32 Notably the use of music differentiated the *Parathavars* and the Christian missionaries from the Muslims with who both had the dispute at the local and global levels respectively.

33 Letter of Francis Xavier from Cochin dated 15 January 1544; he mentions about prayer addressed to Mother Mary.

34 Ibid; from Tiruchendur dated 07 September 1544; one of the village headmen was named Thomas de Motha.

35 Ibid; from Tuticorin dated 20 September 1544; one of the friends of Fr. Xavier was named Antony Fernando. Antony at times cooked food for Fr. Xavier.

36 Ibid; from Manapad dated 08 April 1544; Mathew was an adopted son of Fr. Xavier.

37 Ibid; dated 10 September 1544 and Caesar Frederic p. 115; One of the respectable *Parathavar* persons enquired by Xavier in his letter was named Paulo Vaz. Caesar Frederic informed about the Church of St. Paul in the Pearl-Fishery Coast context.

38 *Jesus Christ* himself was a bachelor who freely mingled with people of varied background and character and was believed to have performed several miracles. As such, he left behind a legacy filled with physical sufferings on the imprint of which the *Catholic Priests* or *Missionaries* were viewed.

39 Letter of Francis Xavier from Nor dated 01 May 1544; Xavier had stated that his health was severely affected and he vomited blood. Similarly, Bishop Robert Caldwell was said to have defecated blood during summers to prevent from which he used to sit in a tub filled with full of water. Since the missionaries came from comparatively cold European countries tropical climate was the major challenge for them.

40 Childhood self-memory of the present researcher that was never successfully clarified by adults until self-learning took place.

41 Akshaya Kumar, Professor of English Literature, Panjab University, in a lecture during a refresher course in social sciences conducted at the UGC-ASC of the same university conducted between 30-11-2010 and 20-12-2010 said that 'before the spread of printing press oral narratives of these kinds of themes dominated most of the societies'.

42 The Church never attempted to the liberate the minds of the people from such beliefs. In fact, the Church itself was responsible for the dissemination of some of the popular miracles and myths. For the Church faith was important at the cost of rationality.

43 Ines G. Zupanov in Sanjay Subrahmanyam (ed.), Op. Cit., pp. 135 – 161; the author of the article demystifies the hagiographical approach of Sebastiao Goncalves in which his tone at times directly blames Francis Xavier. In the field visits conducted at Kombuthurai and Vembar on 02-01-2010 and 14-02-2011 respectively, people identify water bodies that caused the death of young children and subsequently became sacred since Francis Xavier resurrected the children. Nowhere in his letters did Xavier claimed to have resurrected dead children.

44 Letter of Francis Xavier from Tuticorin dated 28 October 1542.

45 Ibid.; from Punnaikayal dated 14 March 1544.

46 For example, the *Maravars*, the *Chavalakarars*, etc. were inter-dependents with the *Parathavars* and the religious identity did not seem to have affected their relationship.

47 Temples at *Thirupudaimarudhur, Tirunelveli*, etc. bear testimony to the contribution of the fishing economy.

48 Ines G. Zupanov in Sanjay Subrahmanyam (ed.), Op. Cit., p. 141.

49 Letter of Francis Xavier from Tuticorin dated 28 October 1542; Jaffna was chosen as the ideal location for settling down the converts as because it was thought to be an easily conquerable place. Plans were also mooted to appoint a ruler exclusively for the Parathavars with a separate head for ecclesiastical affairs. But the invasion failed and consequently, the plans were dropped.

50 A. Sivasubramanian, *Kirittavamum Tamizccuuzalum*, pp. 124–125; the majority people who follow the native religion is usually believed to be tolerant. But the author discusses the emergence of *Vibhudhi Sangams* in later periods that forcibly smeared holy-ash upon the converts.

51 The Pearl-Fishery Coast was once a hotbed of Jainism wherein idea of vegetarianism attained significance. Most often the local disputes between the fisherman and others culminated in the latter avoiding fish in their diet. This was witnessed during the *Mandaikad* riots.

52 R.N. Joe D' Cruz, *Aazhi Sul Ulagu* (Tamil), (Chennai: Tamizhini, 2004), pp. 29 – 31; the tone of the chief characters indirectly reflect the idea of sin involved in fishing.

53 Christianity adopted a flexible approach in this count. Particularly, during Lent period the followers were not supposed to take non-vegetarian foods. But fish was excluded from it.

54 Letter of Francis Xavier from Tiruchendur dated 7 September 1544; the editor was doubtful of whether Xavier was mentioning about barber or boatman. But since the person was depicted as a message carrier, it can be positively assumed as denoting a barber.

55 Interview with Mr. Parabaran (22), Fisherman, Manapad on 8-01-10.

56 Letter of Francis Xavier from Alandalai dated 5 September 1544; particularly during a situation of the crisis caused by the invasion of the Vijayanagara rulers, Francis Xavier was able to achieve the unity of the *Parathavar* people. He freely used the *Tonis* stationed at Punnaikayal and Kombuthurai to help the *Parathavars* elsewhere. Several of his letters bear testimony to it.

57 Interview with Mr. Alangara Michael Nallathambi Fernando (67), President, Parathavar Vadakku Ur, Kottar on 27-11-08.

58 Letter of Francis Xavier from Manapad dated 11 September 1544.

59 Ibid.; from Alandalai dated 5 September 1544.

60 Rowena Robinson, he Cross: Contestation and Transformation of a Religious Symbol in Southern Goa, *Economic and Political Weekly*, Vol. 29, No.3, (Jan.15, 1994), pp. 94–98; in the author's contention, the Catholicism of the Portuguese was feudal in nature as because they viewed other religions as opposed to themselves.

61 Letter of Francis Xavier from Punnaikayal dated 12 September 1544.

62   Ibid.; from Manapad dated 14 March 1544 and from Tuticorin dated 14 May 1544.

63   Ibid.; from Manapad dated 14 March 1544 dated 27 March 1544 and dated 08 April 1544.

64   Ibid.; from Manapad, dated 08 April 1544 and dated 03 August 1544.

65   These were the beneficiaries of the education introduced by the missionaries who at the highest level went up to Goa to pursue religious instruction and possibly helped in the spread of Christianity.

66   Letter of Francis Xavier from Manapad dated 16 June 1544, from Punnaikayal dated 30 June 1544 and from Tiruchendur dated 7 September 1544.

67   Ibid.; from Cochin dated 18 December 1544. *See also* Xavier Kudapuzha in K.S. Mathew, Teotonio R. de Souza and Pius Malekandathil (eds.), *The Portuguese and the Socio-Cultural Changes in India,* (Tellicherry: Fundacao Oriente, 2001).

68   Ibid.; from Punnaikayal dated 23 February 1544, from Tiruchendur dated 7 September 1544 and from Tuticorin dated 20 September 1544.

69   Ibid.; from Manapad dated 14 March 1544 and dated 12 September 1544.

70   Ibid; from Cochin dated 15 January 1544.

71   Purity of body signifies not only taking bath every day but also restraint in sexual conduct. In order to experience sexual pleasure, Adi Sankaracharya trans-migrated his soul into another man's body and prevented his own body from becoming pure. But Christianity laid much stress on the mind. Even if one is provoked of ill feelings it was deemed as sin. But monogamy and remarriage of widows were not looked down upon.

72   Letter of Francis Xavier from Manapad dated 08 April 1544.

73   Ibid.; from Manapad dated 12 September 1544.

74   It appears like soon the Ur returned to its original oligarchic character.

75   In the Hindu temples there were *Dharmakarthas* fashioned on this style. It was prestigious and offered certain privileges to the person who shouldered the responsibility of *Dharmakartha*. But, such positions undermined the powers of the *Ur* and eroded the tribal nature of life.

76   Letter of Francis Xavier from Manapad dated 14 March 1544; Pattangattis were threatened by Francis Xavier of arrest and deport. He derived strength and support from the ecclesiastical quarters located at Cochin in the implementation of his threats.

IX

Latinization at Crossroads:
A Study of Post-Conversion Changes among the Parathavars of the Pearl fishery Coast

Introduction

The merciless behaviour of the natives and the antagonistic dealings of the *Muslims* provoked the *Parathavar* community to adopt *Christianity en masse* with the support and protection of the *Portuguese*. Through conversion, they were given opportunities to share the religious domain with the *Portuguese.* But there always existed a tangible difference between them in terms of physical appearance, language, socio-cultural traits, etc. The *Roman Catholic Church* attempted to evolve uniformity of socio-cultural practices among all its followers. Among several steps, it maintained *Latin* as the universal spiritual language. Further, it also expected the followers to imitate the life pattern of the *Latin* language-speaking people.[1] But, these aims could not be accomplished for the spiritual language failed to appeal to the minds of the followers. Meanwhile, the proponents of the *Catholic* faith such as *Rev. Fr. Henri Henriquez* learned the *Tamil* language and brought out instructional texts in Tamil. In such a context marked by contradictions, whether the conversion of the *Parathavars* caused structural changes in the patterns of inter-caste and intra-class dynamics of the society, as well as religious practices, remains a subject matter for academic and general debate.

Notwithstanding what was mentioned at a social level was also viewed at the level of individuals. A great scholar and insider of the *Roman Catholic Church, Rev. Fr. Lawrence Sundaram* has stated that true conversion can take place only in a context where personal freedom is available for a person to decide his choice of religion.[2] He also underlines the involvement of divine agency in guiding the person opting to convert against selfish motives.[3] If we are to consider the ideas of *Rev. Fr. Lawrence Sundaram,* the very conversion of the *Parathavars* was not genuine for it neither occurred in a context of personal freedom nor was a result of divine promptings. Rather it took place during a period of severe economic crisis and was effectively consolidated by the *Portuguese.* As such conversion into *Christianity* was part of colonialism. Scholars like *Ngugi Wa Thiango* viewed colonialism as a cultural bomb that defaced a man's faith in his living environment, language unity of his society, his personal abilities and potential to struggle against oppression.[4]

147

In contrast to the views mentioned above, scholars like *D.P. Chattopadyaya* have opined that any change in the sphere of religion without a perceptible change in the basic tools of production could not evoke structural change in the socio-religious life of any people.[5] Accordingly, the differences among religions that were in operation in the same economic condition could only be superficial.[6] As far as *Christianity* was concerned, it laid much emphasis on the voice of *God* against physical appearance of *God.* It also expected a deep conviction and commitment to the 'articles of faith' and the 'person of *Christ.*[7] Elements parallel to these are also found in the *Bhagavad Gita,* which is still thought to be the holy book of the *Hindus* by many insiders themselves.[8]

These may sound insignificant for both the convert and non-converts. But, the *missionary* whose chief aim was to establish the truth pertaining to *the external* could not tend to ignore that. Particularly, the beginning of 16th century was marked by the spirit of inquiry that was evoked by *Renaissance, Reformation* and *Counter-Reformation* movements. Therefore, it was essential on his part to study the differences and stress the positive projections of the religion to which he was affiliated. He operated with the clear mandate infused by the *Roman Catholic Church* and attempted to shape the identity of people in definitive terms. But whether they were able to fully implement the principles of the *Church* and make the people adopt a *Latinized* pattern of life that stood on the premise of equality based on religion in the absence of change in the economic sphere and carve out unique identity for the *Parathavars* remains a question because identities tended to change with time both in *Europe* and *India.*[9] They deliberately attempted to put an end to the ideas and practice of *Dharma* and *Karma.*[10]

But one of the authoritative writers of *Parathavar* history, Patrick A. Roche was of the opinion that the *Catholicism* of the *Parathavars* was *Latin* only in form but *Tamilized* in practice. If this can be taken as the central point of the present article, then key factors like *Dharma* and *Karma* have to be studied in correlation with *Catholicism.* The Indian way of life on an average can be effectively understood through the concept of *Purushartha.* Accordingly, there ought to be a balance of values namely *Artha* (material life), *Dharma* (spiritual life) and *Kama* (desire). It was the caste that determined which value shall predominate over others. In the case of the *Parathavars,* since they were traders at the highest level and fishermen at the lowest level, they were associated with *Artha* and *Kama* respectively though by virtue of economic dominance a substantial section remained *Dharmakarthargal* in-charge of temple administration.[11] How far did conversion cause the relocation of these values was another pertinent question before researchers.

Taking into account all of the above-mentioned factors, the present article has been structured in a style inspired by the method employed by eminent historian *Shahid Amin.* By that, the concepts such as *event, metaphor and memory* have been linked and employed to explain the cultural position of the *Parathavars* since conversion. To substantiate this, three events have been picked up and each one contextualizes post-conversion trends in economy, religion and society. The events are the *famine of 1570,* the *martyrdom of Rev. Fr. Criminale in 1549* and the *civil strife* caused by the *Parathavars* at *Tiruchendur* in *1573.* Since the economy is the factor that determines the superstructures like religion and society, it occupies first place. Such an approach will prevent duplication of the works of scholars like Jeyaseela Stephen, Decla, Patrick A. Roche etc. However, strict chronology has not been followed for the study. In the case of the famine, the background that led towards conversion has been given gravity whereas the trends after the martyrdom of *Rev. Fr. Criminale* have been taken for analysis. As far as the civil strife was concerned, both background and post-event developments have been brought under discussion. The views of scholars like K.N. Panikkar, A. Sivasubramanian, S. Decla, etc have contributed to the shaping of the article apart from the views of *Rev. Fr. Lawrence Sundaram* and *D. P. Chattopadyaya.*

Economic Impact of Conversion

The association of the *Parathavars* with the *Portuguese* that culminated in the adoption of *Christianity* by the former was believed to have economically benefitted the community. Some scholars have gone to the extent of stating – though not in the context of the *Parathavars* – that conversion occurred for procurement of a headdress[12] since it symbolized the economic assertion of one community over another. These assumptions were not always true. In the context of the *Parathavars,* they lost their head dress chiefly due to their adoption of *Christianity.* In the beginning, the *Portuguese colonial power* seemed to have given an impression of treating the *Parathavars* at par with them. Particularly, there were concessions in terms of *Stone tax.*[13] Initially, it appeared to be a gift when compared to the exploitations and expediencies of the *Muslims.* While the credit for such concessions was taken by the *Portuguese colonial power,* the *Parathavars* gave their complete loyalty to the *Church.* For them, the *Church* was a culmination of all. Nevertheless, in actuality, there were conflicts of interest between the *Officers, Traders* and the *Church* which the *Parathavars* did not deem important to understand.[14] But, for the constant threats from the *Muslims* and the native rulers in the 16th century, it was highly doubtful whether there could have been any unity among the *Portuguese.*

There were mentionable instances in which the difference between the *monks* and officers to have contributed for division among the people. In such a context, *Rev. Fr. Xavier* took a group of people to the *State of Travancore* and settled in places like *Kottar.*[15] But, otherwise, those who were comfortable under the influence of the *Portuguese officers* remained in their own settlements. However, in the long run, it proved to be negative for those who opted not to migrate though in the case of migrants initially there was the problem of adapting to new professions. The non-migrants were left at the mercy of the *Portuguese officers.*[16] The *Stone Tax* on *Pearls* was increased manifold. On the whole, the tax amounted to 25 per cent during the rule of the *Pandyan Kings.*[17] It was considerably reduced in the brief period that followed conversion.[18] But soon it rose to as high as 75 percent and deeply affected the *Pearl Fishing* enterprise.[19] But the *Muslims* and other natives were able to procure considerable concessions as part of a diplomatic relationship between the *Nayaks* and the *Portuguese.*[20]

With the loyalty of the *Parathavars* at hand, the *Portuguese officials* strengthened the office of the *Jathi Thalaivan* or the caste-headman. He was made the head of the seven important towns known as *Yelu Urs*[21]. He was the head of both spiritual and temporal life of the *Parathavars* symbolizing which he wore a *holy cross* in his neck stated to have been gifted by the *Portuguese King John III.*[22] He was assisted by *Pattangattins* and *Adepans* from every town in the exercise of his judicial and executive powers.[23] Apart from these, they were converted into trade brokers to espouse the cause of the *Portuguese.*[24] It can also be understood as maintenance of an effective hierarchy that ultimately checked the loyalty of the people towards the *Portuguese crown.* But it seemed that the *monks* did not contribute to the consolidation of the authority and power of the *Jathi Thalaivan.*

There were certain lapses in the economic front as left by the *Portuguese official class* that prevented the rise of their authority beyond dispute. There was hardly any trace of the *Portuguese* integrating the *Parathavars* in *horse* and *cotton.*[25] Since the major portion of trade in spices was concentrated on the west coast, they deemed it unimportant to establish factories in the *Pearl Fishery Coast.*[26] Therefore, it could be ascertained that when the *Pearl Fishery* became non-profitable, a substantial section of the *Parathavar* population took to the fishing occupation. It eventually must have led to pressure in fishing occupation caused by overpopulation on the one hand and, on the other hand, contributed to the rise in supply against actual demand. The value of fish was reduced and the frequency of offering to the church in the name of *therippu* increased. But there was neither improvement in the basic tools of fish catch nor any evidence of collaboration to improve fishing although such trends were visible in *Pearl Fishing.*[27] The *Portuguese* introduced among the *Parathavars* the practice of cultivating *chilly, tobacco* etc.[28] But since they compelled the *Parathavars* to sell the produce only to them, the people were not able to have a free hand to fix the price in correlation to their labour.

Factors, as outlined above, affected almost every section of the society and the *Parathavars* encountered a severe famine in 1570. Famines and fall in the standard of living twisted the faces of the humble fishermen towards the direction of the Church. Though the fairness of the *Portuguese official class* was exposed, in view of the political turbulence and want of their military strength they could not be directly opposed. Indeed, the disaffection and dissent were directed towards the authority of the *Jathi Thalaivan.* In consequence, his Sense of Justice was questioned and his judicial decisions were opposed as partial.[29] In such times, the interference of the *Church* was expected by the affected party. The judgment of the *Church* when differed from that of the *Jathi Thalaivan* it caused friction between him and the monks.

The approach of the officers and missionaries tended to differ as far as the development of the colonized land was concerned. The officers did not want to Europeanize the colonized land, and therefore, they even viewed the efforts to introduce education by the missionaries with contempt.[30] But they could not prevent the cross-cultural interaction that occurred in maritime activities which benefitted the trading class of the *Parathavar* society. In the case of the *missionaries,* whatever might be the education they introduced, a substantial section of the *Parathavar* remained fishermen. The missionaries did not realize the importance of teaching the fishermen to protect their livelihood environment or to evolve a corporate character. This education did not help them to physically relocate themselves into agricultural cities as described in *Maduraikanci.*

Apart from affecting the intra-caste dynamics, the religious conversion of the *Parathavars* also affected the inter-caste dialogue as they lost the economic power to patronize the service castes like the barbers and washermen. These service castes were made to adopt *Christianity* or otherwise, they encountered the danger of being ousted from service. In Indian caste system – at the least from one point of time – foreigners have been attributed a status at par with outcastes. Therefore, there remained a danger of the overall caste status to be reduced to those who closely aligned with the foreigners. In such a context, not only was the status of the *Parathavar* community was questioned but also of the service castes. Thus in the second half of 16th Century A.D., a civil strife was caused by the *Nadar* community through which they sought the *Parathavars* to adopt symbols that conform to their low status.[31] This was how the *Parathavars* lost their headdress in the eyes of other communities. Their loyalty to the *Church* was a major hindrance that came between them and the *Dutch* as a result of which they lost the opportunity of reaping the benefit of cotton trade.[32]

The Form of Religion

In India, every sect and sub-sect had its own rituals and castes conveniently sprawled across them. It was the allegiance to any one of these sects that determined the spiritual identity than religion *per se*.[33] Yet, it did not mean a concerted opposition to other sects. The *Parathavars* followed a variety of sects and sub-sects prior to conversion. But conversion in actuality meant giving up all these in favour of *Christianity*. In a context where these people did not know to identify their spiritual belief, the first great change that occurred was the realization of their religion as *Christian*.[34] It was *Rev. Fr. Xavier* who was responsible for that change which he did not deem as significant or success.

The role of *Rev. Fr. Francis Xavier* in the consolidation of the process of *Parathavar* conversion was significant. As said already, he was able to influence the *Portuguese officials* and contribute to the reduction of taxes.[35] He also brought to limelight the corrupt side of the *Portuguese* officials[36] and sought justice for the *Parathavar* people. He was also able to impress upon the native rulers like the *Raja of Travancore*. It remained difficult to classify his character as either official or missionary through his activities. Moreover, if the conversion of the *Parathavars* people could be stated as not based on conviction, then the approach of *St. Xavier* towards them was not based on a deep rooted understanding of their cultural past. Therefore, his conviction like that of any other missionary was that the natives have to realize that they were following something incorrigible and could be rescued through *Christianity*.[37] *Xavier* even seemed to have believed that the people shared his perspective, and therefore, insisted on memorization of prayers than instruction.

Rev. Fr. Xavier championed the cause of social reform and stood against practices such as drunkenness, immorality, and idolatry, etc.[38] But there were hardly few disciples for him to translate these ideas into a consistent movement. One reason behind that was the poor number of priests to serve the people when calculated in terms of the population proportion. Even in the case of availability of priests, the problem of language difference crept in. With the span of time, these priests [39]not only failed to give shape to the reformative ideas of *Xavier* but also thought to elevate his image vis-à-vis the native *Brahmin priests*.[40] They attributed *Xavier* with mysterious and curative powers. In the long run, such attempts failed as that could not make inroads into the 'believed curative powers' of the Mother Goddess. In actuality, the expectation of time from the missionaries was the commitment towards the cause of the people. Such commitment could not be built in the absence of a comprehensive understanding of the people's past.

For a brief period *Fr. Antony Criminale* served the people. In his capacity as *Superior*, he visited the entire coast every month.[41] It was in realization of the fact that there were scores of people who did not get the benefit of listening to a *Holy mass* and children waiting to be baptized. He learned the *Tamil* language and made good attempts to translate *Holy* literature to *Tamil*. However, he died a martyr's death at the hands of the *Telugu* invaders. His death was a phenomenal event that had the virulence of touching the hearts of the converts. A comparable effect was also caused by the martyrdom of *Br. Luis Mendez* killed by a native sometimes between 1549 and 1552 during a punitive expedition by the *King of Travancore* conducted near *Kanyakumari* in the presence of people.[42]

If at all there was a *Catholic priest* who made a thorough understanding of the *Indian* cultural system and patterned his approach accordingly in the context of the *Pearl Fishery Coast*, it was only *Fr. Henri Henriquez*. He not only developed his proficiency in *Tamil* language but also in Indian religious thought.[43] Unlike *Xavier*, *Fr. Henriquez* realized the disaffection that was spread among the *Parathavar* people.[44] Though predominantly illiterate, the people were not altogether ignorant. In the perspective of *Henriquez* there were even signs of response to secular education.[45] But he could not implement many of his ideas possibly because of the distance he maintained with the *Portuguese officials*. He was comfortable in a stationed life what meant dedication to a selected group of people against wandering from place to place. Had he taken efforts to negotiate with the officials to provide tax concessions, it could have resulted only in vain. In such a context, he lacked in ability to contain the non-*Christian* practices. Rather, he compromised on several counts. As a result, the idolatry that was staunchly opposed by *Xavier* found its way into *Christianity*. Along with that, projections of several early forms of worship surfaced.

The temples as an institution were placed beyond the purview of political power for a majority of the people, as well as the rulers, were part and parcel of its spiritual sway. To its contrast, the institutional dimension that was asserted by the Church at the local level necessitated a flexible approach with the rulers and the substantial section of people as only a minority population supported it.[46] Even in the case of the minority population, it was doubtful whether they could be sustained within *Christianity* if there were aspects totally incompatible with it. What emerged was a harmonious dialogue between *Christianity* and the native religions. The colonial religion expanded the boundaries of Hinduism[47] and in turn, its own domain was opened for expansion. The church could not establish absolute control over the local spiritual practices of the *Parathavar* community. In fact, when its interruption was withstood, it only enabled the *Parathavars* to rediscover their own culture.[48]

From time immemorial, the sea was regarded by the *Parathavar* community as a singular complex greater than which nothing exists. With *Christianity*, the veneration towards the sea was associated with the devotion towards *Mother Mary.* Particularly mentionable was the evolution of the icon of *Sindhathiri Matha* located at *Tuticorin.* In this form, *Mother Mary* carried a *Thoni* in her hands.[49] She was regarded as the protector of voyages, and therefore, sailors before venturing into the sea offered prayers to her. During voyages, a specific time was also allocated for praying to God through *Mother Mary.* In her status as guardian, she was also visited by the newly married couple who necessarily dipped their feet in the sea after expressing their devotion to her. Gradually, the *Christian* concept of dividing the world into good and bad found its way into the belief pattern. There evolved a belief that the ship of the *evil spirits* followed the sailors which can be kept away by prayers.[50] Similarly, the native belief that the broomstick could stop storm and rain also continued[51]

Since the *Parathavar* adopted *Christianity en masse*, the totems that marked regional variations disappeared. Though the appearance of sharks and dolphins in the sea were considered to be indicative of *omens,* they lost their spiritual significance.[52] However, turtles continued to receive attention. The oil of the turtle was considered to possess the power to ward off evil.[53] At times of emergency at sea, the sailors attempted to catch a particular type of turtle so that they could be saved. The holy functions of the *Chank* were also reduced to a considerable extent. The blowing of it was stopped. But it continued to be part of house building process, feeding of babies and also formed part of the divine thread worn by females symbolizing wedlock.[54]

Christianity introduced the crab totem. According to folklore, *St. Xavier* dropped his prayer cross while traveling in a boat.[55] It was rescued by a crab and was given back to *St. Xavier.* In recognition of its service, *St. Xavier* blessed it by drawing the cross mark on its back which was embossed forever. The fishermen started treating it as a mark of good omen after this event.[56] Moreover, *Christianity* allowed salt to be part of offerings to God. Such salt was not only thought of having curative power but also believed to increase fish catch.[57]

The concept of devotion to saints in *Christianity* was understood by the people, in general, to be in tune with the native religion that was characterized by pluralistic godheads organized in a loose hierarchy. The importance of these gods was determined by their efficiency to address the problems of the devotee. Particularly, the gods were expected to make the devotees feel their magical powers. It was also believed that the gods could perform miracles only when provoked by the devotees to do so. As far as the *Christian* converts were concerned, they predominantly employed the same native methods to please the *Saints.*[58]

The *Catholic Priests* attempted to check the native practices corrupting the form of *Christianity* of the period.[59] They established control over the *Ur* organization and punished the defaulters. Rev. Fr. Henri Henriques printed the doctrines of *Christianity* and circulated them. Since the conversion of the *Parathavars* was not based on a deep conviction, efforts like these did not find wide appreciation. The priests realized the possibility of alienation within *Christianity* in case if principles of puritan life were excessively articulated. They introduced dramatic performances like *Kallarai Vasapu Nadagam*[60] through which they propagated the basic tenets of the religion such as *death, removal of sin, resurrection, Kingdom of God*, etc. These the *Priests* believed would help in the retention of people within the *Catholic* fold. But these ideas did not prove effective in a situation where they were not able to offer a remedy to physical problems such as chickenpox as in the native system. Practically it remained difficult to retain people secretly visiting temples to perform rituals to safeguard them.[61]

The *Catholic monks* relied more on the side of the faith of the followers than rationality when teaching the tenets of *Christianity*. But they appealed to the rational side of the followers while practices of other religions were brought to the discussion. They also realized that the average mind of the native was not spiritually ingrained and could not distinguish between the myths of *Christian* and native religious forms. They did not prevent the spread of false folkloristic information that tended to move towards iconography than canonization. Thus several myths about miracles in the name of *St. Xavier,* was freely allowed to spread which gradually found its way into the chronicles issued in the church. This is a kind of absorption and assimilation of indigenous religious belief. By doing so, they tried to integrate the foreign with the native, where to the foreign it was new, whereas to the native it was common.

Similarly, the dominance of Mother Goddess worship was well realized by the *Catholic priests,* and therefore, they introduced the devotion to *Mother Mary.* As a matter of logic, they chose the vibrant *Tuticorin* town to establish the *Church of Our Lady of Snow.*[62] The *Sancta Maria* title of *Mother Mary* image was locally believed as the establishment of the parallel to *Santhana Mari,* one of the prominent *Mother Goddesses* of the region.[63] Paradoxically, a *Mother Mary* image placed in the *Church of Kottar* was believed to have been installed by *Rev. Fr. Xavier* himself though he championed against *idol-worship*[64]. As one found in native practice, She was symbolized with motherhood and venerated with the offering of milk. Moreover, the dead virgins in the families were considered *she-angels* who derived divine power from *Mother Mary.*[65] Not only these dead females were accorded divine status, but to a lesser extent the ancestors of the family also. It was the responsibility of the females of the family to look after the timely performance of certain rituals to these family-divinities. The *Church* which was able to establish its control upon the *Ur* was not able to stop these practices in the family.

Society

The mechanism of control established by the *Roman Catholic Church* gave impressions of being absolute. It prescribed certain universal rites for all of the members irrespective of difference based on language, nationality, etc. Most important among such rites was *baptism* which required the presence of *God-parents* apart from regular parents. In many cases, the *Parathavars* had *Portuguese God-parents* and they were made eligible for taking family names of the latter. At several instances, the *monks* also shared similar names. In *Hinduism,* apart from the handicap of a *non-Brahmin* being ineligible to enter the sacred altar, he could not take titles taken by the *Brahmin* priests. But *Christianity* did not impose such hindrances. Similarly, the *Christian monks* – particularly from *Europe* – lived a life of piety and humility and took food offered by the people, selflessly served the lowest of them, came forward to offer their lives in defence of them and withstood physical hardships caused by climate.

These egalitarian gestures gave a revolutionary outlook for *Christianity* which found its easy reach among the humble fishermen.

In spite of the revolutionary elements in *Christianity* and *Portuguese* sailors coming forward to be *Godfathers,* these were not sufficient to break neither the walls of racism nor of casteism. There were hardly a few matrimonial alliances that actually took place between the *Portuguese* and the *Parathavars,* on the one hand, and on the other, the *Parathavars* were not willing to accommodate the lower castes at par with them. Possibly, there could have been some alliance between the *Parathavars* and the descendants of *Casados.*[66] However, the *Parathavars,* the *Portuguese* and the *Casados* together made the lives of the slaves worst. The Catholic Church, therefore, compromised on these issues and even distributed the space within its premises accordingly.[67] When the *Church* served by selfless monks like *Rev. Fr. Henri Henriquez* was willing to compromise on egalitarian principles, it was not without the realization that the original humanitarian spirit propagated by *Lord Jesus Christ* was lost. The result was that *Christianity* failed to ingrain special values in the social life of the natives, especially among the *Parathavars.*

It was not to undermine the potential of either *colonialism* or its agents like the *Church* in interrupting the lives of the natives. Rather it meant that the rich culture of the native people withstood the colonial interruption and contributed to the emergence of certain values within the premise of which the people relocated themselves.[68] For instance, the veneration with which they viewed the social system based on the *Brahminical* hierarchy gave way to status based on the relationship with the *Portuguese.* Every caste irrespective of adhering to *Christianity* or not indulged in such a process and the *Christians* were only pioneers in that.[69] On their part, the *Europeans* accorded higher social status to *Christians* than others.[70]

Such a tendency found expression among the *Parathavars* as early as the third quarter of the 16th century A.D. In an event that took place at *Tiruchendur* in 1573, the *Parathavars* were stated to have provoked the anger of the *Brahmins* by dropping a dead fish in the well from which the latter drew water.[71] The incident caused a civil strife between the *Parathavars* and the *Hindus* at large and resulted in the commitment of the *Portuguese* officers to punish the culprits. This incident would not have occurred but for the *anti-Brahmin* propaganda – as outlined already – in which the *Catholic monks* were indirectly involved.[72] Nevertheless, it marked the departure of the Parathavar community in terms of relating themselves in the *Sanskritic mode* of social segmentation. It was also suggestive of the availability of alternative social pattern for the *Parathavars* to relate themselves which was thought at the least by the perpetrators of the mischief to be comparatively better.

The fundamental premise of the alternative social life out of *Sanskritic pattern* rested in the assuming of *Portuguese* family names. But the assumption of family names caused further damage to the fabric of the *Parathavar* society. Families with corporate success tended to turn inwardly and they cherished the history of their family. Their status was acknowledged by the *Church* and the *Jathi Thalaivan* who honoured them by offering food in the table. It resulted in the emergence of the class of *Mesakkarar* above all members of *Parathavar* community. The humble fishermen seated in sheets of cloth were mentioned as *Kamarakarar* and those who made the livelihood from non-fishing jobs were categorized into *Menakadar*.

The members of the *Mesakkarar* class came to believe that it was below their prestige to move hand-in-hand with those who were economically positioned lower. Nevertheless, *Kamarakarar* and *Menakadar* considered prestigious to enter into a matrimonial relationship with them. They even did not bother much about the actual economic position of the *Mesakarar*. At times, such bridegrooms lived a life of mere dependency on the income of the *Kamarakarar*. Not only had it prevented the tribal element, but also the linkage of faction. The factions that existed at village level were linked to factions formed by these families and they together at times contested the power of the *Jathi Thalaivan*.[73] Most often than not, the *Church* either directly or indirectly questioned the authority of the *Jathi Thalaivan* with the support of a few *Mesakkarar families*.[74] Since economic status was the major criteria for social negotiation, there were intermarriages between the *Mesakkarars* and the *Sinhalese* people. Many of the women remained unmarried owing to the *family status* consciousness of the *Mesakkarars*.[75]

Christianity in the region attempted to strengthen the status of women through redefining their moral belief. For long, the minds of the women were socialized with patriarchal notions and they maintained an extraordinary commitment towards men and family. They stood ineligible for inheriting parental property and were expected to perform *Johar* at the death of the husband. Polygamy was widely prevalent. The *Roman Catholic Church* in its various meetings urged to reform these practices among *Christians*.[76] The *Church* took positive measures to prevent the practice of alcohol consumption and restricted the movement of men in private places meant for women in a settlement.[77] It gave particular freedom for women insofar attending the *holy mass* during periods that followed delivery of a baby and from husband while assisting a woman who delivered a child were concerned.[78]

These measures were not sufficient to make a breakthrough in the social status of women. The greatest property that a fisherman hoped to earn was a boat. If at all, it was to be inherited the taboo that barred women from venturing into the sea for fishing made the inheritance useless. In such cases, it became a dowry and the *Parathavar* society subsequently left scope for problems that pertained to dowry. Similarly, the initiatives of the Church to integrate the women folk with it through favourable treatment did not meet with total success. The first domain of worship for them was the home wherein devotion to ancestors was common. The native practice of observing of puberty taboo was common while worshipping here though the *Church* did not impose such predicaments.

Conclusion

The potential to introduce change in the basic tools of production remained with the *colonial officers*, who did not always work hand-in-hand with the missionaries. Their aim was to build *Portugal* as a powerful state and the *Parathavars* who had been accorded citizen status were thought to share similar sentiments. Therefore, a huge share of the proceeds of the *Pearl Fisheries* was transferred to *Portugal* in return for which military protection was given to the *Parathavars*. The *Portuguese officers* refrained from linking the converts to the profitable slave trade that took place with *Batavia*.[79] Otherwise, the modernization of the fishing industry happened to wait for the arrival of the Indo-Norwegian project in the twentieth century.

The arrival of St. Xavier gave impressions of an orthodox Christianity being introduced among the Parathavars. But later missionaries like Rev. Fr. Henri Henriquez understood the limitation of the foreign religion when introduced among a people who were used to pluralistic methods of worship. The native religion expanded to accommodate the features of the new religion. It contributed to a dialogue and consequently, Christianity also was influenced by the native religion. Therefore, the major ideas of the native religion such as idol-worship, Karma and several other superstitious beliefs found their way into Christianity. Socially, it let way for the unchristian practices such as cross-cousin marriage to continue.

The realization of the importance of the native language by *missionaries* like *Fr. Henri Henriquez* that culminated in the founding of a Tamil School maintained the faith of the *Parathavars'* in their language. As a result, scholars like *Anthony Kutty Annaviar* and others emerged as poets in the 17th century A.D. They were able to realize the problems based on their language identity which was accepted and taken for struggle despite the economically assertive class from among the *Parathavar* society took a different stand. The kind of division like *Mesakarar, Kamarakarar* and *Menakadar* though caused by colonial interruption was only a way of rediscovering of culture wherein people relocated themselves. It was not only the *Christians* but also a substantial section of the population adapted to a way of life introduced by the colonial powers. In view of such a context, the *Parathavars* were able to retain their original culture. Thus as *Roche* said the Christianity that was introduced in the region can only be dubbed as *Tamilized Christianity. Latinization* was only a myth and it did not reach the cultural core. Therefore it can be effectively stated that it is standing only in crossroads.

Endnotes

1   T.K. Oommen and Hunter P. Mabry, *The Christian Clergy in India Vol. I, Social Structure and Social Roles,* (New Delhi: Sage Publications, 2000), p.43, these two sociologists who have authored the book intend to develop the concept *Latinization* parallel to the idea of *Sanskritization* of M.N. Srinivas.

2   Lawrence Sundaram in ______ (ed.), *Christianity in India: Its True Face,* ( ), p. 46.

3   Ibid., pp 47–48.

4   K.N. Panikkar, Coloniamum Panpattu Matramum (translated in Tamil by K.R. Sankaran) *Ungal Noolagam,* January 2012, p. 80; *Ngugi Wa Thiango* is an African poet and author of the book 'Decolonizing the Mind: The Politics of Language in African Literature.

5   D.P. Chattopadyaya, *Madhamum, Samugamum* (Tamil), (Chennai: New Century Book House, 2009), pp. 23–47.

6   Ibid.

7   Lawrence Sundaram, Op.Cit, p. 49.

8   Though any text cannot be exactly said as the Holy text of the Hindus, of late a predominant number of people belonging to the religion believe that the Bhagavad Gita as their holy book.

9   Interview of Romila Thapar to IDRCCRDI entitled *Romila Thapar: India's Past and Present – How History Informs Contemporary Narrative* posted on Youtube and viewed on 04-04-2013; since she is also a Marxist like D.P. Chattopadyaya it can be assumed that her views are only further explanations to his views and not contradictory statements. It is to say that with every tangible change in the sphere of economy, there occurred changes in other spheres independently in India as also in Europe.

10 Teotonio R. De.Souza, From Christianization of Karma and Luso-Tropicalism and Lusosphere, *Seminar 630* (Feb. 2012), pp. 23–24.

11 A. Patrick Roche, *Fishermen of the Coromandel-A Social Study of the Paravas of the Coromandel,* (New Delhi,: Manohar, 1984), p. 22.

12 A. Sivasubramanian, *Kirittavamum Tamizccuuzalum* (Tamil), (Nagerkoil: Kalachuvadu Pathipagam, 2010) p. 77.

13 N. Athiyaman, *Pearl and Chank Diving of South Indian Coast (A Historical and Ethnographical Perspective)* (Thanjavur: Tamil University, 2000), p. 71; the writer states that at the initial stage, the tax was discriminatory to the disadvantage of the Hindus and Muslims.

14 In fact, when a mechanism like *Padroado* was in place, there was no meaning for such a division.

15 Britto Vincent (ed.), *Thooya Saveriar Kadithangal* (Palayamkottai: FRRC, 2002), Letter of Francis Xavier from Tuticorin dated 14 May 1544.

16 Ibid.

17 L.F. Benedetto (ed.), *The Travels of Marco Polo*, (New Delhi: Asian Educational Services, 1994), p. 293.

18 N. Athiyaman, Op. Cit., p. 63.

19 A. Sivasubramanian, *Kirittavamum Tamizccuuzalum,* p. 77.

20 N. Athiyaman, Op. Cit., p. 63; the *Portuguese* agreed to allow the *Muslims* to dive freely in the Kayalpatnam region. In turn, they were allowed to move their articles of trade inland.

21 The seven towns are Vembar, Vaippar, Tuticorin, Punnaikayal, Veerapandyanpattinam, Alandalai and Manapad. However, since these seven towns were the chief axis of other 23 villages, they also gave their signal allegiance to the Jathi Thalaivan.

22 Unpublished manuscripts of Capt. Berchmans Motha, Grandson and Successor of Parathar Jati Thalaivanmor, referred at his home in Tuticorin on 21/04/2010; he was offered a special seat in the *Church of Our Lady of Snow.* In the absence of the bishop, he acted in his place.

23 Ibid.

24 S. Decla, *Muthukulithuraiyil Porchukeesiyar* (Tamil), (Chennai: New Century Book House, 2009), p. 109.

25 A. Patrick Roche, Op. Cit., p. 45.

26 Ibid.

27 O.A. Alphonsa, *Socio-Economic Transformation of the Parava Community in the Pearl Fishery Coast,* Unpublished Ph. D. thesis submitted to Kerala University, 2002, p. 131; she hints at the Portuguese technology but does not explain what exactly it is.

28 A. Sivasubramanian, *Kirittavamum Tamizccuuzalum,* p. 78.

29 Anonymous Author (ed.) Besse, *The Chronicles of the Pearl Fishery Coast,* __________, p. 20.

30 K.N. Panikkar, Op. Cit., p. 83.

31 Anonymous Author (ed.), *The Chronicles of the Pearl Fishery Coast,* p._.

32 Unpublished Manuscripts of Capt. Berchmans Motha; the *Jathi Thalaivan* shot a *Parathavar* man dead when he came out of the Protestant Church after taking Baptism there. Nobody was able to effect an action against the *Jathi Thalivan.* Thereafter, no Parathavar man dared to associate himself with the Dutch.

33 Romila Thapar, Op. Cit.; she stated that during the early census operation many people could not tell exactly about the religion they followed. They celebrated the festivals of one religion and attended the proceedings of another religion. Hence identity based on religion remained loose.

34 Letter of Francis Xavier from Tuticorin dated 28 October 1542.

35 Joseph Velinkar in K.S. Mathew, Teotonio R. de. Souza and Pius Malekandathil (eds.), *The Portuguese and the Socio-Cultural Changes in India,* (Tellicherry: Fundacao Oriente, 2001) p. 532.

36 Letter of Francis Xavier from Alandalai dated 5/09/1544; he wrote to his friend Francis Mansilhas about the corrupt interests of a *Portuguese* captain. It was natural that such a type of information was spread from one person to other.

37 In a national workshop entitled Towards a Theoretical Understanding on Tamil Society: Text/Praxis/Memories conducted at St. Xavier's College, Palayamkottai, between 10-11-2008 and 16-11-2008 Mr. A. Sivasubramanian delivered a lecture in which he stated that the Protestant Missionaries predominantly employed the words 'manamthirumbinargal' and 'meetkapattargal' meaning 'change of heart' and 'rescue' respectively.

38 Joseph Velinkar, Op. Cit., p. 532.

39 Anonymous Author (ed.), *The Chronicles of the Pearl Fishery Coast,* pp. 11–14; Fr. John de Lizanza, Fr. Coelho (Indian), Fr. Alphonso Cypriano, Fr. Nicholas Lancillotti, Fr. John de Beira, Fr. Antony Vaz, Fr. Paul de Valle and Fr. Antony Diaz were among some of the important catholic priests of the time.

40 Joseph Velinkar, Op. Cit., p. 532.

41 Anonymous Author (ed.), *The Chronicles of the Pearl Fishery Coast,* p. 12.

42 Ibid., pp. 15–16.

43 S. Viswanathan, Tamilology and a German Quest, *Frontline,* ________ ; in general, it was believed that only from the time of Bartholomaeus Ziegenbalg (1683–1719) and after the recognition of the native knowledge was made. But prior to him, *Henriquez* seemed to have made some

attempts to understand the native knowledge system. Possibly like Ziegenbalg he also observed that the natives discussed the same philosophical themes as the savants of Europe.

44 A. Sivasubramanian, *Kirittavamum Tamizccuuzalum,* p. 77.

45 T. John, *Then Thamilagathil Katholikam,* (Tirunelveli: Selvi Pathipagam, _____) p.126.

46 The *Brahmins* and their monopoly on spirituality were so dominant in the realization of which *Rev Fr Robert de Nobili* thought that if a handful of *Brahmins* accepted *Christianity* then the complete population can be brought within its fold.

47 K.N. Panikkar, Op. Cit., p. 83.

48 Ibid.

49 A. Sivasubramanian, *Thoni* (Tamil), (Palayamkottai: Folklore Resource and Research Centre, 2007) pp. 85–91.

50 Ibid. p. 84.

51 Ibid.

52   Joe d'Cruz, *Aazhi Sul Ulagu,* (Tamil), (Chennai: Tamizhini, 2004), p. 106.

53 Ibid. p. 182.

54 James Hornell, The Indian Chank in Folklore and Religion, *Taylor and Francis,* Vol. 53, No. 2 (Jun, 1942), p. 120.

55 Mr. Alangara Michael Nallathambi Fernando (67), President, Parathavar Vadakku Ur, Kottar: 27-11-08.

56 Ibid.

57 A. Sivasubramanian, *Uppittavarai,* (Chennai: Kalachuvadu Pathipagam, 2009) p. 84.

58 At *Manapad* there is a cave in which *St. Francis Xavier* is said to have lived. The place has attained a sacred status. Today at the entrance one can see a rope to which several clothes symbolizing cradles have been tied. This is a native practice wherein people seek progeny to God by tying cradle in a tree or rope. There are several similar practices that have become part and parcel of *Christianity.*

59 T. John, Op. Cit., p. 123; St. Xavier is said to have ordered to ablaze a house of an idol-worshipper.

60 A. Sivasubramanian, *Kirittavamum Tamizccuuzalum,* p. 96.

61 Interview with Mr. Parabaran (22), Fisherman, Manapad on 8-01-10; the informant said even today if affected by chickenpox the residents secretly attribute some rituals for the Mother Goddess located at Kulasekharapattinam.

62 A. Patrick Roche, Op. Cit., pp. 52–53.

63 Interview with Mr. Sukumaran (47), Resident of Kottar on 27/03/2010.

64 Mr. Alangara Michael Nallathambi Fernando (67), President, Parathavar Vadakku Ur, Kottar: 27-11-08.

65 Ibid.

66   S. Decla, Op. Cit., p. 36; these *Casados* were the Indo-Portuguese descendants. The Portuguese were encouraged to marry only Muslim and Brahmin women as they had attractive skin texture like Europeans. These *Casados* seemed to have entered the *Pearl Fishery Coast* for business and there was the expectedly matrimonial relationship between them and the *Parathavars*. Possibly, the bright skin for which many *Parathavars* are known owed to this reason.

67   A. Sivasubramanian, *Kirittavamum Tamizccuuzalum,* pp. 55–69.

68   K.N. Panikkar, Op. Cit., p. 82.

69   As M.N. Srinivas rightly points out, the Brahmins started westernizing themselves when such a crisis irked them.

70   Until independence, the *Parathavars* were considered as a 'forward caste'. In the post-independence era they demanded lower status because of the benefits that may accrue from caste reservation followed by the government.

71   Anonymous Author (ed.), *The Chronicles of the Pearl Fishery Coast,* p. 27.

72   Ibid.

73   A. Patrick Roche, Op. Cit., p. 55; he provides evidence from a Jesuit Parish diary of 1623 placed at Virapandianpattinam and states about the plot of a Rector to elevate a rival against the *Jathi Thalaivan.*

74   Unpublished Manuscripts of Capt. Berchmans Motha.

75   R.N. Joe d'Cruz, *Aazhi Sul Ulagu,* p. 146.

76   S. Decla, Op. Cit., p. 102.

77   Ibid., pp. 102–104.

78   Ibid.

79   P.J. Sanjeeva Raj, Baggage that Weighs Heavily on Mind, *The Hindu* dated 23 Aug. 2013 (Madurai Edition), p. 9.

Conclusion

Though presented in nine chapters, the central focus of the commonly linkable abstract concept maintained as 'between water and fire' can be said as conversion and change thereafter. Water was symbolic of dynamism effected by contact via sea and fire of static represented by land and the stagnant cultural core. The present researcher made an inquiry based on the theoretical arguments of *D.P. Chattopadyaya* that stated 'the needs of the new economy which emerged after the discoveries of 6th Millennium B.C. conditioned the shape of all religions as merely the correspondence between the spirits of God and man.' *D.P. Chattopadyaya* did not distinguish among religions. The three religions that emerged in *West Asia* including *Christianity* stressed on the *Voice of God.* But there was hardly any realization of such basic principles among the *Parathavar* converts. In fact, the missionaries drew parallels from the native life to spread *Christianity* as because the *Parathavar* society of that time had subordinated spirituality to economic interests. Therefore, adoption of *Christianity* was only a change of fellowship. Hence religious conversion of the *Parathavars* was found only to be a directed social action evoked by the needs generated in the sphere of economy.

Parathavars adopted *Christianity* en masse. Yet their cultural practices did not depart much from that of the non-convert *Tamils.* The difficulties in compromising at the cultural level took the present writer to trace the roots of the *Parathavars.* The projections of the prehistoric native life, impressions of civilizations such as *Mesopotamian* and *Indus* and cultures like that of the *Aryans* have gone into the gradual forming of *Parathavar* culture. By virtue of their location in the coast, the *Parathavar* people were constantly exposed to various lifestyles of the globe. All these not only made the culture to be complex but also contributed to its adaptive character although they formed part and parcel of the larger Tamil society as evident from the studies on genetics, kinship pattern and sharing of common myths. The engagement with the *Portuguese* was brief and insufficient to bring forth strides of change in the cultural element. Even the *Catholic Church* presented itself to suit the needs of the natives. In the field based ethnographic observations the cultural continuities prior to the adoption of *Christianity* tended to remain dominant. Thus religious conversion did not bring forth structural changes in the cultural-core of the *Parathavar* people.

Economic development espoused by trade had caused migration among *Parathavar* people. Settlements of the *Parathavars* emerged in the trade routes and coasts of Malabar and Sri Lanka.

However, there were socio-religious mechanisms that required the return of the members of a locality from time to time. Though people in the *Pearl Fishery Coast* did not directly rely on the land for the livelihood, they took pride in associating themselves with the place where their ancestral roots stemmed. They deemed prestigious to continue as members of the *Ur* (village) and participate in the holy activities of the guardian deity. Thus the pattern of migration did not take a chaotic course. Since these people carried religion with them to places of their settlements its historical geography of the spread can be mapped. Thus it is evident that the adoption of a new religion by a defined group of people can be geographically mapped.

Migration among *Parathavar* people was a pointer that marked the departure of the geographical isolation. The frequency of migration was linked to the quantum of production output. Salt and dry-fish were the chief surpluses produced from the coast that found circulation among all people irrespective of geographical variation. Apart from that evolved the *chank-cutting industry* and *pearl-fishing* enterprise. The proceeds of these were utilized to procure wood from the forest and derive the services of skilled personnel in the art of boat and ship-making. The *catamaran* and *vallams* were made for the fisherman whereas *Thonies* were built for the traders. Port cities emerged and articles of value moved towards it. Further, it attracted traders from abroad. Locally it was thought better to encounter the foreigners in unison. The *Portuguese* were just one of such foreign trading groups but not a power which civilized the natives in general and *Parathavars* in particular. Therefore, it goes to state that prior to adoption of *Christianity* the *Parathavar* people had an independent and vibrant economy.

The needs of the economy provoked the *Parathavars* to comprehensively and constantly engage themselves with nature. The elements of frightening nature were deified, and therefore, the sea in its comprehensive form was venerated. Subsequently, the totems that were thought to represent the resources of the sea were identified as ancestors and were also treated as sacred. With further knowledge of coastal resources the *Parathavar's* command in the sphere of economy consolidated and it created several dependent castes that included *Brahmins*. The *Brahmins* received a share in the proceeds of the *Pearl Fisheries* and bestowed higher social status to the *Parathavars*. Temples like *Tiruchendur, Tirupudaimarudhur, Kanyakumari* etc. bore testimony to the contribution of the coast. The local cult worships and totems of the *Parathavars* were given explanations in the *Brahimical order* and were linked with gods like *Varunan, Murugan, Vishnu* and *Sivan*. These gods were independently worshiped at the port towns with the support of the *Brahmins*. Hence access to *Brahminical* gods was within reach for the *Parathavar* people before conversion into *Christianity*.

The economic assertion, on the one hand enabled the process of Sanskritization by deriving the services of castes like *washer-men, barbers, carpenters, goldsmiths* and *Brahmins* whereas on the other hand divided the *Parathavar* society internally into classes. It also divided the social domains of men and women. But since the very philosophy of the coast was 'assertion of death over life' uncertainty and chaos determined the social relationship of people alongside materials. It was manifested in the authority of the *Ur* which attempted to deface the class differences. It commanded the fishermen to defend the traders during periods of contingency. It also took best efforts to compensate for loss. Even the wealthy traders who met with misfortune were absorbed as fishermen through the interference of the *Ur*. The social life remained tribal despite economic development.

In the first quarter of the 16th century A.D., serious differences crept between the *Parathavars* and the *Muslims*. Though the native *Muslims* traced their origin from the *Parathavars*, at a time of crisis it was not sufficient to establish harmony. The fellow natives of other castes unleashed vengeance when the *Muslims* instigated them with money. There were already scars of the invasion of the *Vijayanagar* army upon the *Parathavars*. They had no option than to negotiate with the *Portuguese* officers and seek protection. The latter expected the former to adopt *Christianity* so that their absolute loyalty can be derived. There were optimistic trends within *Christianity* for the *Portuguese* governors like *Albuquerque* paved way for an egalitarian outlook within the religion by provoking his sailors to marry *Indian* women. But this was not sufficient condition to prompt *Parathavar* conversion. *Islam* that entered the region far ahead of *Christianity* had similar features but failed to attract the *Parathavars*. Thus the religious conversion of the *Parathavar* has to be viewed in the light of the crisis they encountered wherein their life and property were put to threat and not on the benevolence of the *Portuguese*. Therefore, it can be effectively stated that the liberal approach of the *Portuguese* towards the natives was instrumental in causing religious conversion.

Adoption of *Christianity* remained just symbolic in the periods for nobody was familiar with the basic tenets of the religion. It necessitated the arrival of trained priests and *St. Xavier* was most important among them. He observed the continuation of native practices among the newly converted *Christians*. He made best attempts to purge *Christianity* of idol practices. But the grounds of such reforms were weakened when he and other priests introduced devotion to Mother Mary and other Saints for such initiatives took the *Parathavars* closer to the spirit of *Bhakthi Movement* than *Christianity*. Moreover, the ordination of sainthood upon *St. Xavier* caused the germination of several myths that were structurally native. Thus, there were identifiable parallels between the Bhakti Movement and the activities of St. Francis Xavier that provided space for the latter to consolidate the natives and their faith.

The missionary activities did not cause close negotiation between the *Portuguese* and the *Parathavars* in the economic sphere. Though the *Catholic order* received a share in the revenue of the *Pearl Fisheries*, there was hardly any change in the basic tools of production that pertained to the *Parathavars* and the *catamarans* and *vallams* continued. However, the engagement of the *Portuguese* with the *Parathavars* contributed in the consolidation of the division of society into *Mesakarar*, *Kamarakarar* and *Menakadar* with *Portuguese* family titles classifiable under each category. Though the titles were symbolic, they were important among the chief factors that derived the loyalty of the community towards the church. Therefore, when the *Dutch* asserted control over *Tuticorin*, their provocation to reap the benefits of cotton trade after reconversion to *Protestant* denomination went unheard. Subsequently, the *British* also maintained only a professional relationship with the members of the *Parathavar* community. With the spread of *Catholicism* in regions beyond the coast, the access to benefits that flowed from the Church such as education was hampered. Therefore, the community did not largely undergo the change in its internal structure due to the adoption of *Christianity*. Since there was no substantial change in the basic tools of production, the socio-cultural changes evoked by religious conversion were only marginal.

Index